ICONS OF STYLE

BTS

First published in 2026 by Welbeck
An Imprint of HEADLINE PUBLISHING GROUP LIMITED

1

Cataloguing in Publication Data is available from the British Library

ISBN 978 1 03543 529 6

Printed in China

MIX
Paper | Supporting responsible forestry
FSC® C104740

Headline's policy is to use papers that are natural, renewable and recyclable products and made from wood grown in well-managed forests and other controlled sources. The logging and manufacturing processes are expected to conform to the environmental regulations of the country of origin.

HEADLINE PUBLISHING GROUP LIMITED
An Hachette UK Company
Carmelite House
50 Victoria Embankment
London EC4Y 0DZ

The authorised representative in the EEA is Hachette Ireland, 8 Castlecourt Centre, Dublin 15, D15 XTP3, Ireland (email: info@hbgi.ie)

www.headline.co.uk
www.hachette.co.uk

ICONS OF STYLE

BTS

The story of the K-pop fashion icons

Kati Chitrakorn

WELBECK

TIMELINE

2010–2013 Pre-debut

2010 and **2011** Auditions held by Big Hit Entertainment

2012 Final line-up of seven members established

13 June 2013: Debut with the release of their single album *2 Cool 4 Skool* and the lead single "No More Dream"

2013–2014 School Trilogy: *2 Cool 4 Skool, O!RUL8,2?, Skool Luv Affair*

2014 *Dark & Wild*

2015–2016 Youth Trilogy: *The Most Beautiful Moment in Life pt. 1, The Most Beautiful Moment in Life pt. 2* and *Young Forever*

2016–2017 *Wings/You Never Walk Alone*

2017–2018 Love Yourself Trilogy: *Her, Tear, Answer*

2019–2020 Map of the Soul Duology: *Map of the Soul: Persona, Map of the Soul: 7*

2020 *Be*, including "Dynamite"

2021 "Butter" CD single inc. "Permission to Dance"

2022 *Proof*

2026 *Arirang* album and world tour

OPPOSITE The members of BTS wore maroon Gucci suits at the 2020 *Billboard* Music Awards in Los Angeles, California.

OVERLEAF BTS on the late-night talk show *Jimmy Kimmel Live!*, on 15 November 2017. They played six songs, finishing up with "Fire".

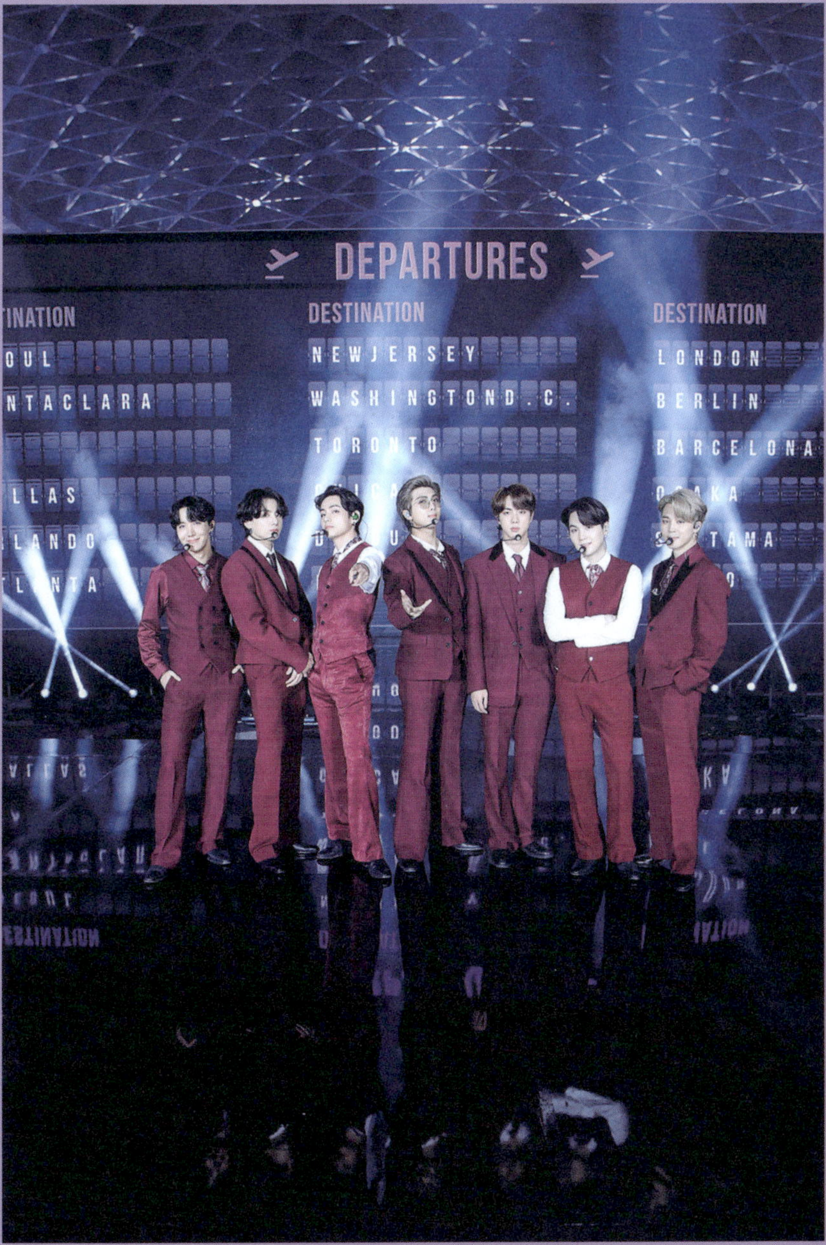
DEPARTURES
DESTINATION
NEWJERSEY
WASHINGTOND.C.
TORONTO
DESTINATION
LONDON
BERLIN
BARCELONA

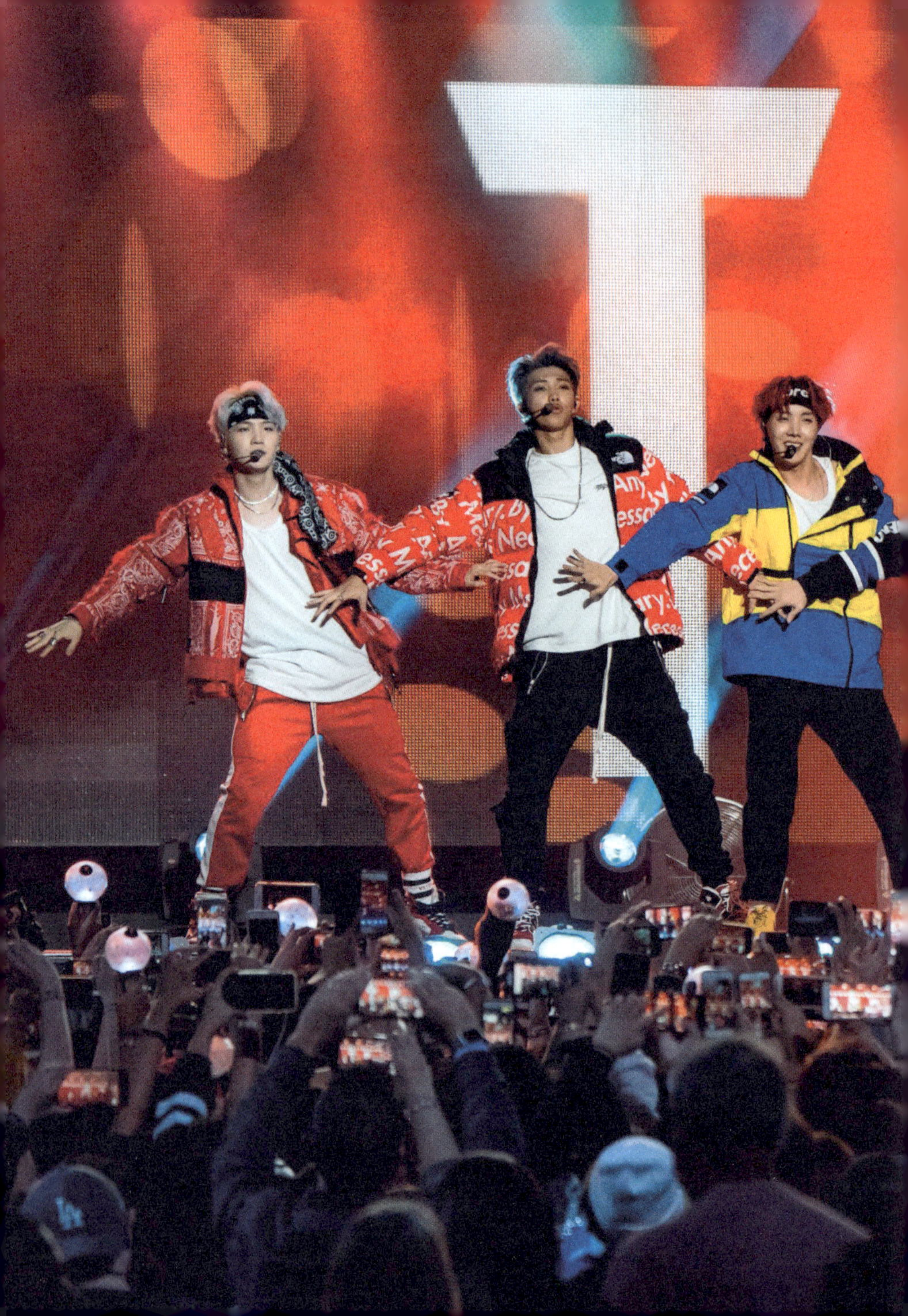

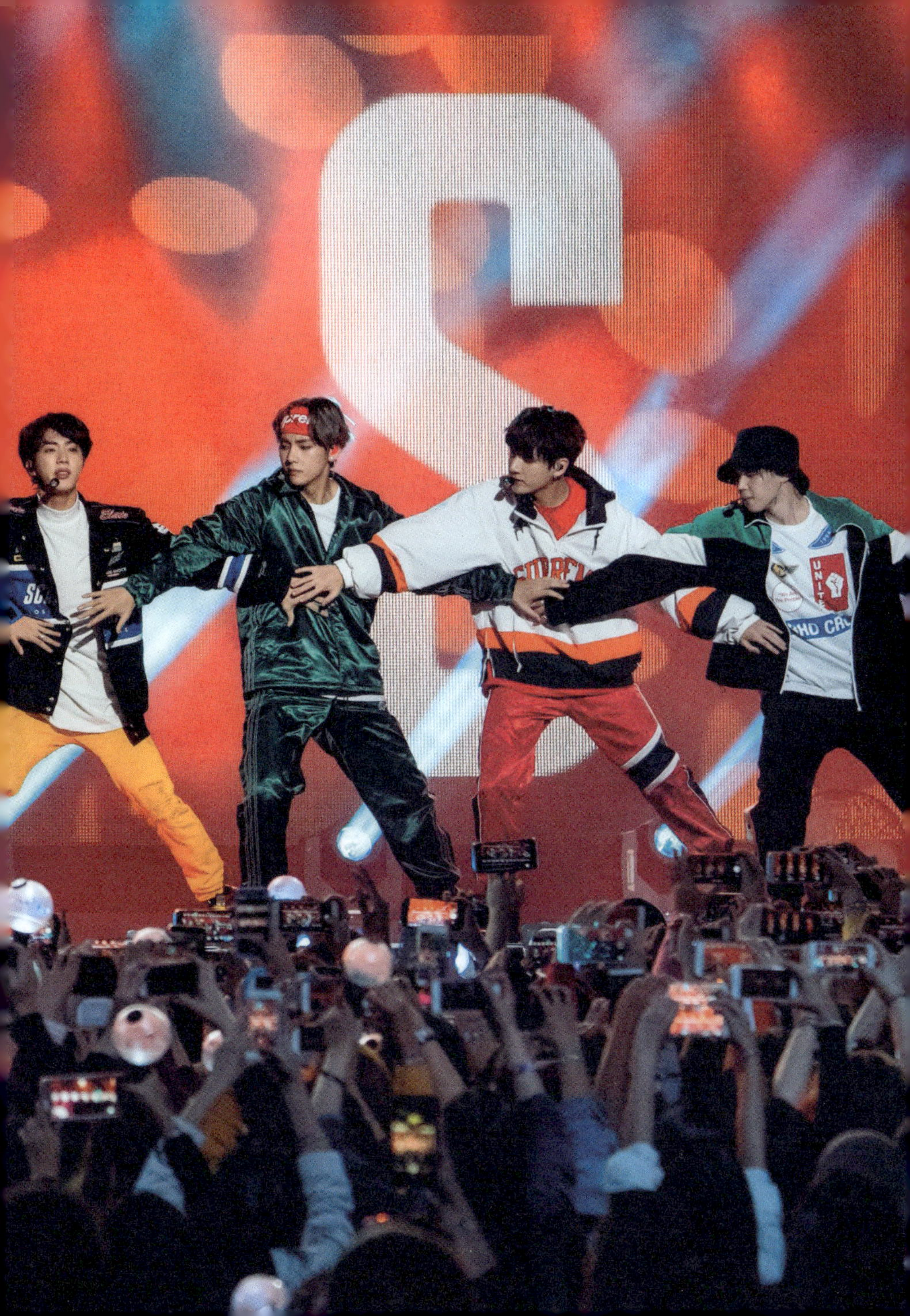

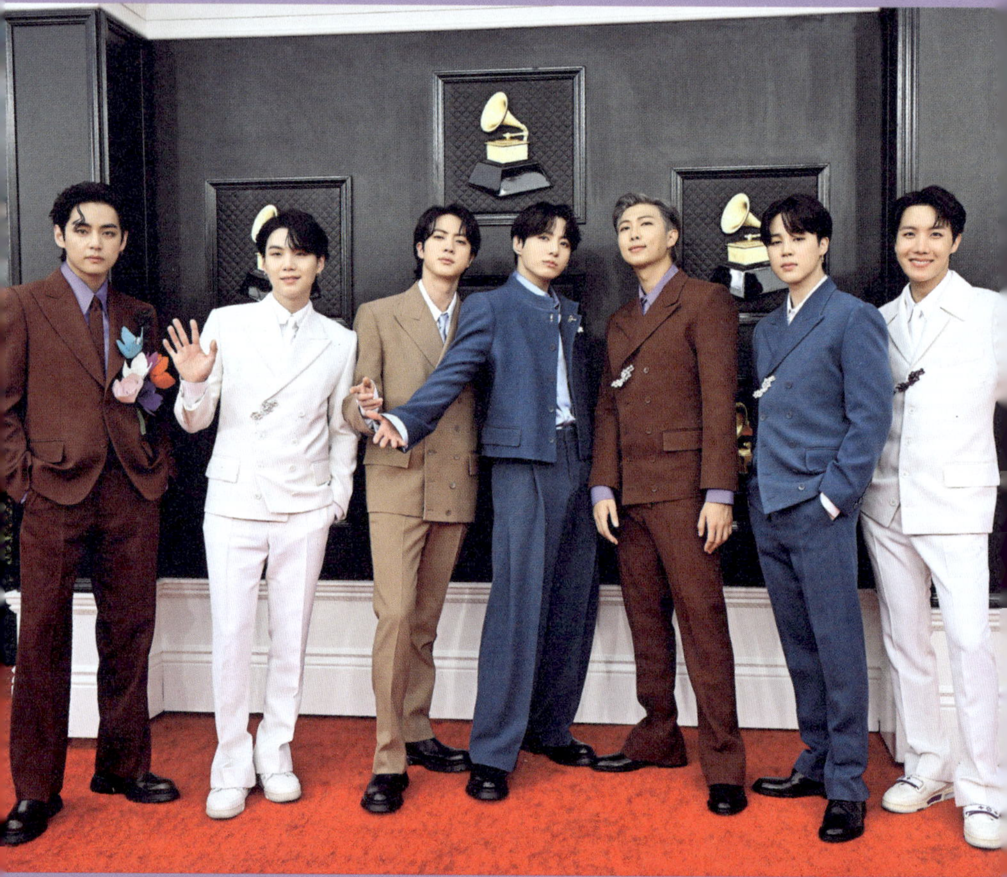

V, Suga, Jin, Jung Kook, RM, Jimin and J-Hope in custom-made Louis Vuitton at the 64th Annual Grammy Awards in Las Vegas, Nevada in April 2022.

INTRODUCTION: "THE BANGTAN BOYS"

The rapid ascent and widespread appeal of Korean culture is remarkable in its speed and influence. Whether it is the unprecedented international recognition of the South Korean film *Parasite*, the first non-English language film to win the Academy Award for Best Picture, or the global adoption of innovative Korean beauty products such as BB cream, cushion compacts and sheet masks, the impact of South Korea's cultural exports – known as "hallyu" or the "Korean Wave" – can be felt widely.

Yet, even as the country's cuisine, entertainment and beauty products gain favour globally, it is K-pop that continues to be the most recognized symbol of South Korean culture. The 2025 Global Hallyu Survey, based on 2024 data, conducted by the Ministry of Culture, Sports and Tourism (a central government agency in South Korea) and the Korean Foundation for International Cultural Exchange, showed that 18 per cent of 26,400 respondents with prior experience of Korean culture said that pop music was the first thing they associated with the country – keeping K-pop in the top spot for an eighth consecutive year.

Leading that front is BTS, which continued to be the most popular K-pop act for the seventh year in a row at 25 per cent, followed by girl group Blackpink at 12 per cent, according to the survey.

The members of BTS are RM, Jin, Suga, J-Hope, Jimin, V and Jung Kook, and the initials stand for the Korean phrase "Bangtan Sonyeondan" (Korean: 방탄소년단), which translates literally as "Bulletproof Boy Scouts". It later became a backronym for "Beyond The Scene", to encompass the idea of personal growth and the evolution of BTS as a group.

A worldwide sensation with mainstream appeal beyond Asia, BTS dominate the music industry, much like The Beatles – to whom they are often compared – did almost six decades prior. While the two groups have obvious differences, they have inspired devoted fan bases and generated chart-topping success, including three No. 1 albums on the *Billboard* 200 chart in less than a year. BTS was also the first K-pop band ever to top the US album chart, has been No. 1 on iTunes in over 100 countries, and has over 80 million subscribers on YouTube. These are astounding feats considering that their songs are mostly in Korean.

And then there are the live concerts. Interest in BTS tours has always been high, with tickets selling out in minutes for many shows and creating fierce competition among fans. Their Love Yourself World Tour, for example, which ran from 2018 to 2019, was the highest-grossing tour by a K-pop group at the time, according to *Forbes*, and attracted over two million attendees. The Wings Tour, a year prior, in 2017, also had rapid sell-outs in various locations, including North and South America.

OPPOSITE As the youngest member of BTS, Jung Kook is often referred to as the "Golden Maknae" (he's good at *everything*). Pictured here wearing Versace while performing at the 2022 football world cup in Qatar.

OVERLEAF BTS performing on Mnet's *M! Countdown* show in July 2013, shortly after their official debut.

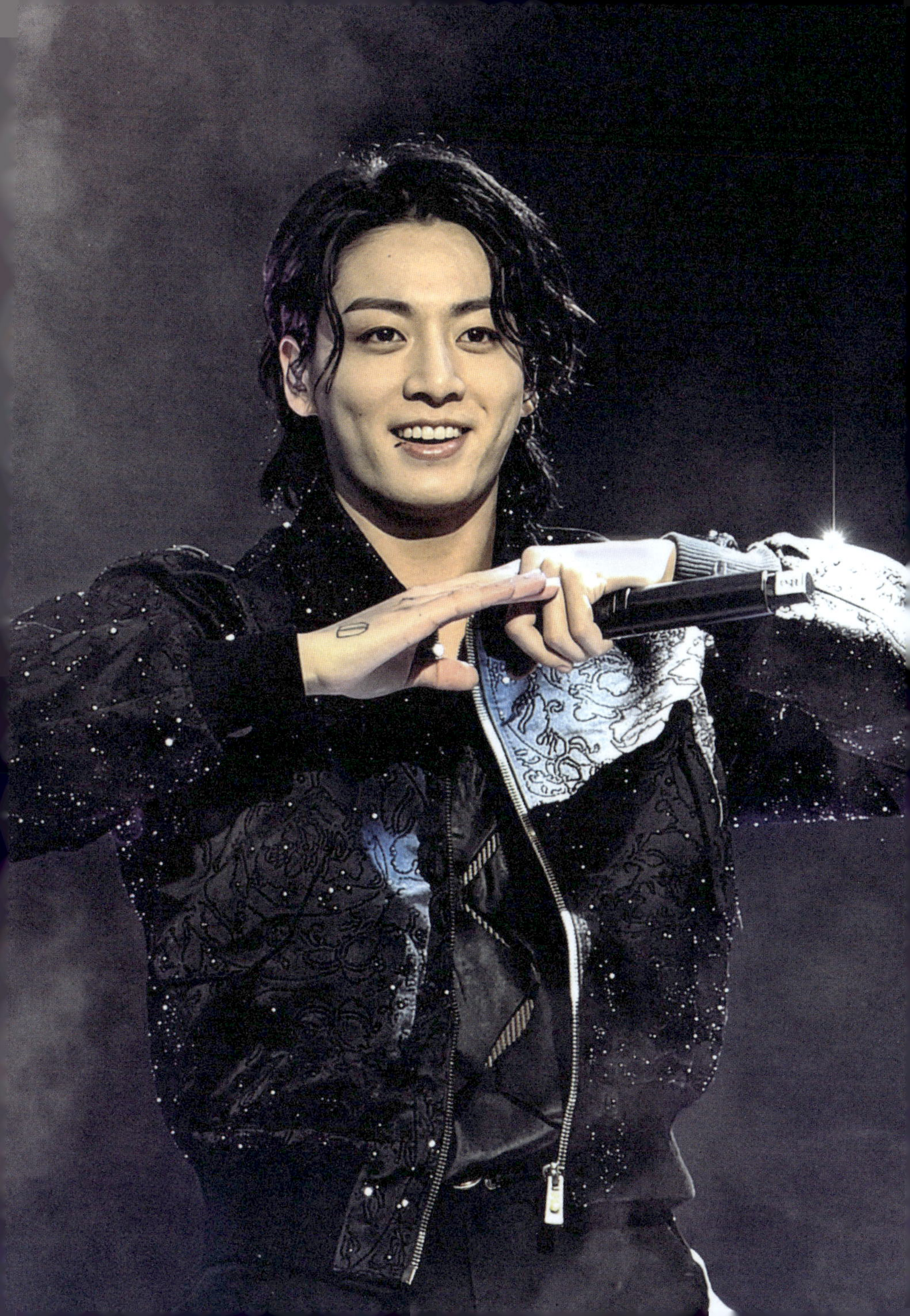

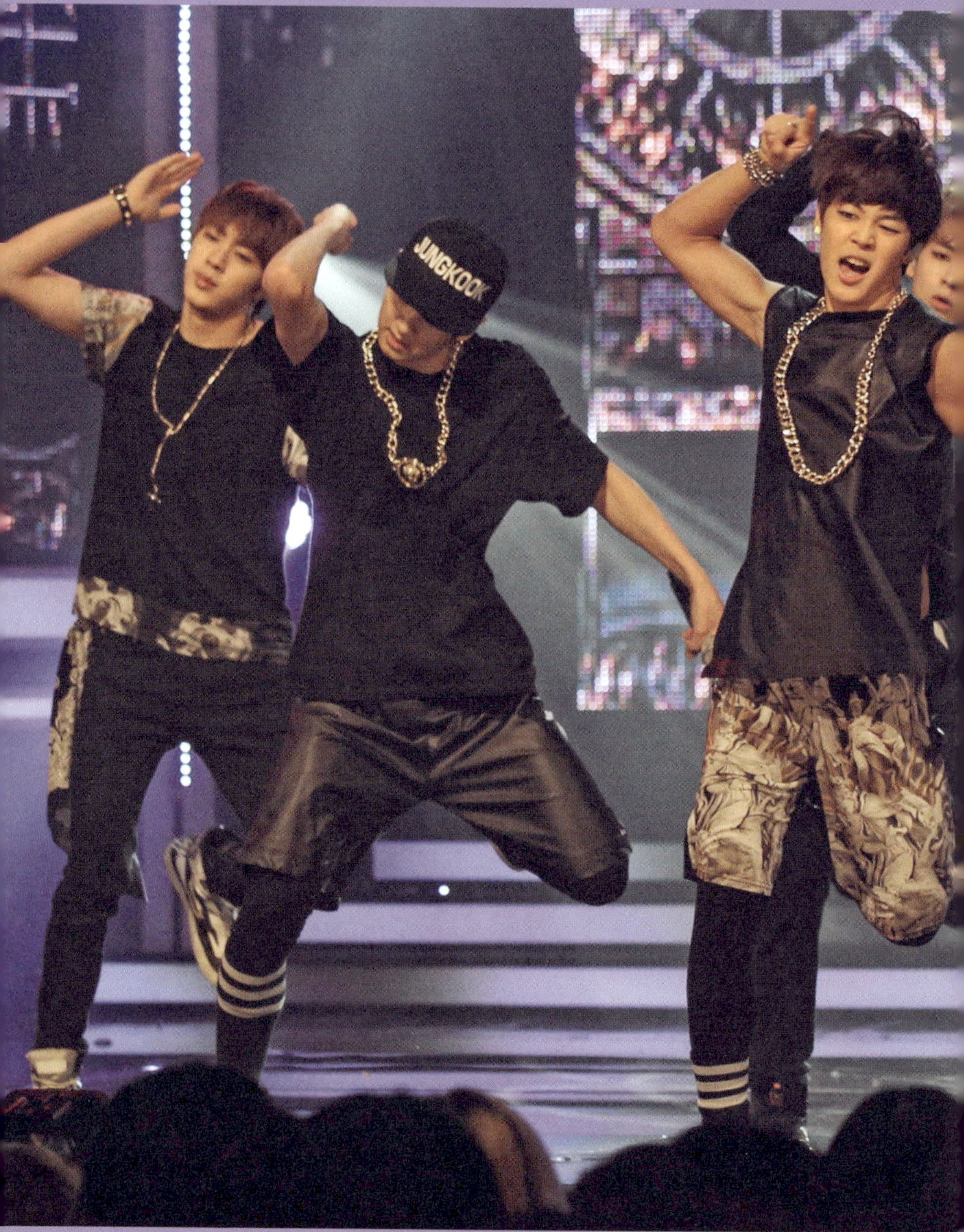
JUNGKOOK

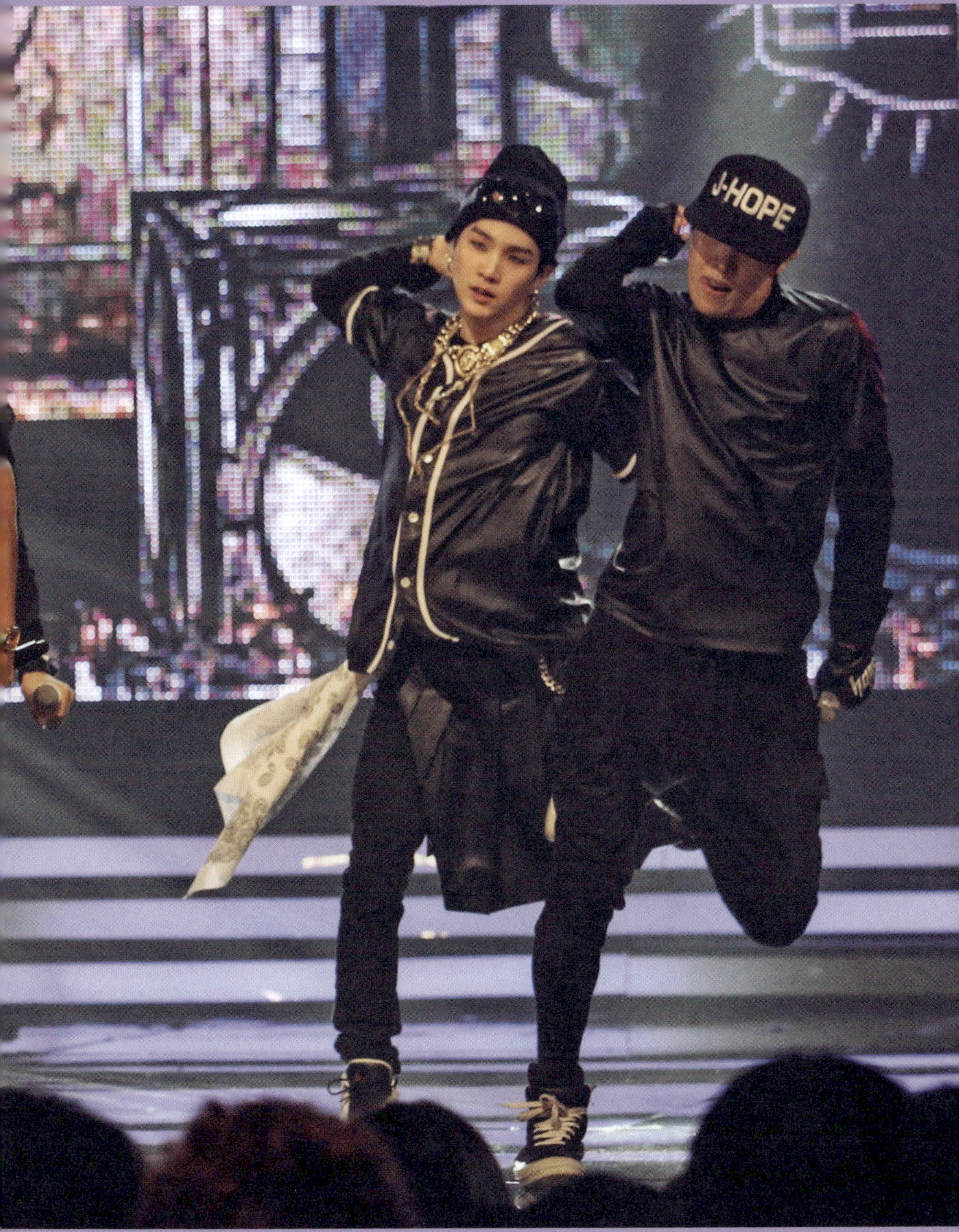
J-HOPE

"BTS isn't just the biggest K-pop act on the charts. They've become the biggest band in the world – full stop."

TIME MAGAZINE, 2020

BTS at the 61st Annual Grammy Awards at the Staples Center, Los Angeles in February 2019.

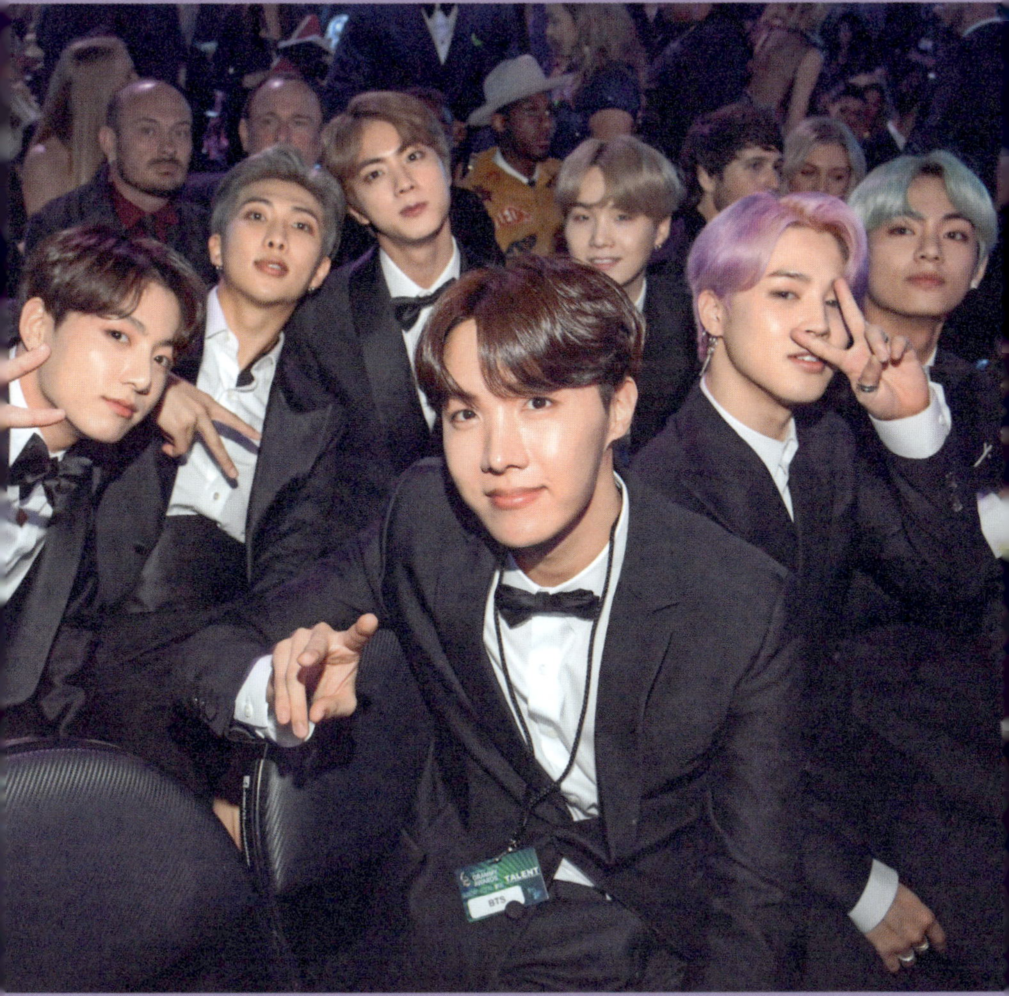
TALENT
BTS

BTS was described by *Forbes* in 2019 as "easily the biggest and most successful name in K-pop in the world" that can "do things no other name in their genre can". Meanwhile, *Time* magazine gave them the nickname "Princes of Global Pop" in a 2022 interview. But beyond their musical achievements, the members of BTS have also become known for their stylish appearances, that challenge traditional gender stereotypes and boundaries.

Whether at red carpet events or through their off-duty looks, the BTS approach to fashion has become almost as striking and influential as their music. Their style – which feels coherent as a group, yet maintains an individuality that is unique to each member – has since been recognized by fashion establishments in Korea and overseas, through magazine covers and editorials with *Vogue, W, Harper's Bazaar, GQ* and *Esquire*, among others. All seven members have signed deals with international luxury brands including Louis Vuitton, Valentino, Calvin Klein, Bottega Veneta, Dior, Gucci, Celine and Cartier.

By the end of 2025 it had been over three years since BTS made a united public appearance. The band had been on hiatus due to their mandatory military service in South Korea; the members had been gradually enlisting since December 2022, with the last one, Suga, completing service in June 2025. Despite this, some individual group members – for example, Jung Kook – still ranked in the Top 10 most popular K-pop acts, demonstrating their enduring appeal, according to the Global Hallyu Survey.

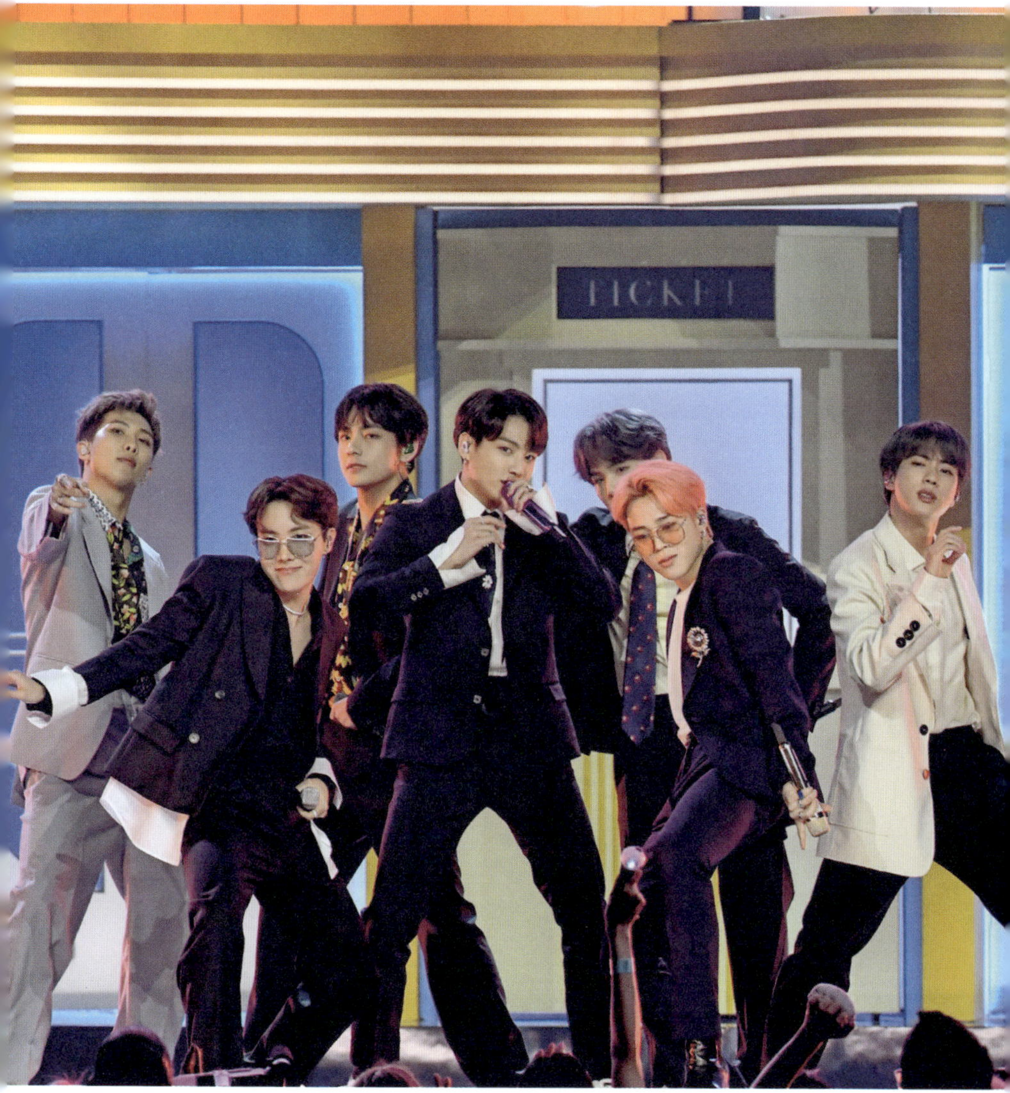

BTS performed "Boy With Luv" live for the first time during the 2019 *Billboard* Music Awards at the MGM Grand Garden Arena, Las Vegas in May 2019.

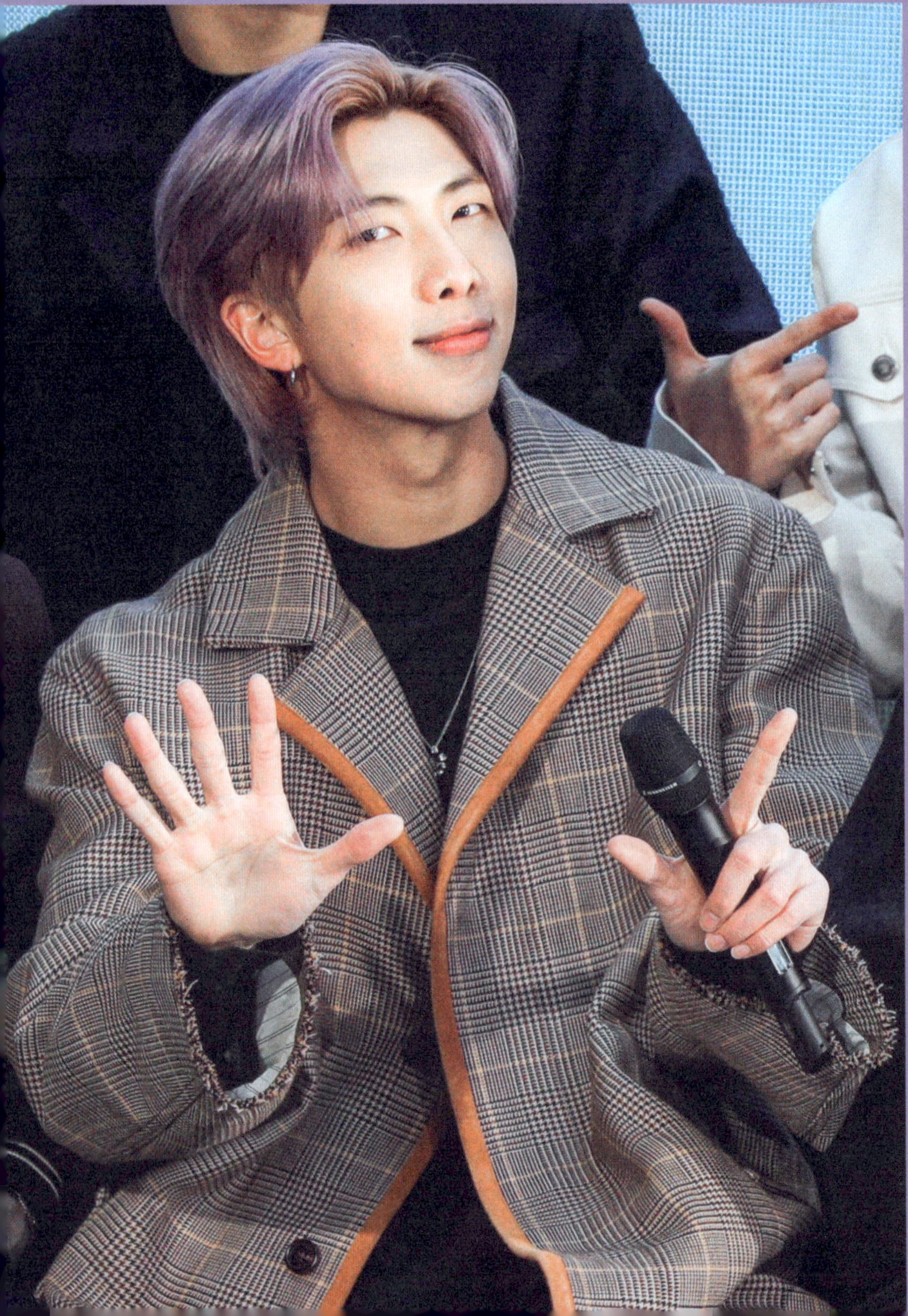

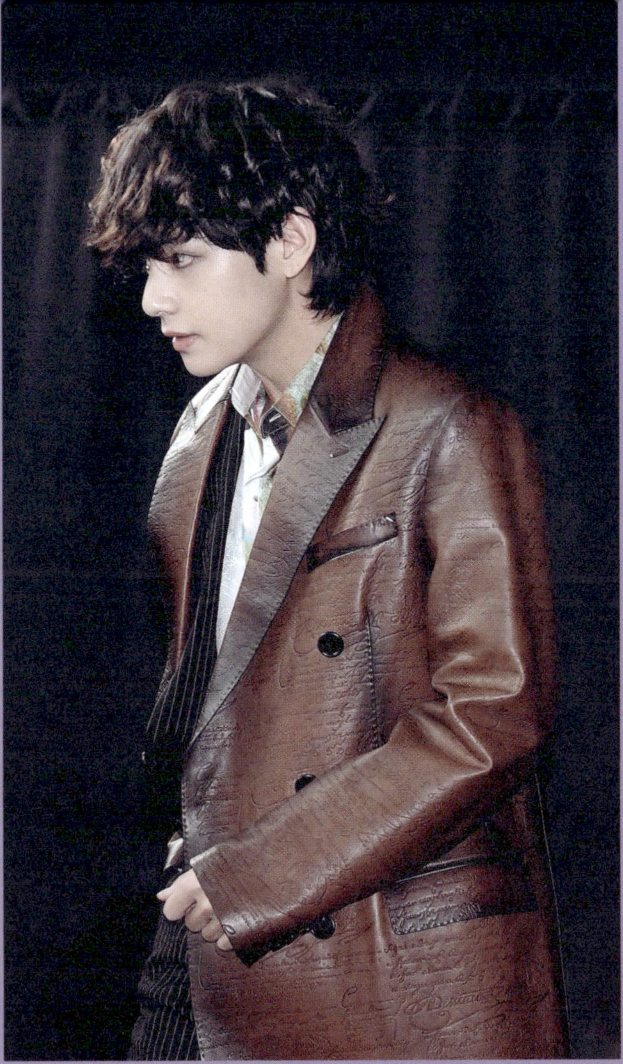

ABOVE V wearing a long brown leather jacket
at the 2019 SBS Gayo Daejeon in Seoul.

OPPOSITE RM on *The Today Show* at Rockefeller
Plaza in New York City, February 2020.

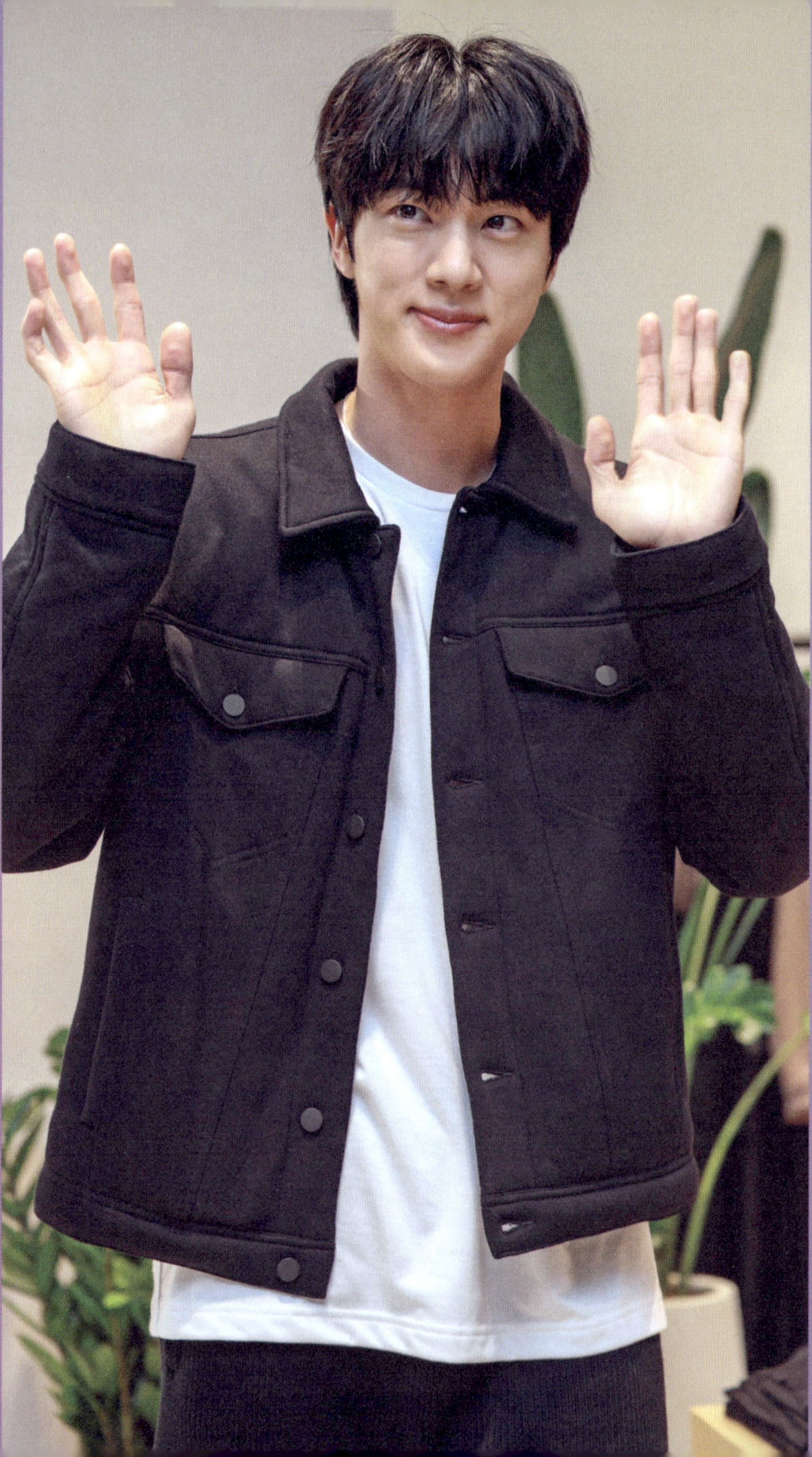

Outsized interest and high demand is expected to continue for future tours, especially with the anticipation surrounding their comeback. In July 2025 the K-pop superstars confirmed they would return to the spotlight with a new album and a world tour in 2026. It was the band's first world tour since their Permission to Dance on Stage Tour in 2022. The new album was the band's first full-length release since 2020.

"We'll be visiting fans all around the world, so we hope you're as excited as we are", the band said of their reunion on fan platform Weverse.

BELOW A fan's smartphone decorated with a picture of the BTS band members.

OPPOSITE Jin was present at the opening event for Alo's Asian flagship store in Gangnam-gu in Seoul, July 2025.

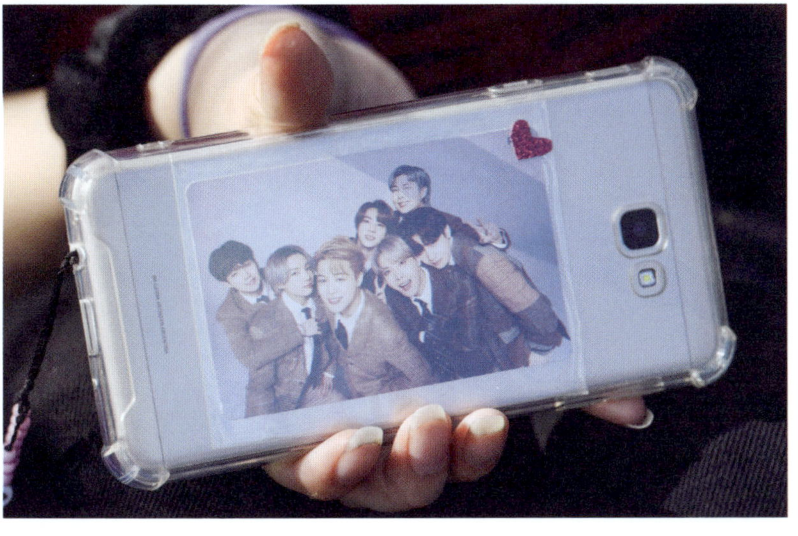

PRE-DEBUT

CHAPTER 1

DAYS

PRE-DEBUT DAYS

The fact that BTS consists of seven members may have initially seemed unusual, given that the most established boy bands that came before them – Backstreet Boys, The Jacksons, NSYNC, Take That and One Direction, to name a few – all had five.

RM, Suga, J-Hope, Jin, Jung Kook, V and Jimin have been singing and dancing together since 2012, when South Korean music mogul Bang Si-Hyuk, aka "Hitman" Bang, pieced the group together at the Big Hit Entertainment record label he founded in 2005. It is now one of the pillars of the colossal K-pop industry, valued by Bloomberg at $10 billion in 2024.

Bang, who studied aesthetics at South Korea's prestigious Seoul National University, started his career at JYP Entertainment, one of the "big three" corporations in K-pop. The idea of BTS first formed in 2010 when Bang set out to independently create a hip-hop group.

The members of the newly formed BTS pose for photographs in June 2013 as they make their debut.

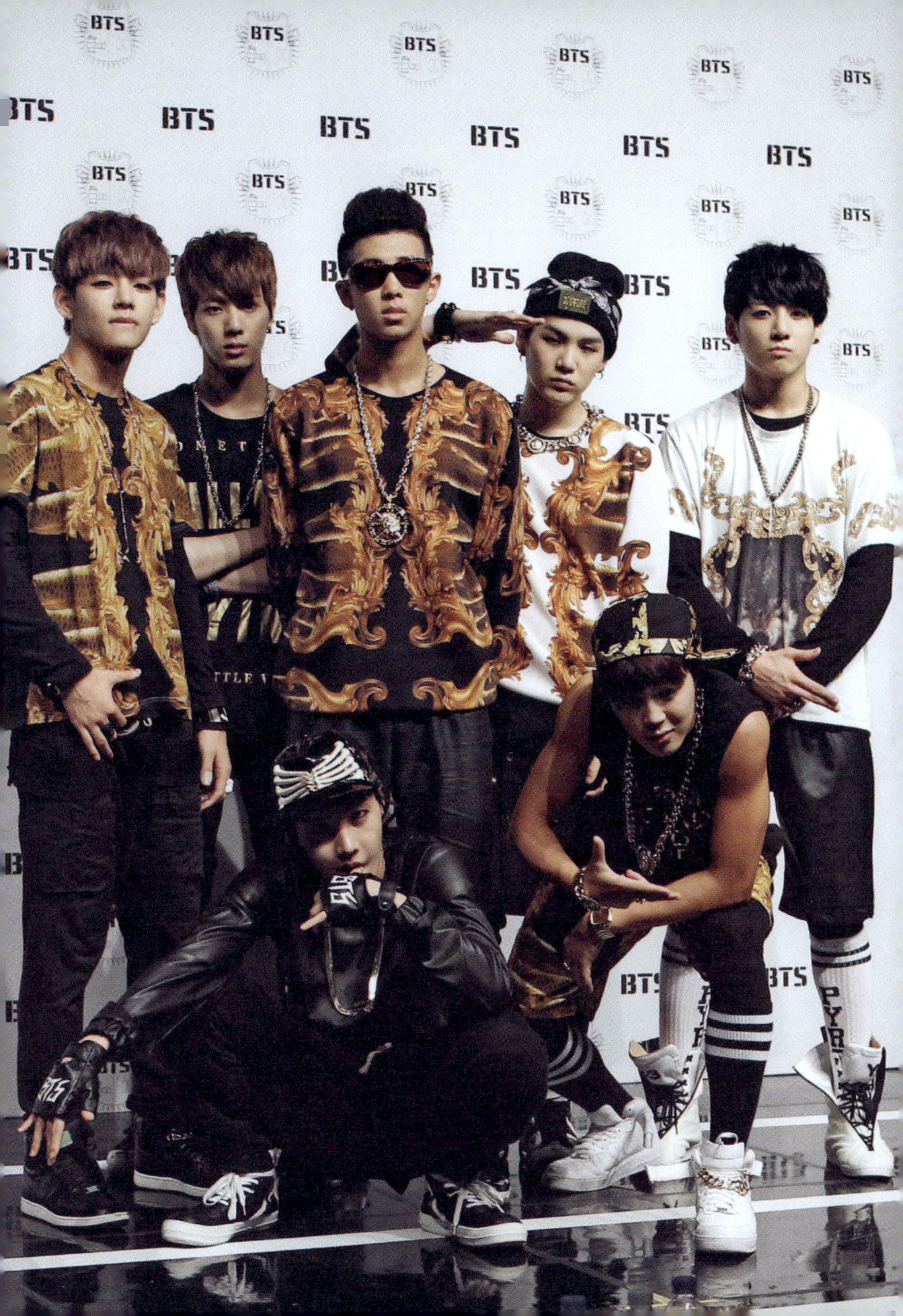
BTS

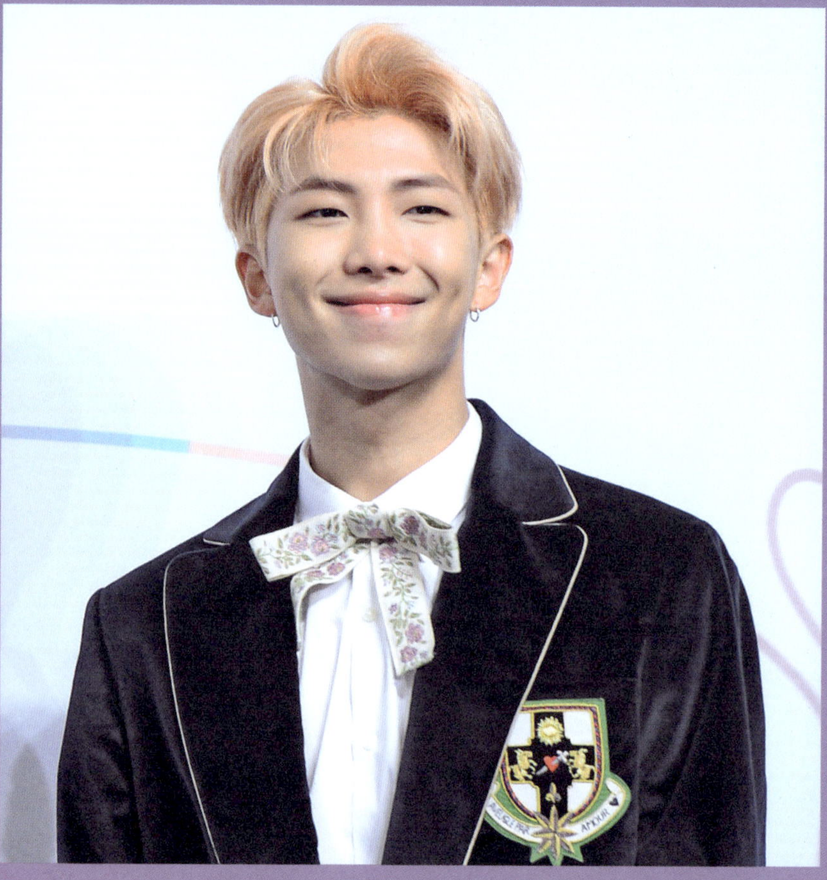

RM is known for his smart and sensible style. At the press conference for the new BTS album *Love Yourself: Her* in September 2017, he wore a preppy blazer with crisp white shirt and bow tie.

The first member to join BTS was RM (Kim Nam-joon), who was scouted and auditioned in 2010, aged 16. RM (short for Rap Monster) had begun rapping three years prior and went by the name Runch Randa. During this time, the Seoul-born teenager was active in local amateur hip-hop circles, such as Jungle Radio, an underground hip-hop cafe. As well as his native Korean he was also an English speaker. He taught himself by watching reruns of the popular New York-based TV sitcom *Friends*.

A South Korean rapper named Sleepy first met RM at a rapper crew audition. The former has spoken of this on multiple talk shows, including SBS Power FM's *Cultwo Show* in 2017 and MBC's *Radio Star* in 2018. One day, Sleepy had told Pdogg, a Big Hit producer, that he knew of a talented high school-aged rapper and started playing RM's underground music. Impressed by what he had heard, Sleepy took the demo songs and played them for Bang, who subsequently signed RM to the label, he shared in a 2019 interview with *Time*, despite there not being a trainee plan in place for a boy group called BTS at the time.

"I listened and it was killer", Pdogg recalled of RM's music to the niche technology blog *Tongue Technology* in 2013. "At that time, the direction that BTS would go in wasn't fixed in detail. At first, we wanted to make a hip-hop group, rather than an idol group", Pdogg said.

The idea of Bangtan was first revealed to the public in August that year, with promotions for Hit It!, the first audition round to directly recruit for BTS members. The first two trainee members were revealed to be RM and Iron (Jung Hun-cheol), a young Seoul-born rapper who was known for participating in the third season of the popular reality TV rap contest *Show Me the Money* (he ended as runner-up). Shortly afterwards, South Korean rapper Supreme Boi (Shin Dong-hyuk) was also revealed to be a trainee. By September 2010, Bangtan released their first group track, "Hook Gayo", featuring RM, Iron and Supreme Boi.

What follows thereafter is not clear. Varying accounts have been documented and it has not been addressed by Bang in interviews. There is speculation that the original Bangtan debut was cancelled in favour of moving the group away from being solely a hip-hop crew. Thus, a second Big Hit! audition was scheduled, which led to the finalized BTS line-up that we know today. Iron and Supreme Boi did not debut as part of the group.

OPPOSITE Clockwise from back left: Jung Kook, V, Jin, J-Hope, Jimin, Suga and RM in conversation at the Grammy Museum in Los Angeles, September 2018.

OVERLEAF BTS on MBC Music's *Show Champion* in Ilsan, South Korea in September 2014.

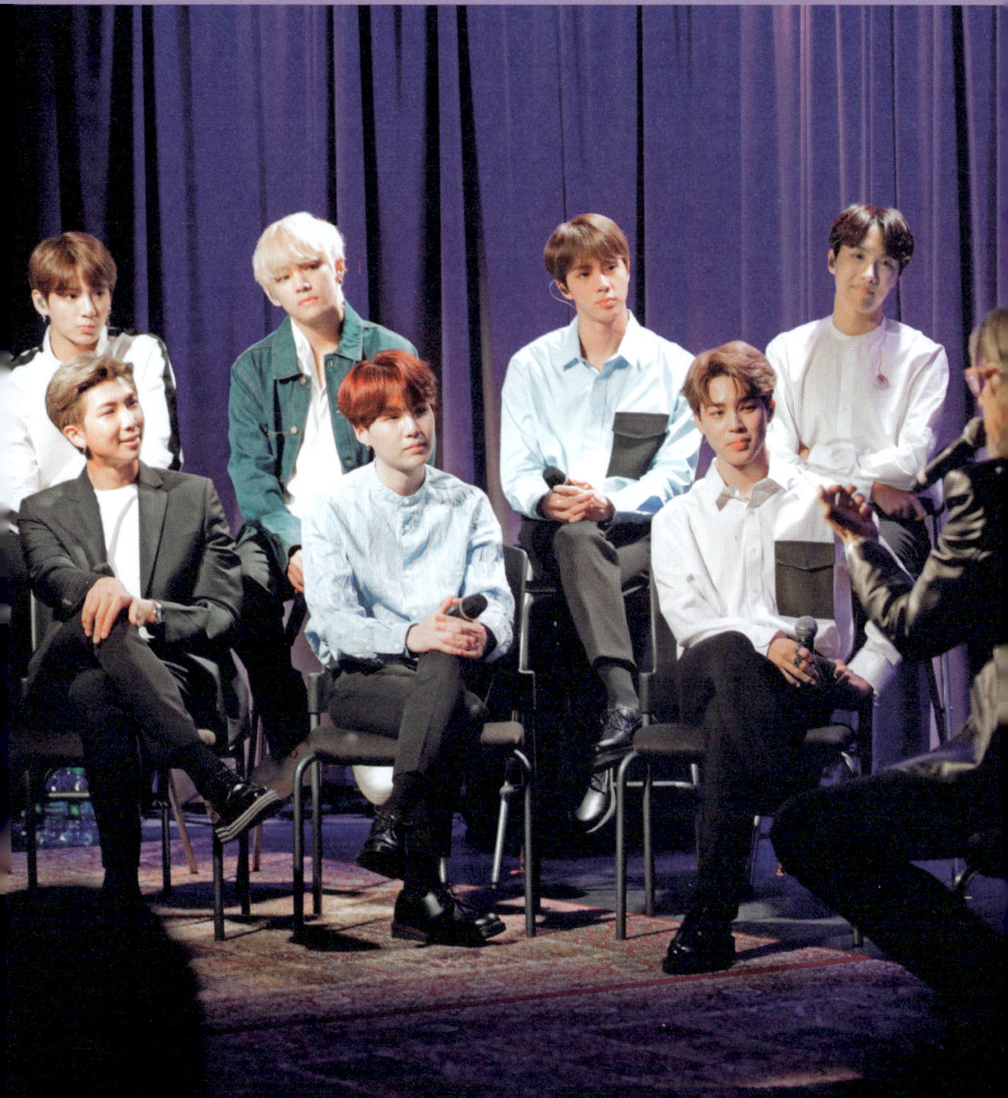

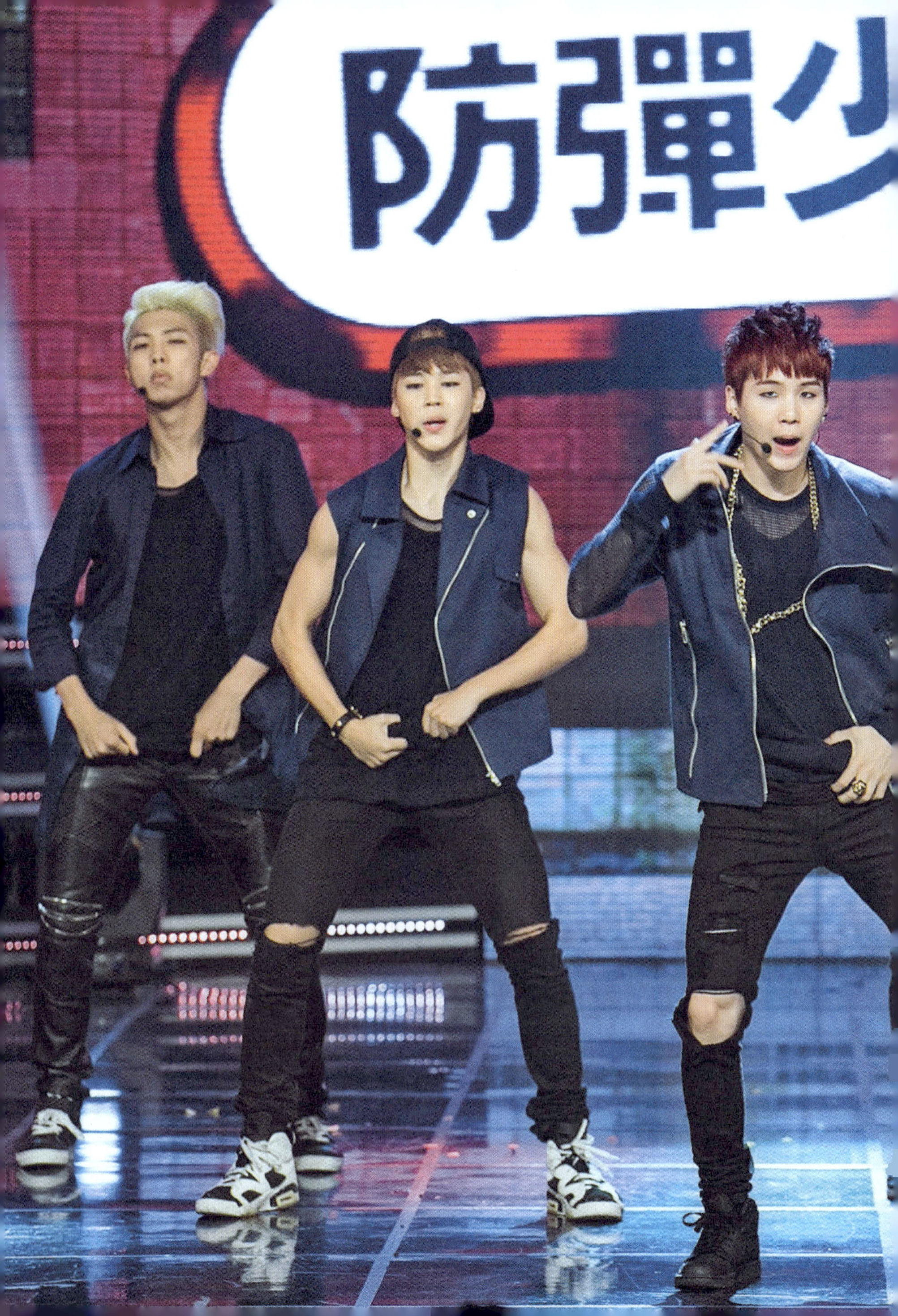
防彈少

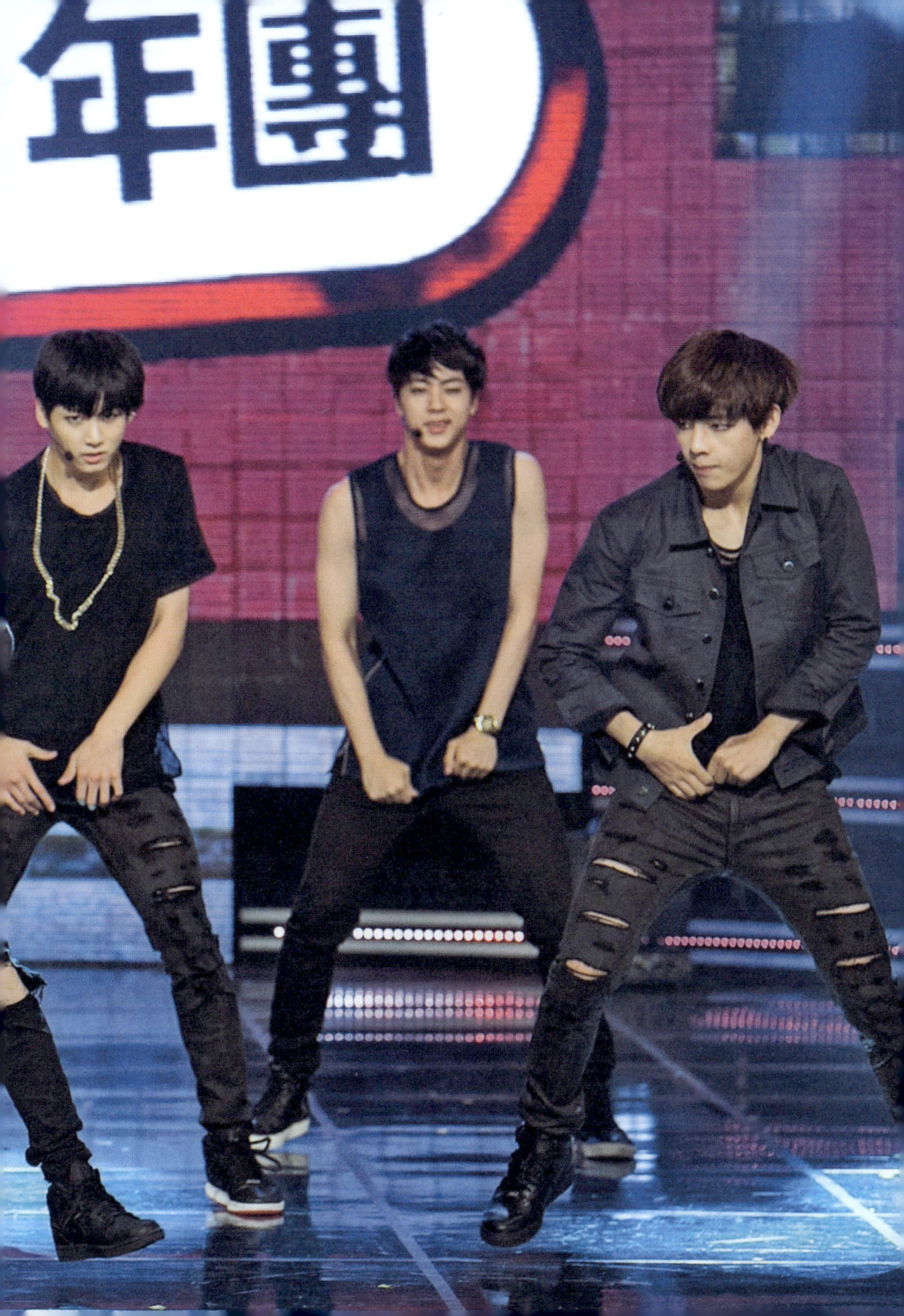
年團

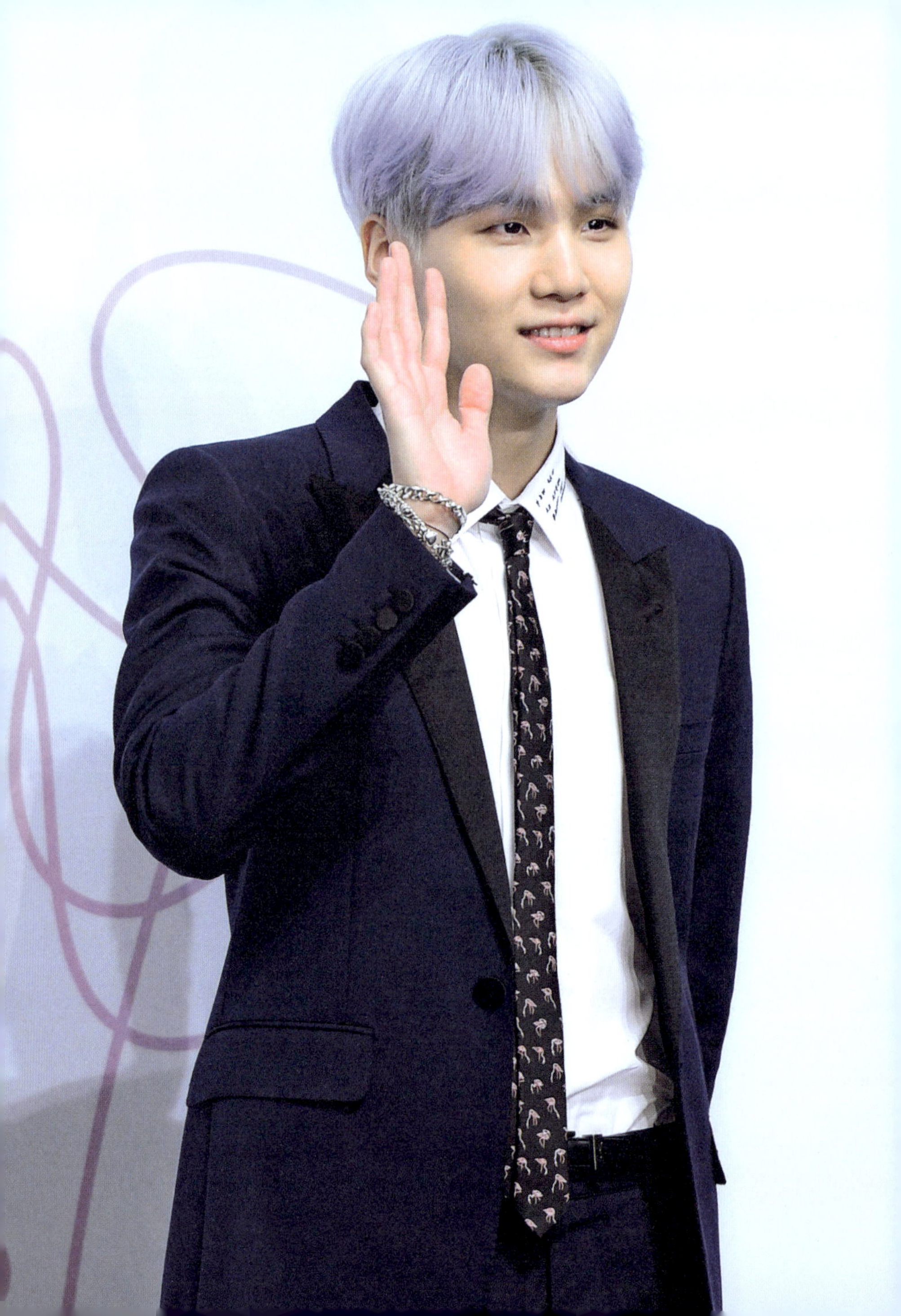

On Bangtan's move away from hip-hop, Pdogg explained to *Tongue Technology* that it wasn't intentional, but simply organic: "It was just like, we can't bury kids like these. The friends Rap Monster had around him were all born in '94 and '95. But they all did really well", he said. "I saw all these talented kids and said as much to [Bang] Si-hyuk. At first we called them the Bangtan Crew. Then after they gradually started to change direction towards idol-dom, we reorganized them, and dance and performance aspects started to come in."

That second audition is how BTS got its second member, Suga (Min Yoon-gi). He hailed from Daegu, where he worked as a part-time delivery boy and was also an underground rapper known as Gloss. He chose the name because it was close to the meaning of his birth name, Yoon-gi, which translates as "to shine". He joined BTS after his successful audition in 2010.

J-Hope (Jung Ho-seok), a talented street dancer from Gwangju, became the third member to debut as part of BTS. Due to his training at the Gwangju Music Academy and involvement with the city's underground dance group Neuron, J-Hope had gained recognition for his dancing skills and had won various local prizes, including first place in a national dance competition in 2008. His ability to rap was a fitting advantage.

Suga is regarded by fans and critics a highly artistic and deeply emotional member of the band. Pictured here at the *Love Yourself: Her* press conference in September 2017.

"I saw all these talented kids and said as much to [Bang] Si-hyuk. At first we called them the Bangtan Crew.

Then after they gradually started to change direction towards idol-dom, *we reorganized them, and dance and performance aspects started to come in."*

**PDOGG,
BIG HIT PRODUCER**

Jin (Kim Seok-jin) and Jung Kook (Jeon Jung-kook) followed next. Jung Kook, who was born in Busan, joined BTS as a trainee in the summer of 2011. Earlier that year he had taken part in *Superstar K*, a South Korean talent show similar to *American Idol*, which resulted in casting offers from seven entertainment companies, as Jung Kook said on Mnet's *New Yang Nam Show*. He eventually chose to become a trainee under Big Hit Entertainment after seeing RM – now his fellow band member – perform.

Jin joined around the same time as Jung Kook, but, unlike his counterparts, he was originally scouted by SM Entertainment (one of South Korea's largest entertainment companies) while on the streets of Anyang, his hometown. In a TV interview, Jin said he decided to pursue a theatre major (at Konkuk University), with the hope that through acting he "would learn and experience lots of different things". But, he conceded, "I became an idol instead and experienced and learned even more than I could've ever imagined."

Sharing a similar fortuitous turn of events, in 2011 V (Kim Tae-hyung) originally attended an audition for Big Hit Entertainment not for himself, but to support a friend that was trying out, he has since revealed on talk shows including *The Tonight Show Starring Jimmy Fallon*. The son of a farming family in Daegu, V didn't actually intend to try out for the group, but a team member at Big Hit Entertainment saw him and encouraged him to audition, he revealed to Jimmy Fallon. He succeeded in advancing to the next round.

J-Hope's reputation as the group's mood-maker stems from his bright personality and has earned him the nickname "sunshine" among fans and fellow members.

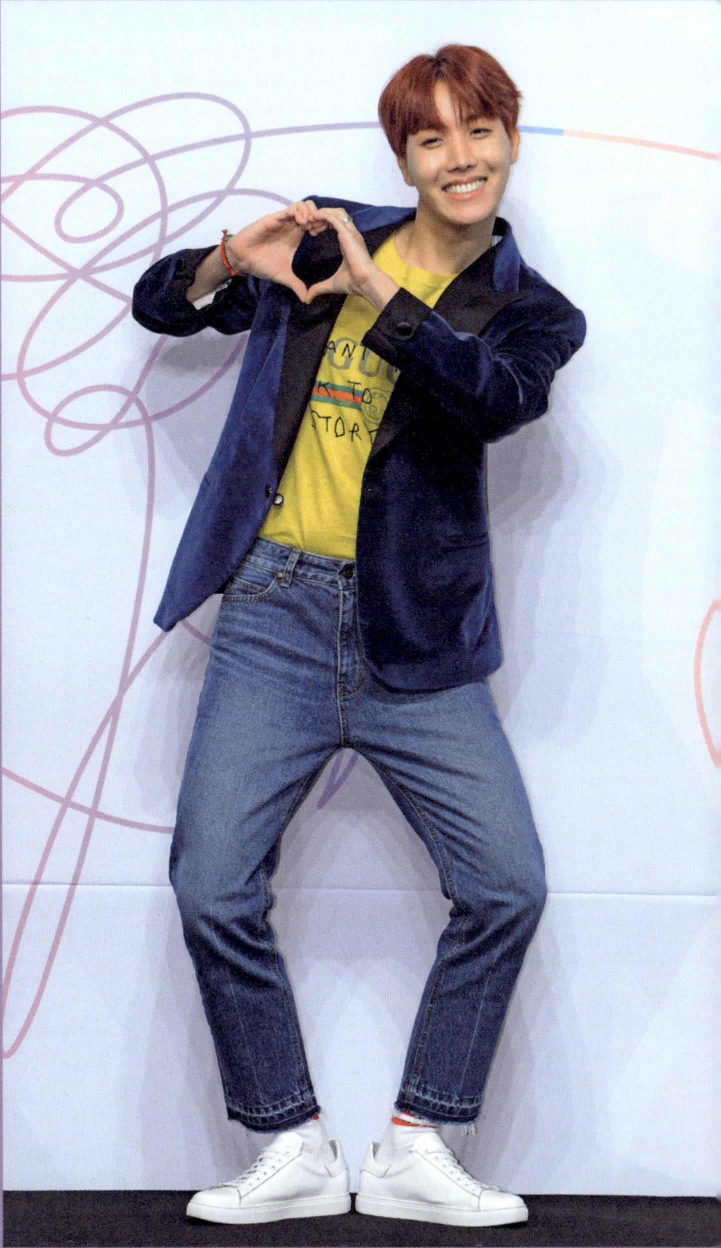

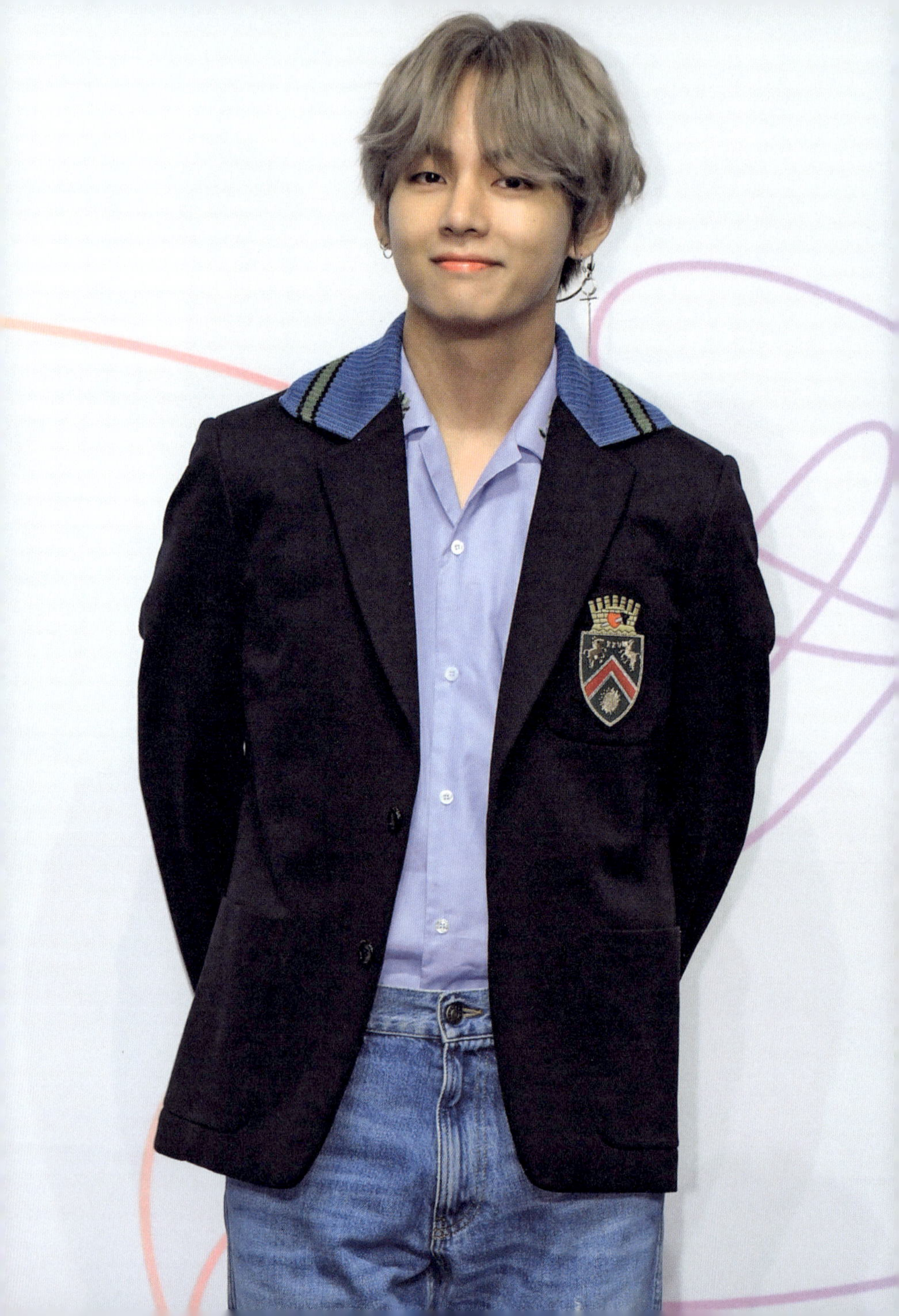

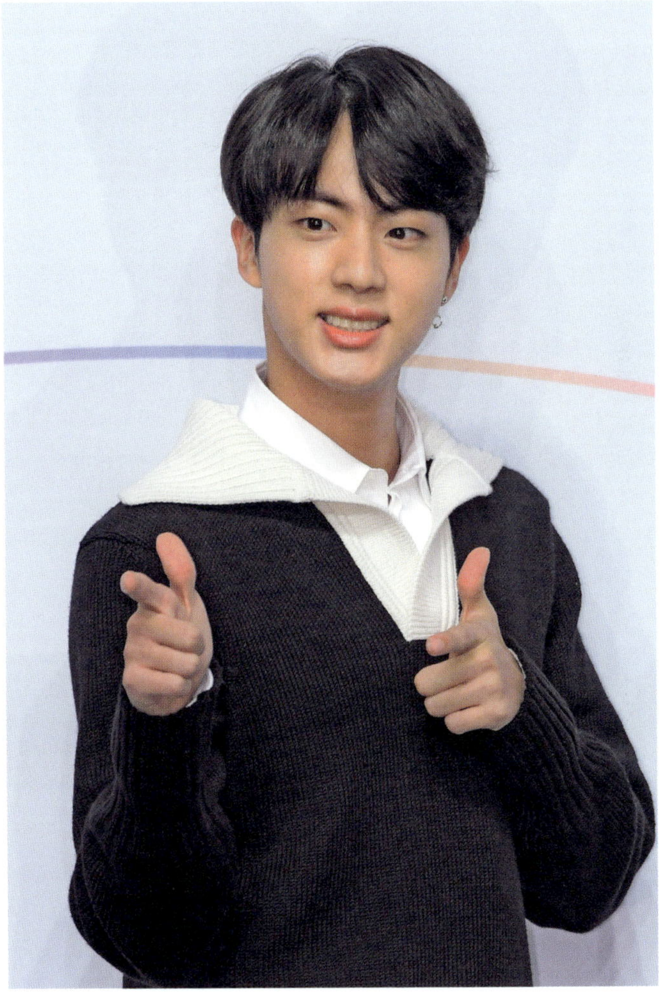

ABOVE The eldest in the group, Jin is one of the more private BTS members and is seen as a supportive, older brother figure.

OPPOSITE Best known for his distinct vocals and charismatic presence, V, wearing a jacket by Gucci, is recognized for his ability to charm and attract new fans.

In 2012 the seventh member was admitted to the group: Jimin (Park Ji-min), who subsequently had the shortest training period of his peers before debuting. Prior to BTS, Jimin was a student in the modern dance department at Busan High School of Arts before transferring to Korean Arts High School.

"When I first joined the agency as a trainee, I didn't have any ambition to be on the team because I didn't think [BTS] was my team", he admitted on Suga's online talk show *Suchwita* in March 2023. However, it was Suga who convinced him to stay on. "I still remember the lights were off, and we were in our beds. I think we woke up because [RM] was snoring, and you were on the top bunk", Jimin recalled of the shared moment in their dormitory. "You [Suga] said, 'You're a good singer and I really want you to be on our team'. That was when my ambition sparked."

"I knew what your tone and your voice would sound like when you sang. No one else on the team had that tone", responded Suga, speaking of Jimin's vocals. "I felt that you could become a singer with a unique voice."

And with that, BTS was complete. On 13 June 2013, all seven members debuted with the song "No More Dream" from their first single album *2 Cool 4 Skool*. The track focused on breaking free from societal expectations and not following the dreams of parents or teachers, but your own, even though the path may be unclear. In the accompanying music video, which has surpassed 300 million views on YouTube, the band's clothing style was edgy and rebellious, reflecting the song's theme of challenging societal expectations.

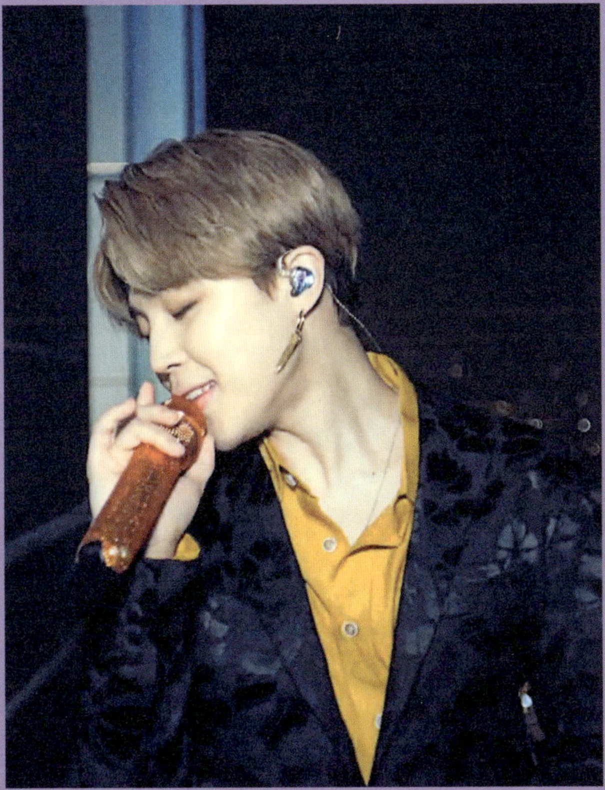

Jimin performing onstage during the 63rd Annual Grammy Awards in 2021. BTS sang "Dynamite".

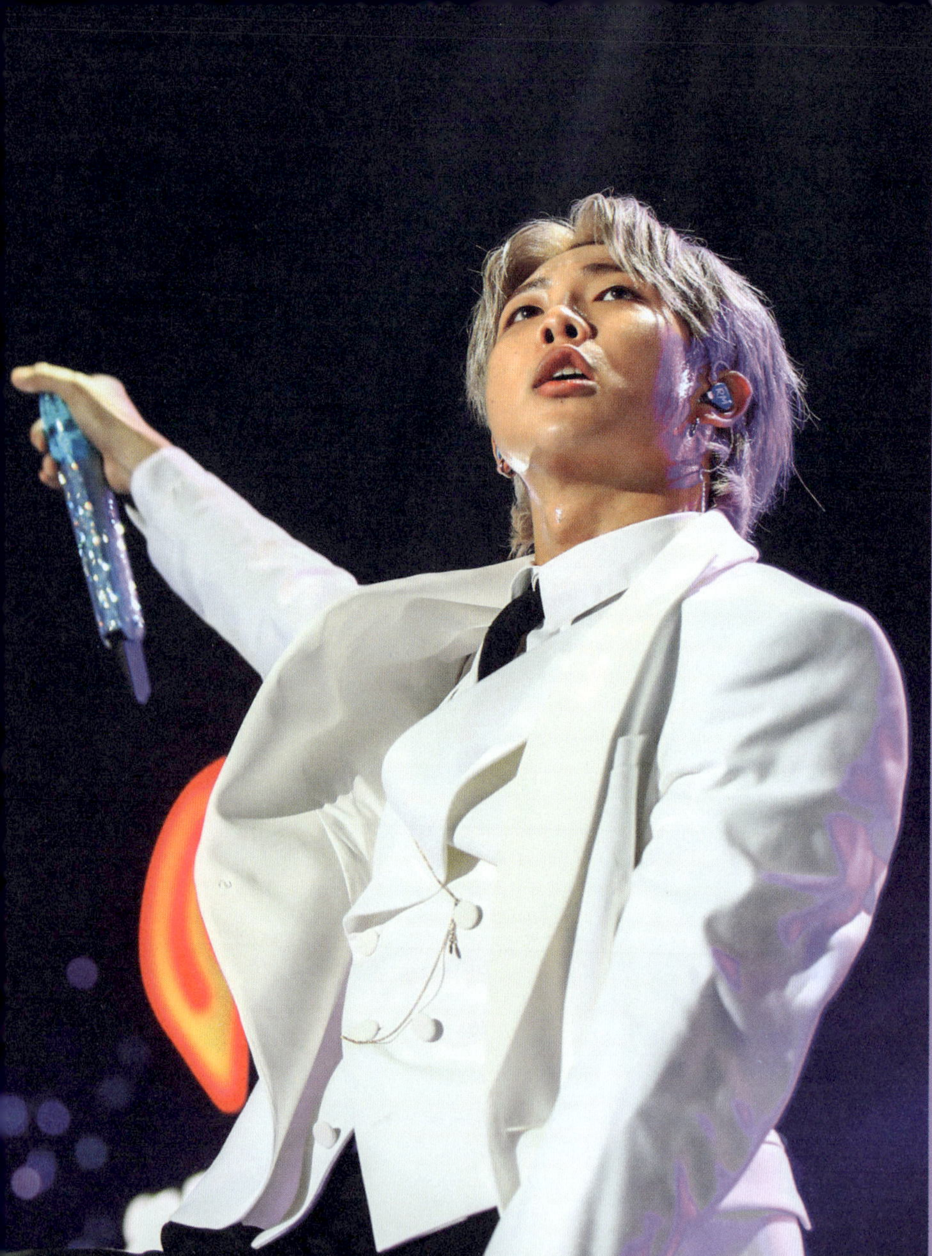

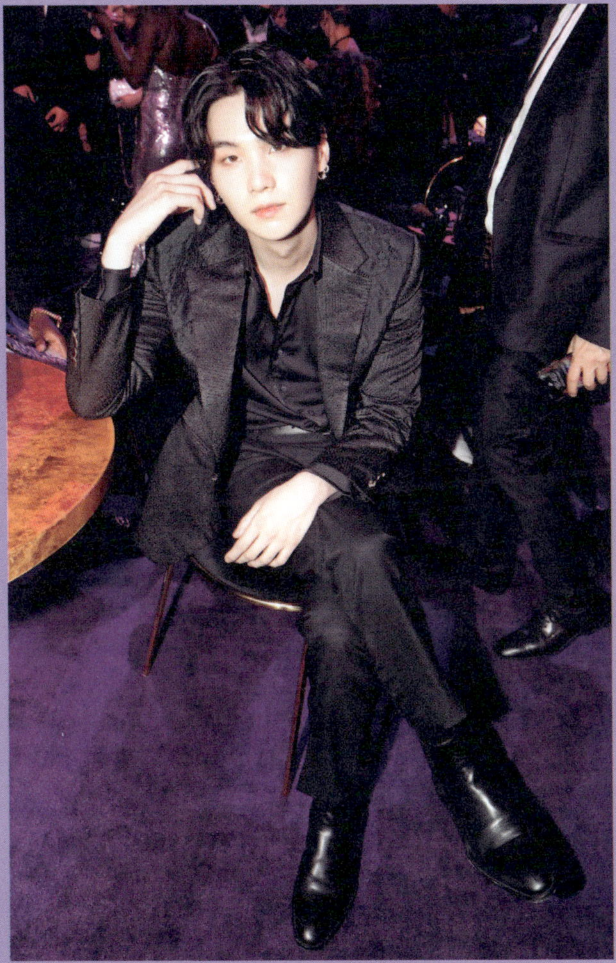

ABOVE Suga sharply dressed at the 64th annual Grammy Awards in April 2022.

OPPOSITE RM performing at the 102.7 KIIS FM Jingle Ball 2019, in Los Angeles, California.

Notably, in the video, BTS members appear to be heavily influenced by American hip-hop style and music icons such as The Notorious B.I.G. and Wu-Tang Clan. It is evident in the bold accessories such as snapbacks, chains and bandanas, which are worn with baggy, monochromatic clothing – many of which were reportedly by insider-favourite streetwear labels of the time, such as Hood By Air, Kokon To Zai and Pyrex Vision. The latter was founded by the late Virgil Abloh, who was also the visionary creator of Off-White and former head of Louis Vuitton menswear. Each member sported a smoky eyeliner look applied to both their upper and lower lash lines. Some also had shaved designs in their hair, adding to the anarchic vision.

While some fans have observed that the "No More Dream" era make-up and styling was in distinct contrast to some of their later, more refined styles, it demonstrated that BTS had exceptionally modern attitudes to fashion early on in their formation – and an experimental dress sense that would continue to evolve.

V and Jin in Louis Vuitton at the 64th Annual Grammy Awards in Las Vegas, Nevada, April 2022.

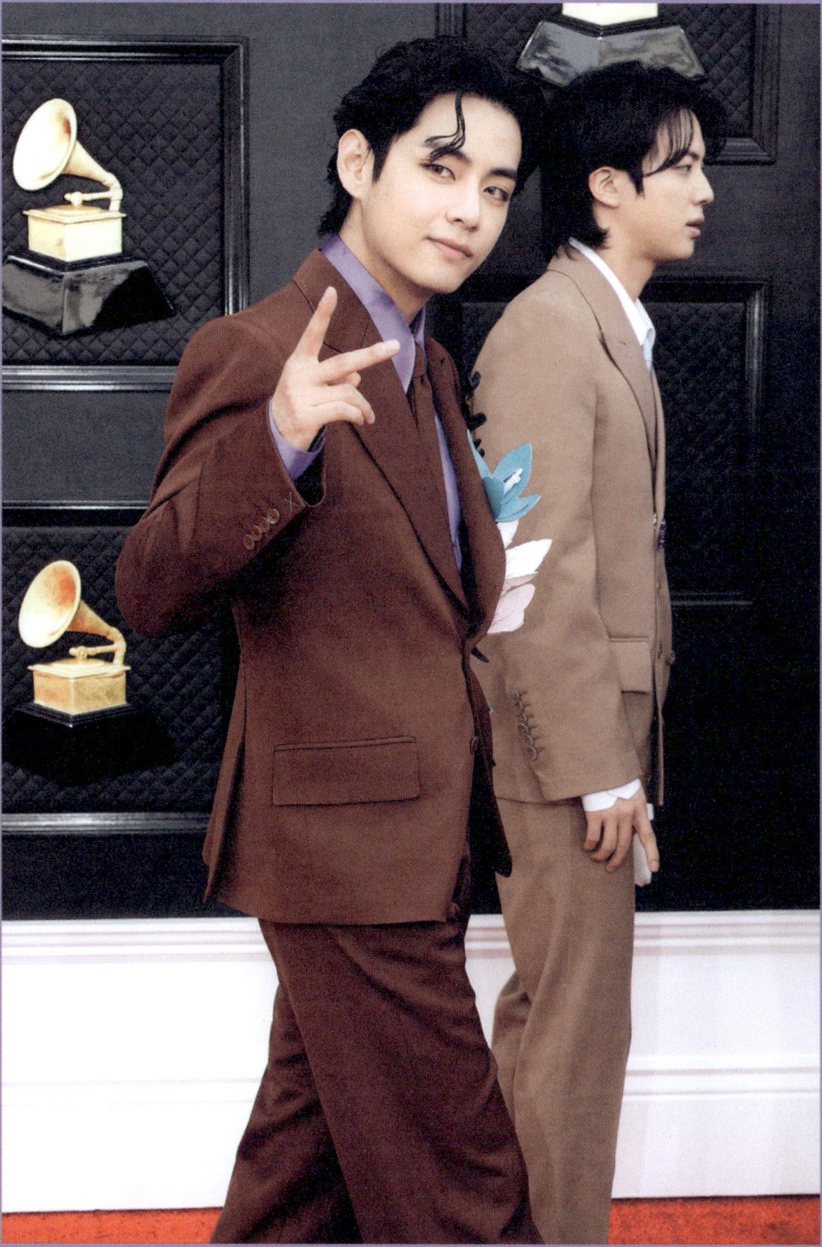

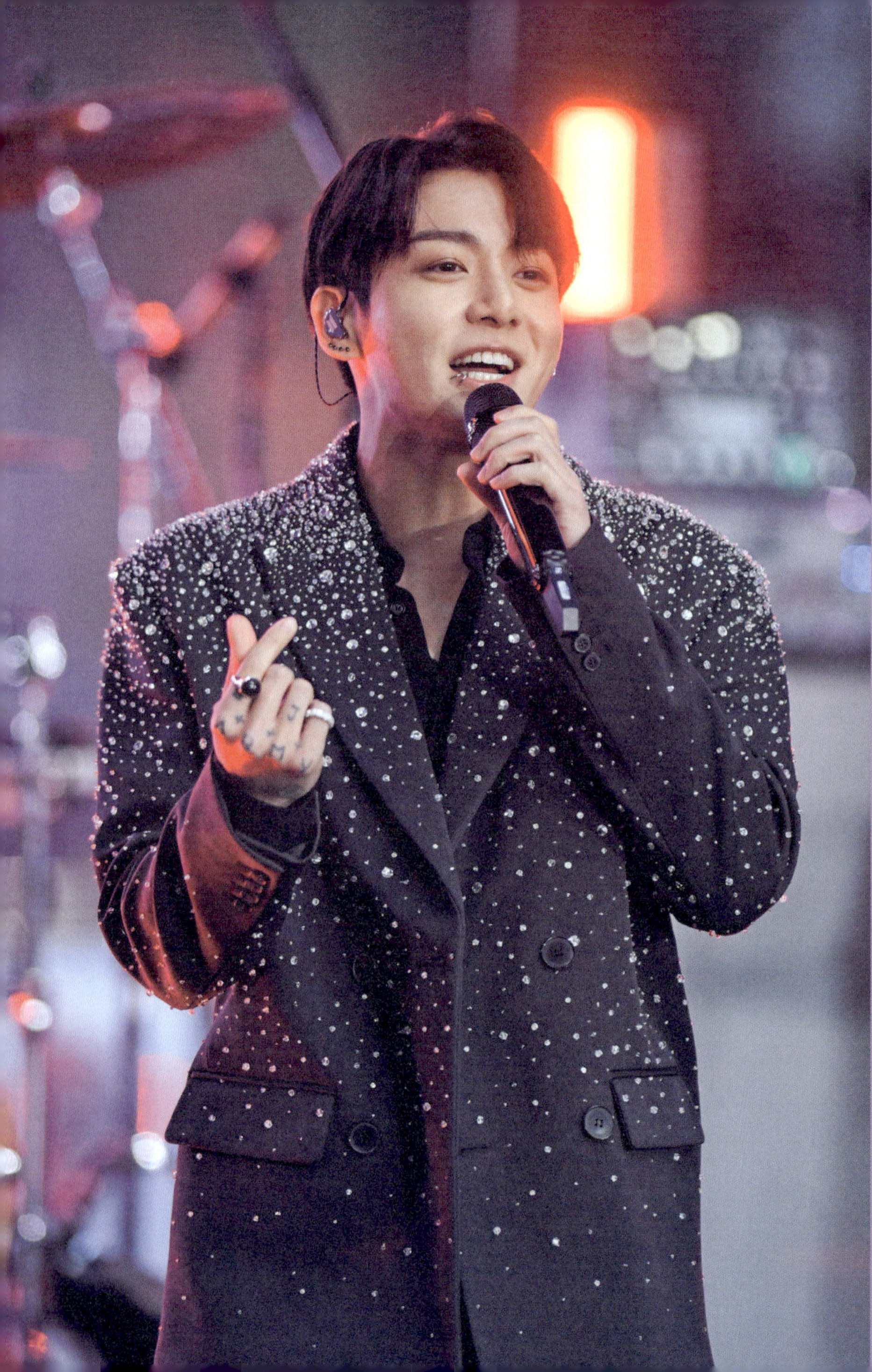

“Frankly speaking, I was confident, *but this is beyond my imagination.”*

JUNG KOOK, *THE TONIGHT SHOW STARRING JIMMY FALLON*, 2023

OPPOSITE Jung Kook performed on NBC's *Today* show at Rockefeller Plaza in New York City, November 2023.

OVERLEAF BTS on the *Good Morning America* Summer Concert Series in 2019. The band also performed in 2021 and 2023.

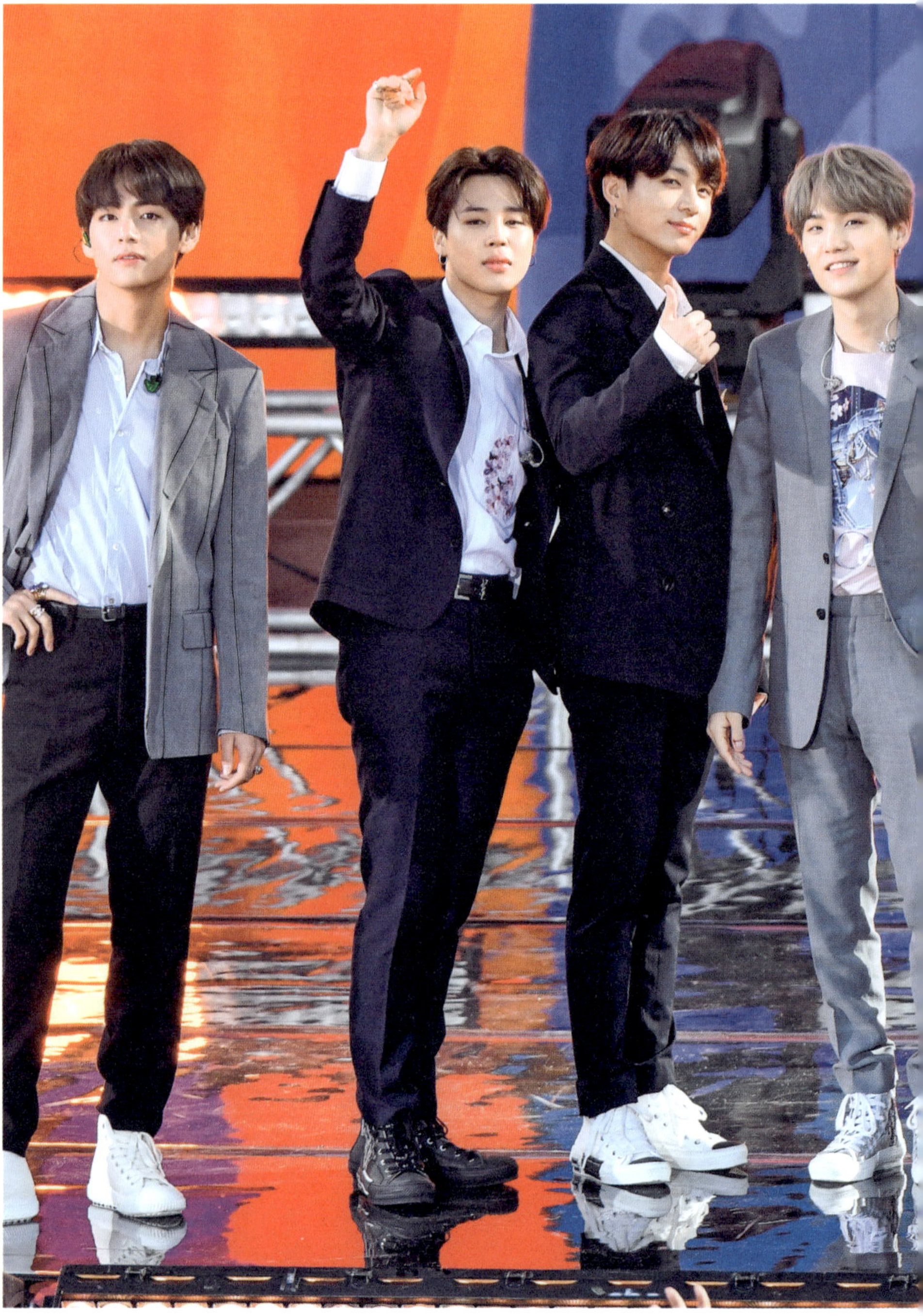

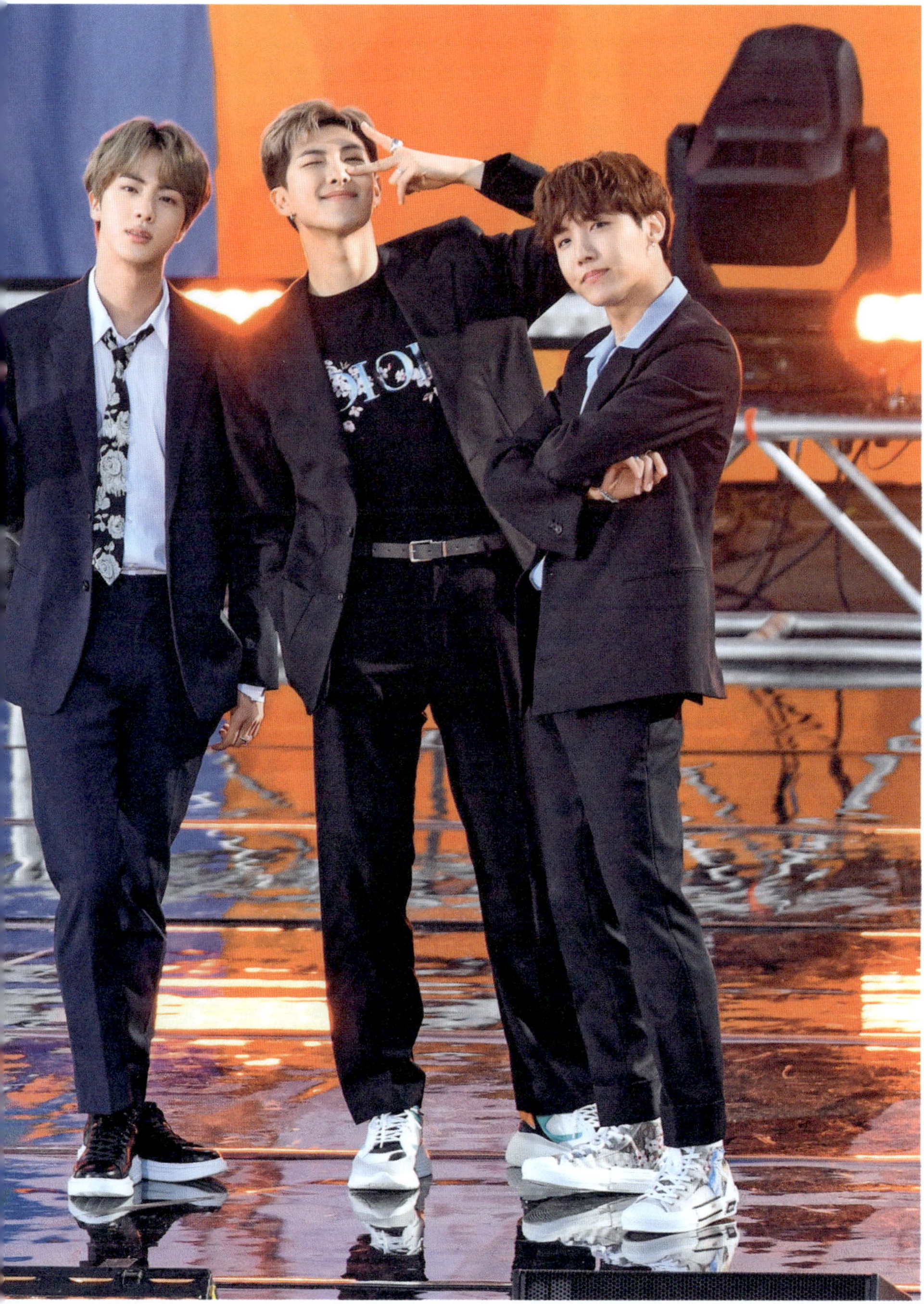

BOOSTING THE

CHAPTER 2

KOREAN WAVE

BOOSTING THE KOREAN WAVE

The prominence of cultural staples such as BTS has been an invaluable asset for South Korea, whose soft power reached new heights in 2020, according to the Carnegie Endowment for International Peace, a non-partisan international affairs think tank.

Following the country's democratization in the late 1980s and the Asian financial crisis of the 1990s, South Korea's former president Kim Dae-jung – whose inauguration was attended by the late singer-songwriter and dancer Michael Jackson – saw an opportunity to invest heavily in culture. Compounded with the relaxation of censorship and lifting of travel restrictions (the South Korean government banned overseas leisure trips for its citizens until 1983), the push to diversify the economy contributed to the global spread of Korean culture – the Korean Wave – which has inadvertently boosted tourism and economic growth.

Once considered by some as emotional and "low culture", the Korean Wave is now a core component of the nation's economic competitiveness. First ignited by the flourishing of local TV dramas, such as *What is Love* and *Star in My Heart*, exported primarily to China and Japan in the early 1990s, Korean culture has since become more visible through the advancement of pop music, smartphones, cosmetics, fashion, food and games.

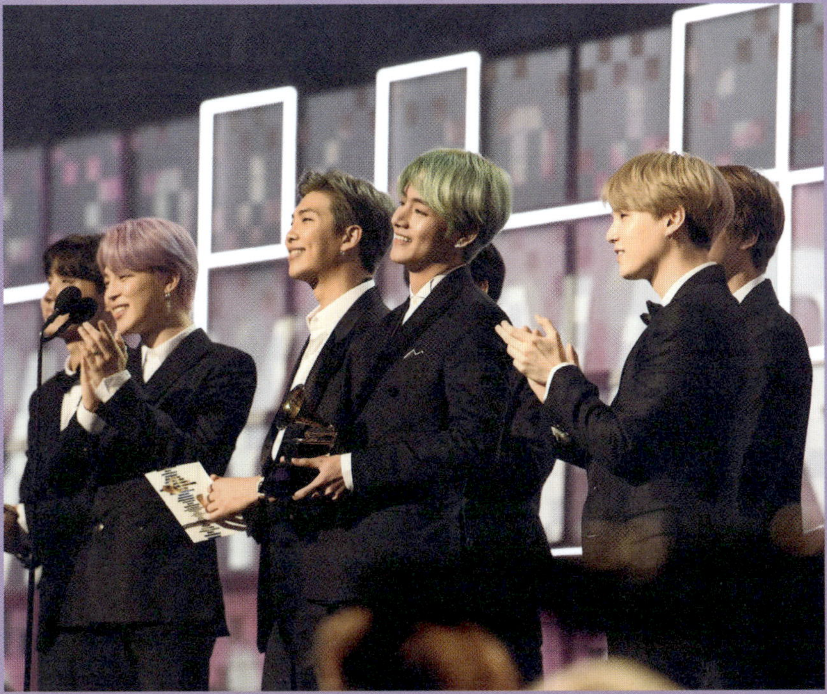

A combination of formal attire – suits by Korean designers JayBaek Couture and Kim Seo Ryong – and colourful hair for BTS at the 61st annual Grammy Awards in February 2019.

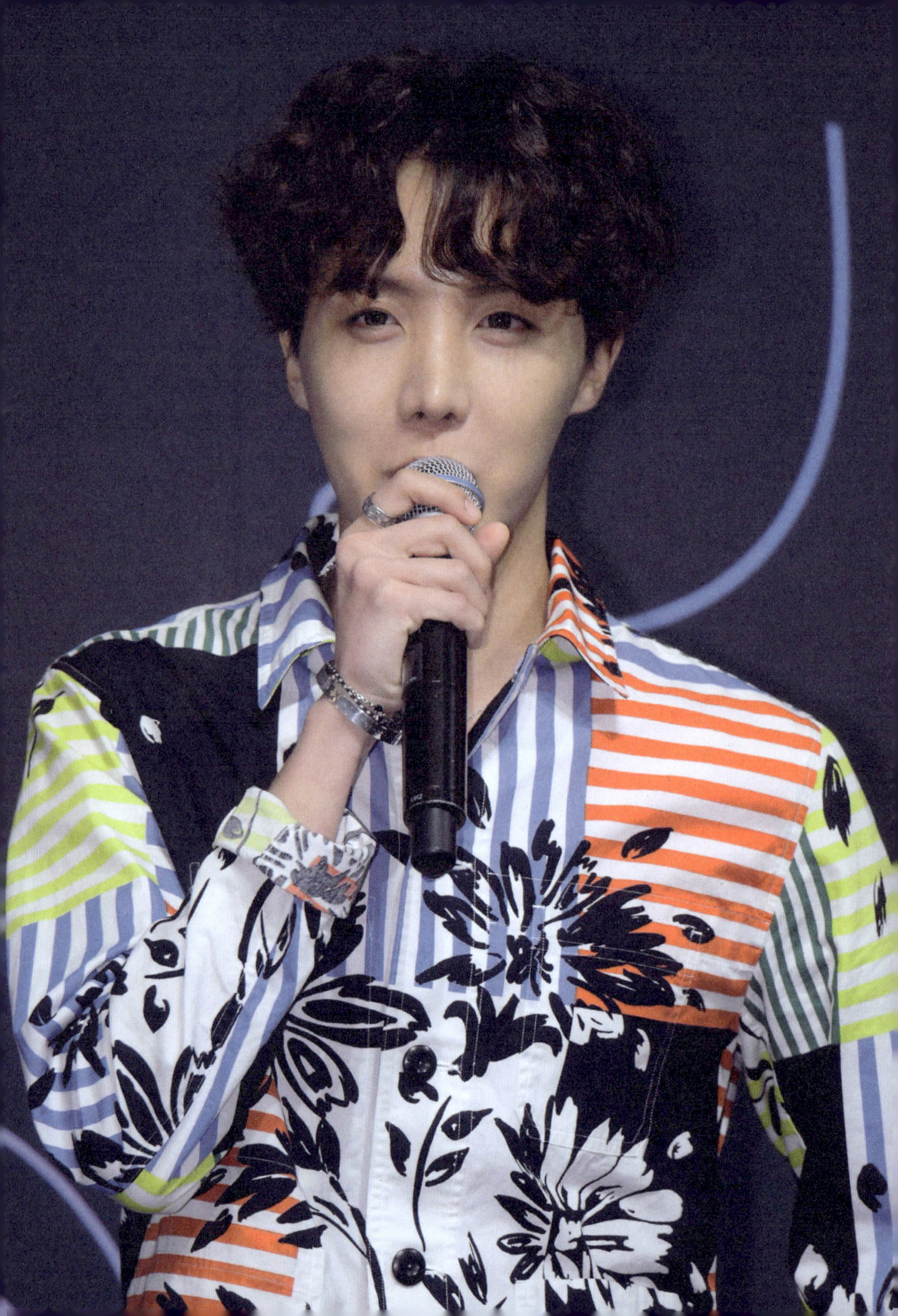

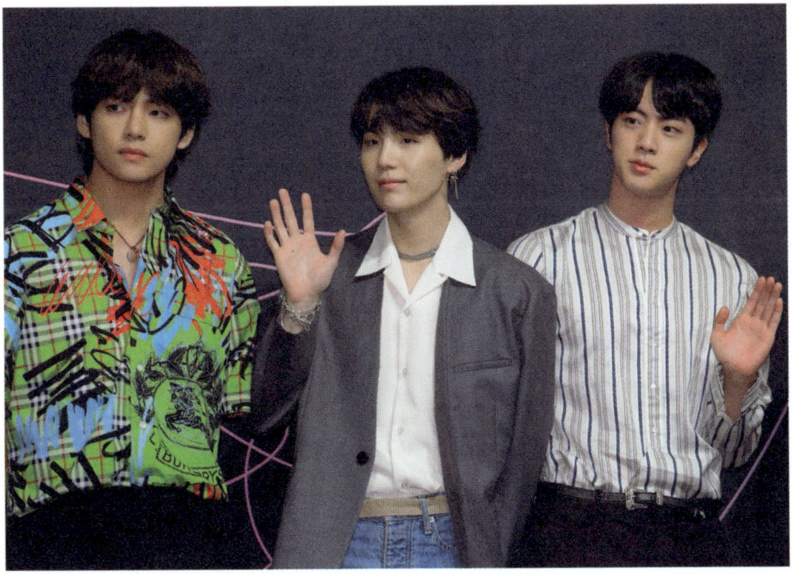

ABOVE V, Suga and Jin at the press conference for the new album *Love Yourself: Tear* in May 2018.

OPPOSITE J-Hope in a jazzy Burberry shirt at the *Love Yourself: Tear* press conference, which was held at the Lotte Hotel in Jung-gu, Seoul.

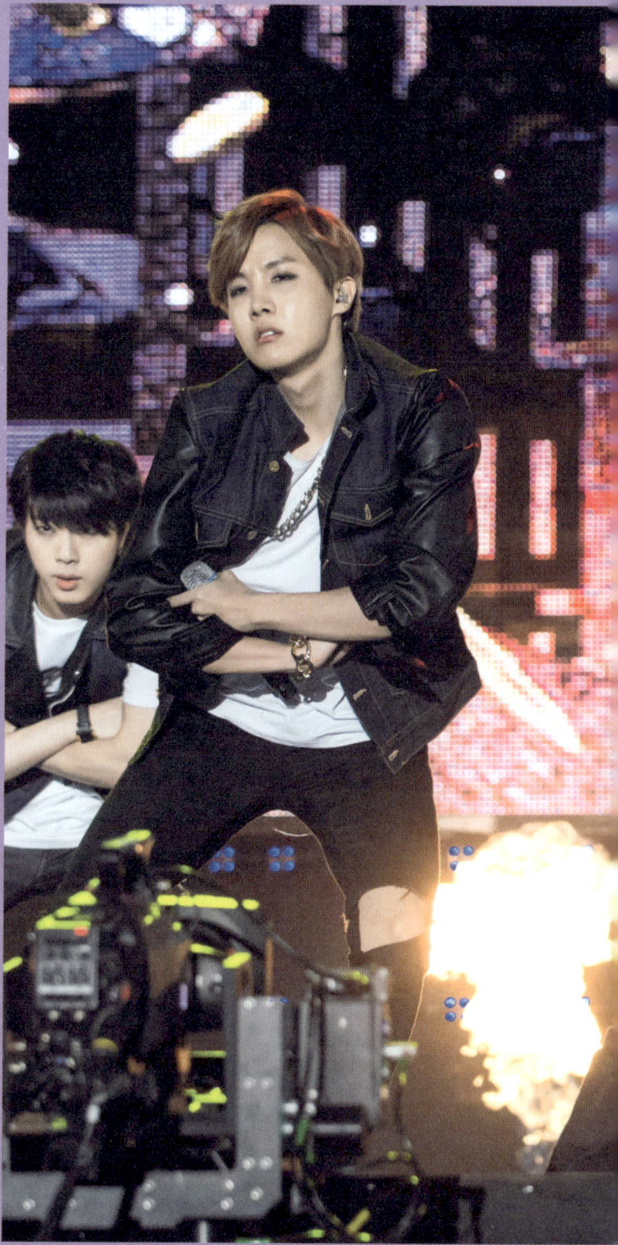

BTS took inspiration from grunge, such as ripped jeans and check shirts tied around waists, when they performed at the 2014 K-pop Expo in Incheon, South Korea.

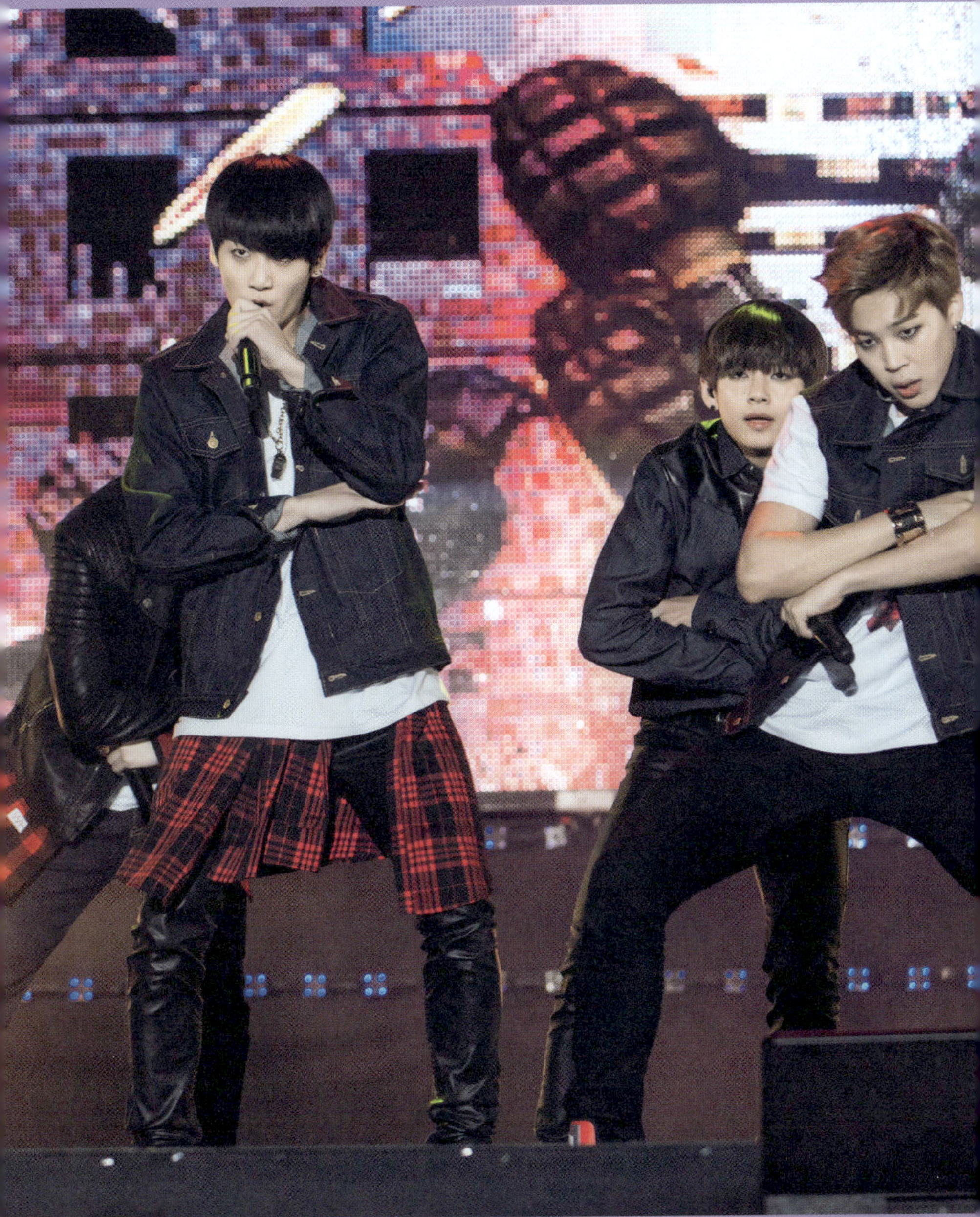

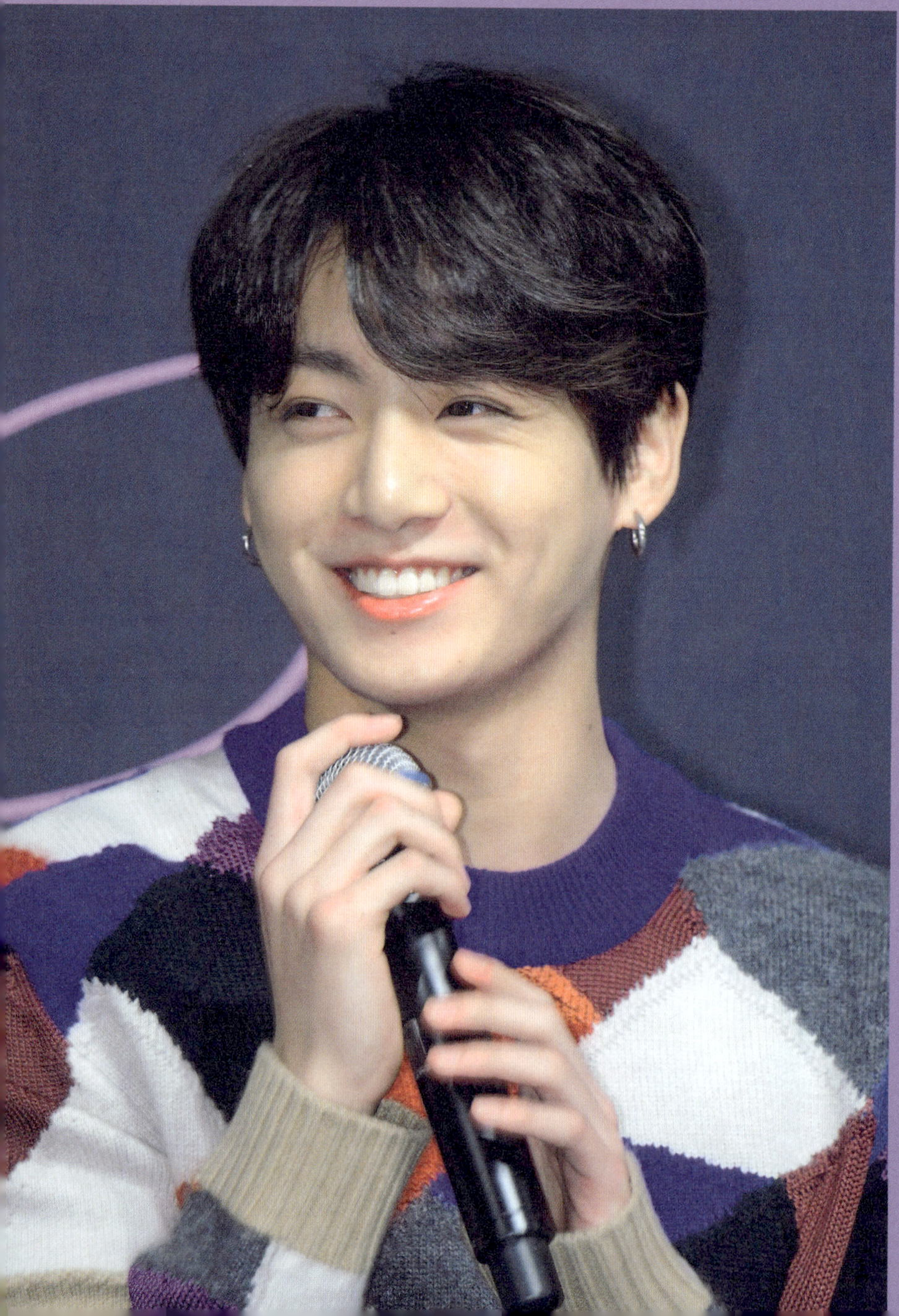

The trend's popularity in the early part of the decade was concentrated predominantly in neighbouring Asian regions, but it now routinely reaches the Americas, the Middle East and Europe. Modern K-dramas such as *Crash Landing on You* and newer offerings such as *The Glory, Squid Game* and even the dating reality TV show *Single's Inferno* have captured the hearts of viewers worldwide, while the rise of global streaming services such as Netflix has widened the reach and popularity of these programmes.

While the South Korean government isn't alone in using culture as a deliberate tool of soft power – several countries, including Saudi Arabia, invest in cultural affairs and exchanges partly to strengthen diplomatic ties and to boost their international reputation – success has been remarkably quick and effective.

Speaking to *The Korea Times* in 2021, Lee Gyu-tag, a professor of cultural anthropology at George Mason University Korea, said: "Today, K-pop is not only for Koreans. Stars and their companies are setting their sights on the global market."

Jung Kook wore a colourful patterned Burberry jumper at the press conference for the band's third album, *Love Yourself: Tear*, released in May 2018.

"In 2005 I was just an elementary school kid and I just wanted to be a rapper."

RM, *ROLLING STONE*, 2022

RM opted for a bright blue jacket at the *Love Yourself: Tear* press conference in May 2018.

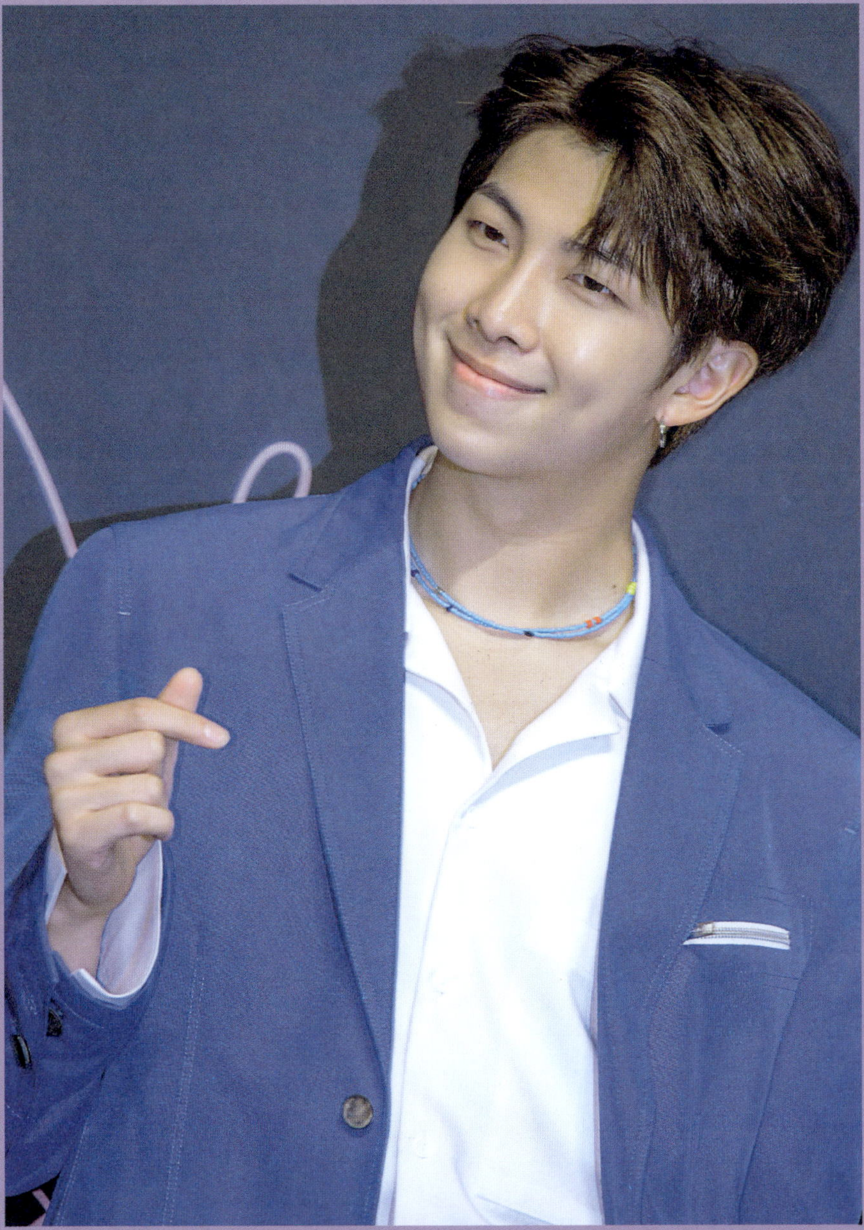

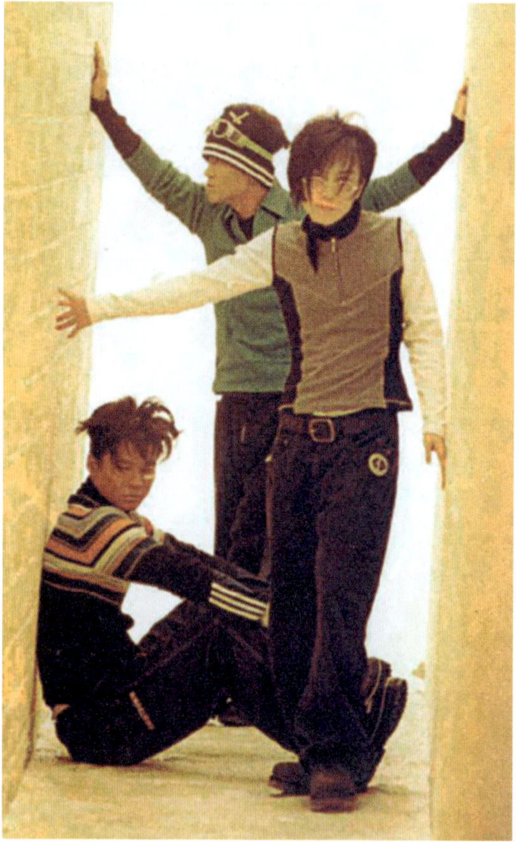

LEFT Trailblazing K-pop band Seo Taiji and Boys (Yang Hyun-suk and Lee Juno) pose for a photograph, circa 1990, in South Korea.

OPPOSITE Psy performed the global hit "Gangnam Style" at the 2022 Seoul Festa "K-Pop Super Live" concert.

One of the first global mainstream Korean pop hits was the 2012 song "Gangnam Style" by South Korean singer-songwriter and rapper Psy. Inspired by the nouveau riche lifestyles associated with the Gangnam district of Seoul, the viral tune and its accompanying music video served as an introduction to K-pop for many global audiences who weren't previously familiar with the genre of music. But Psy was, in fact, already a third-generation K-pop star. To date, there have been at least four different K-pop generations.

The first generation of K-pop is believed to have begun in the early 1990s and lasted until around 2004. Among that initial wave was Seo Taiji and Boys, a South Korean group that consisted of composer and producer Seo Taiji, and vocalist and dancers Yang Hyun-suk and Lee Juno. From 1992 to 1996 the trio experimented with several different genres of Western music and is credited by *Vulture* as being one of the artists who pioneered the use of rap in Korean pop songs.

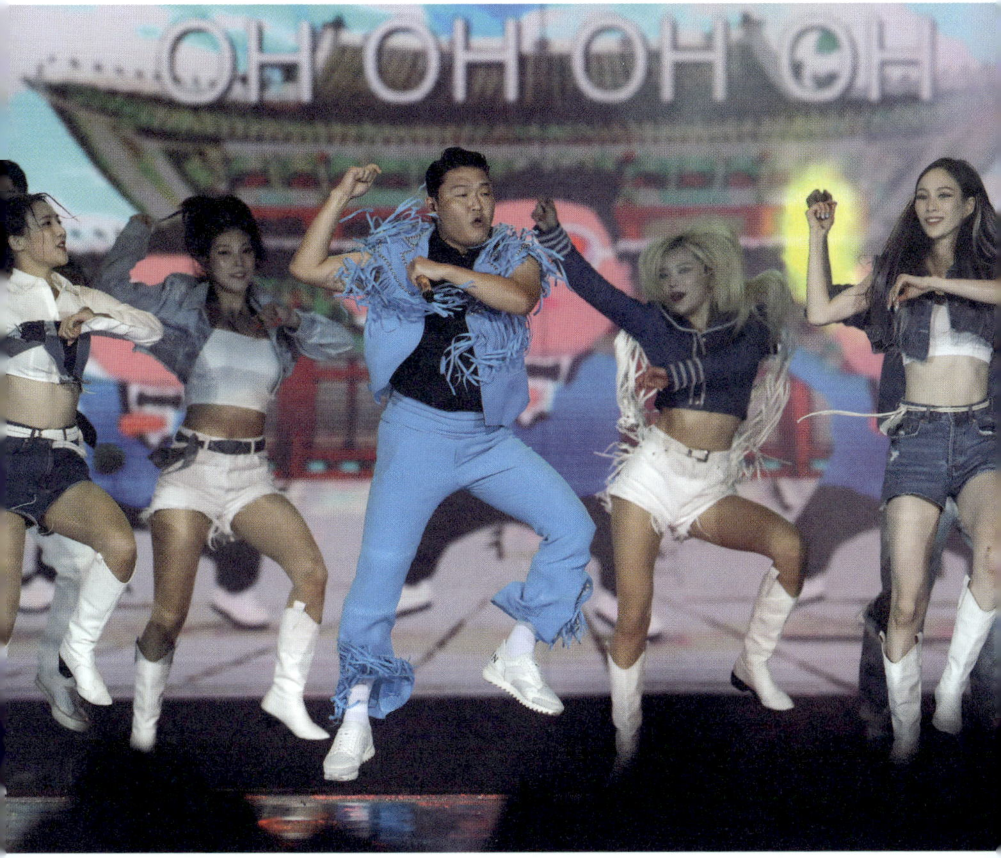

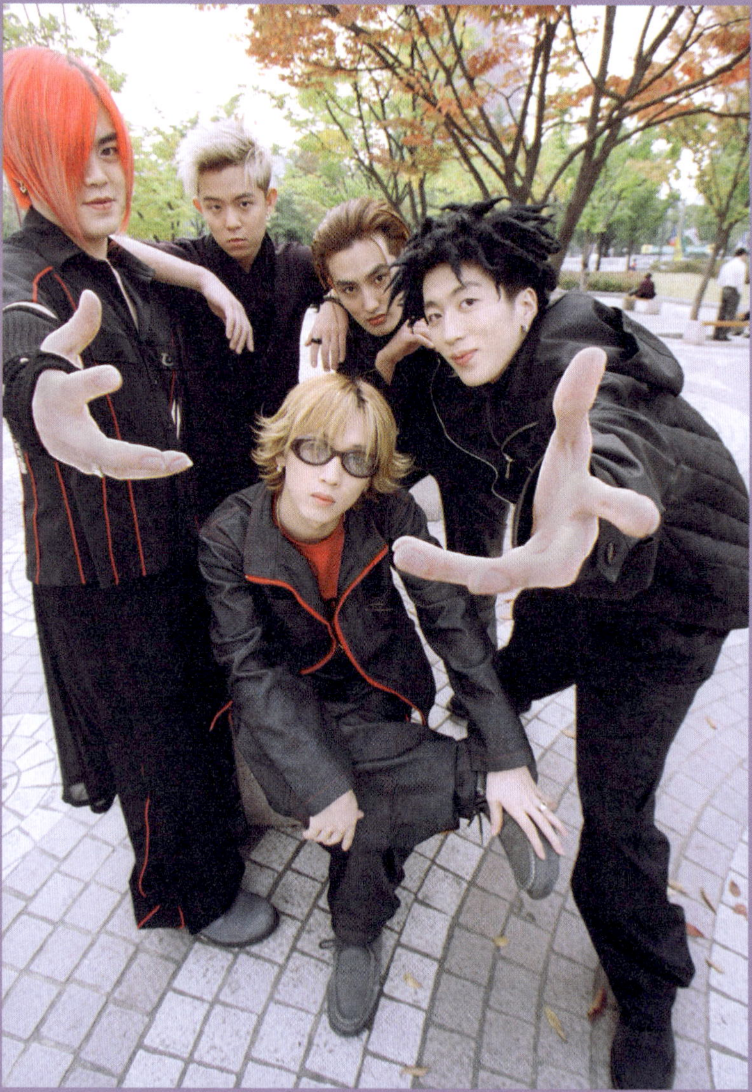

Members of the boy band H.O.T. – one of the first
Korean idol groups – pose for a photo in 2000.

But it was the 1996 debut of South Korean boy band H.O.T. that is widely considered to be the birth of the first Korean idol group. An acronym for "Highfive of Teenagers", H.O.T. launched under the record label and entertainment giant SM Entertainment and had five members: Moon Hee-joon, Jang Woo-hyuk, Tony Ahn, Kangta and Lee Jae-won. And although Seo Taiji and Boys achieved significant popularity in the same decade, it was the idol formula – a focus on perfectly choreographed dance performances and extremely polished visual images – that was established by H.O.T. and which became a defining aspect of K-pop.

Both groups paved the way for many new music acts that also experimented with sound and incorporated choreography into their performances. But as the second-generation era of K-pop stars emerged around 2003 – including Super Junior, 2Ne1, BigBang, Shinee and Girls' Generation – the genre started to expand beyond South Korea and resonate throughout China and other neighbouring Asian countries. With its catchy melodies, synchronized dance moves and relatable lyrics, the K-pop model became heavily commercialized and the idea that it could be a very profitable business was cemented.

By the third generation of acts, from 2013, which included Psy as well as Blackpink, Twice and Red Velvet, K-pop became better known worldwide and the training periods required to debut became all the more intensive. Trainees were expected to spend years practising their dancing, singing, rapping, acting and more, while simultaneously going to school – all in the hope of honing their skills enough to debut and achieve "idol" status. Surprisingly, recruited members were no longer necessarily required to be Korean.

For example, while Blackpink members Jennie and Jisoo are from South Korea, Rosé was born in New Zealand and raised in Australia and Lisa is from Thailand. This international composition has contributed to their widespread popularity and appeal across different countries and cultures.

As K-pop continues to expand, a global presence has become compulsory and fourth generation groups – including Stray Kids, Tomorrow X Together, Enhypen, I-dle, Aespa, Le Sserafim and NewJeans – are expected to communicate with fans globally. Today, idols can audition from practically anywhere in the world, including the United States, Canada, Australia, the UK, Indonesia, Thailand, Japan, China and more. Increasingly, songs are also sung in English or have English catchphrases woven in. And as many standard idol contracts in South Korea have historically spanned seven years, a new generation of K-pop stars, along with any significant roster changes, would emerge on a roughly septennial cycle.

In 2021 Bang hired Scooter Braun, the music manager who made his name launching the careers of Justin Bieber and Ariana Grande, as CEO of the US branch of Hybe (the name Big Hit Entertainment rebranded as that year) and announced a ten-year partnership with Universal Music Group. In 2024, the Netflix docuseries *Pop Star Academy: KATSEYE* aired, featuring the casting and formation of Katseye – the world's first mainstream multiracial girl group modelled on the K-pop framework – under Hybe and Universal division Interscope Geffen A&M Records. The band's single, "Touch", sung entirely in English, came complete with TikTok-friendly choreography and quickly landed on Spotify's Top Hits playlist.

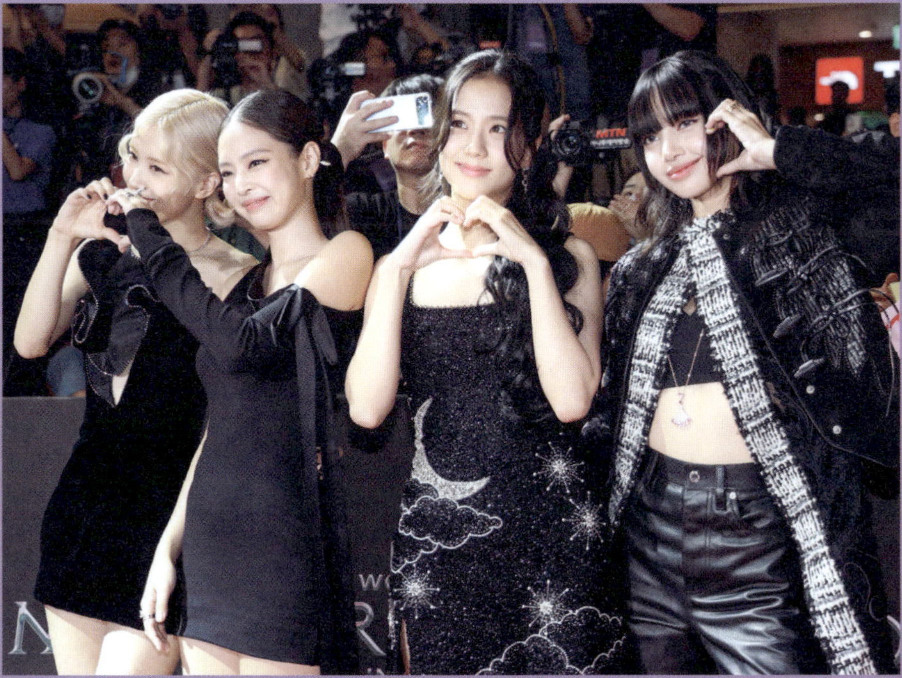

Blackpink at the premiere of their concert film *Blackpink World Tour: Born Pink*, released on 31 July 2024.

"I think BTS really opened the floodgates. Although BTS weren't the first to open the doors

to K-pop worldwide, they were the first to become mainstream."

HELENA KOSINSKI, NIELSEN MUSIC'S GLOBAL VICE PRESIDENT, 2019

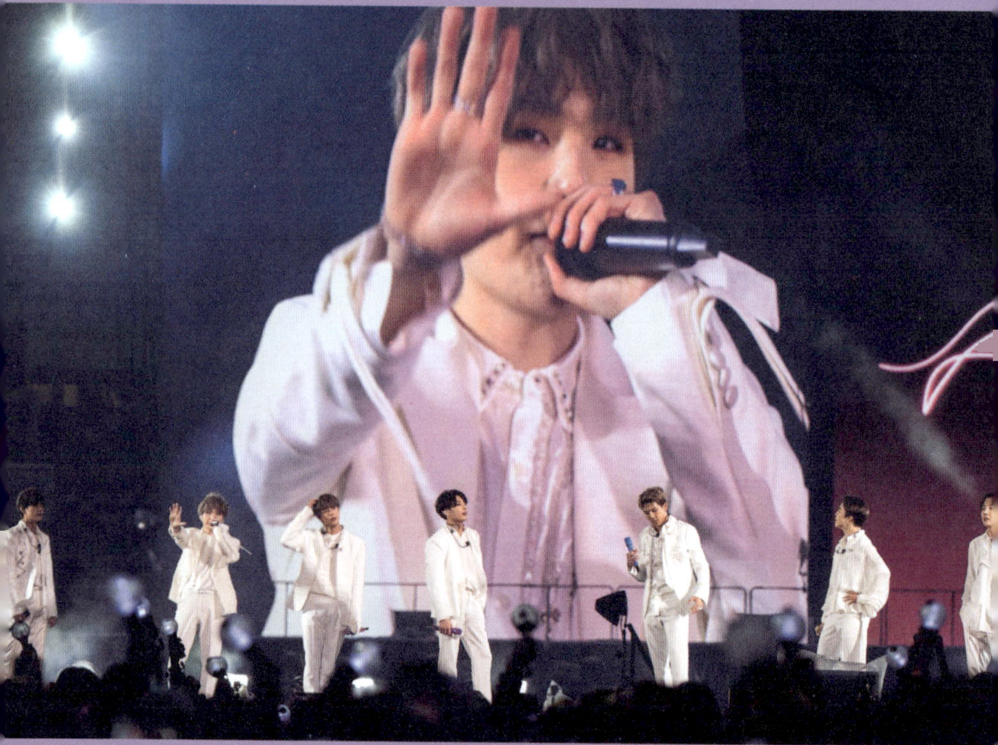

ABOVE BTS performing at Soldier Field, Chicago in May 2019 as part of the *BTS World Tour: Love Yourself*.

OVERLEAF BTS, in Louis Vuitton, all pose during a showcase for the new single "Butter" at the Olympic Hall, Seoul in May 2021.

Indeed, K-pop has evolved from a niche genre to an elaborate global industry, with new talent continually coming to the fore. Yet, BTS – considered to be part of the third generation of K-pop stars – has maintained its status as the most popular boy group, not only in South Korea but across the world, contributing at least $4.9 billion to the country's GDP, according to Youna Kim in her 2022 book *The Soft Power of the Korean Wave: Parasite, BTS and Drama*. And while K-pop has traditionally been dominated by the "big three" entertainment companies (SM, YG and JYP) since the mid-1990s, BTS (which continues to operate under Hybe) has created a global phenomenon that is more widely recognized and influential.

"Although BTS weren't the first to open the doors to K-pop worldwide, they were the first to become mainstream", said Nielsen Music's global vice president Helena Kosinski in 2019, as reported on koreaboo.com.

"We have to consider ourselves not just better [than other K-pop acts], but the best", RM said in an interview with Seth Abramovitch in *The Hollywood Reporter* that same year. "When we're out there on that stage, we're there to conquer. We think we're the ones."

BTS started to gain real traction in the USA around 2017 and grew from there, helped by collaborations with international performers including Halsey, Nicki Minaj, Ed Sheeran, Coldplay and Charli XCX. Their ability to stay competitive is also due to their loyal fans. The internet has played an enormous part in the success of the group, with social media in particular allowing BTS members to connect with their audiences on a personal level – something almost unheard of among the polished and often remote K-pop acts that preceded them.

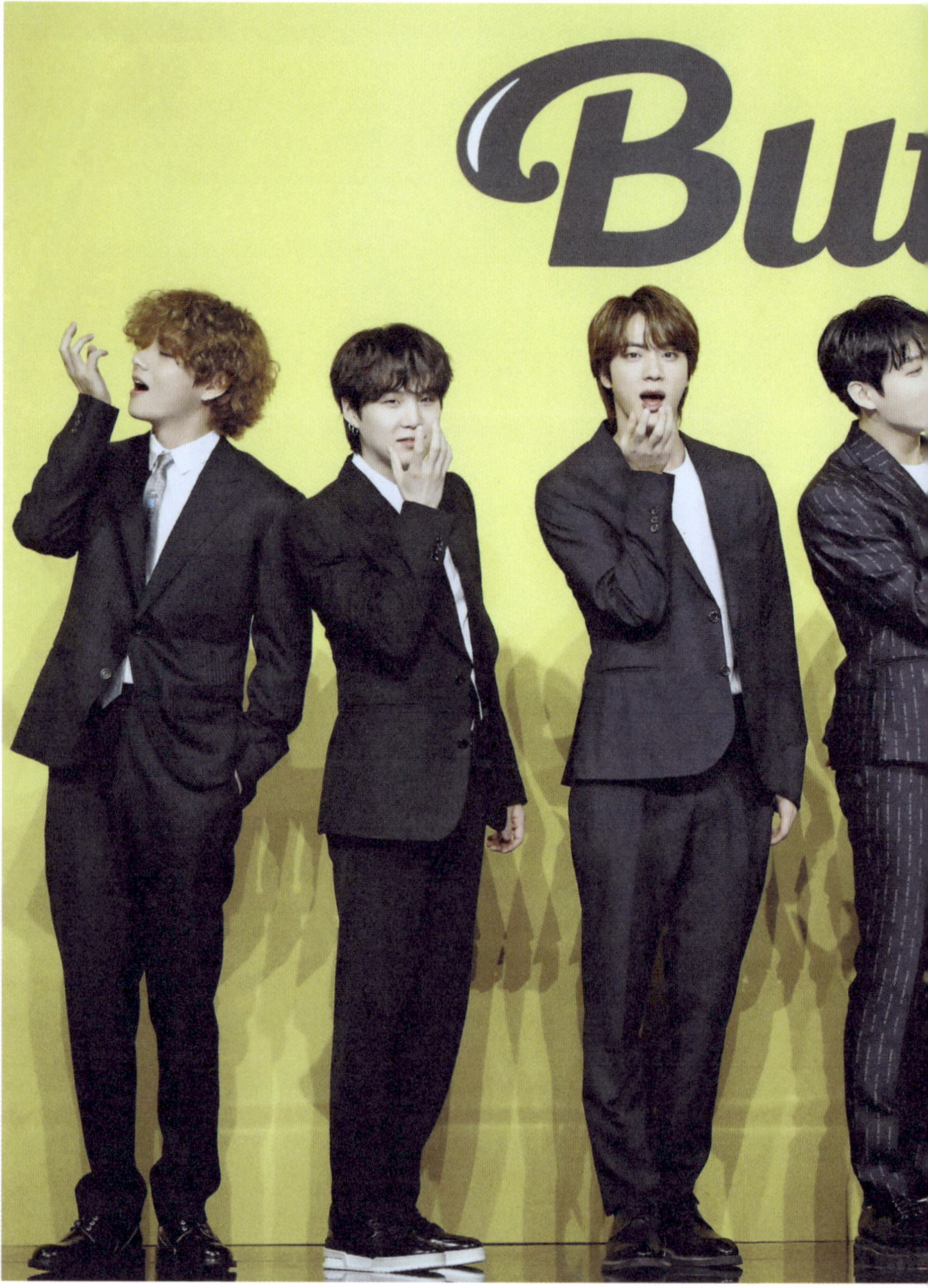

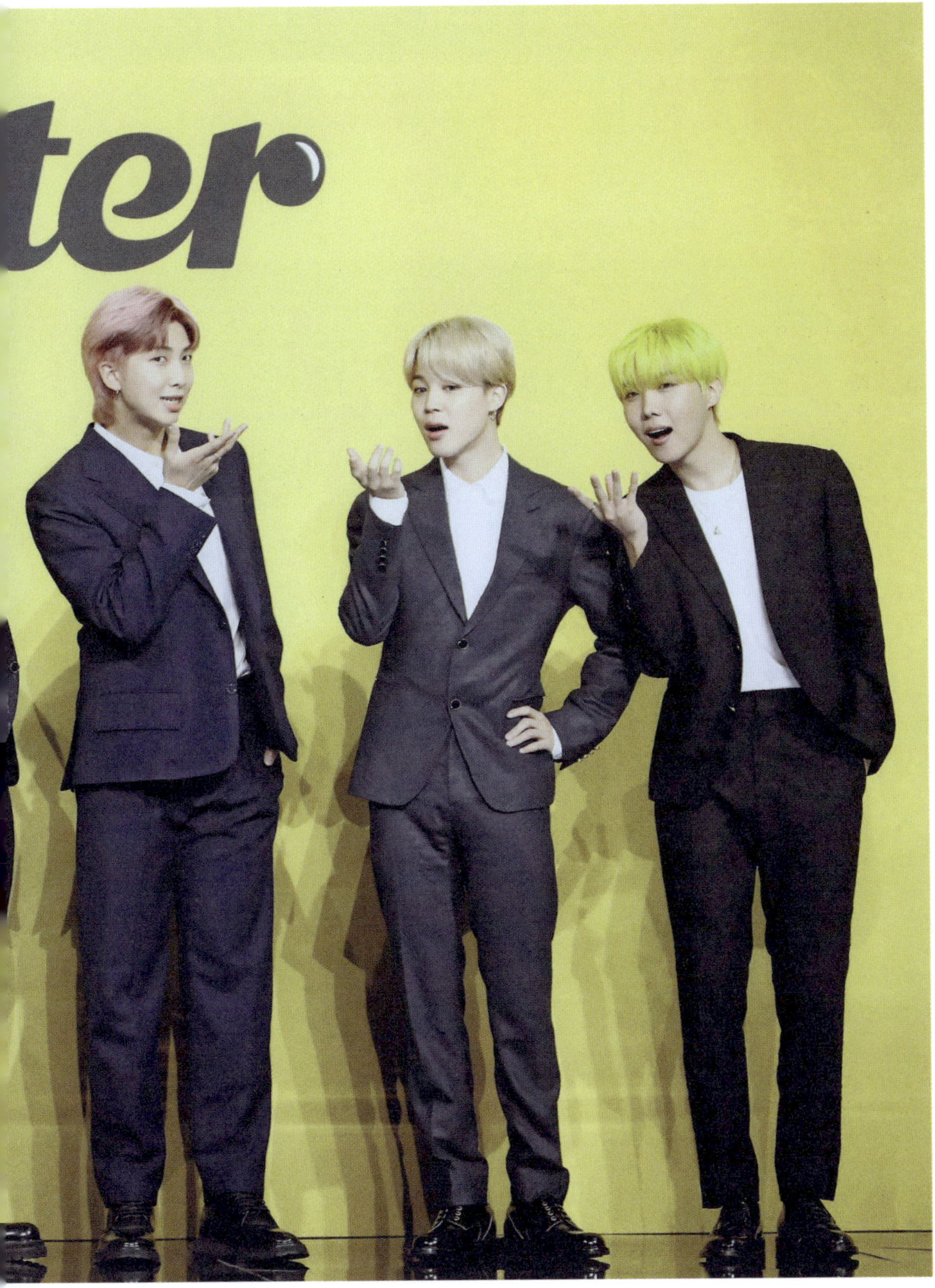
ter

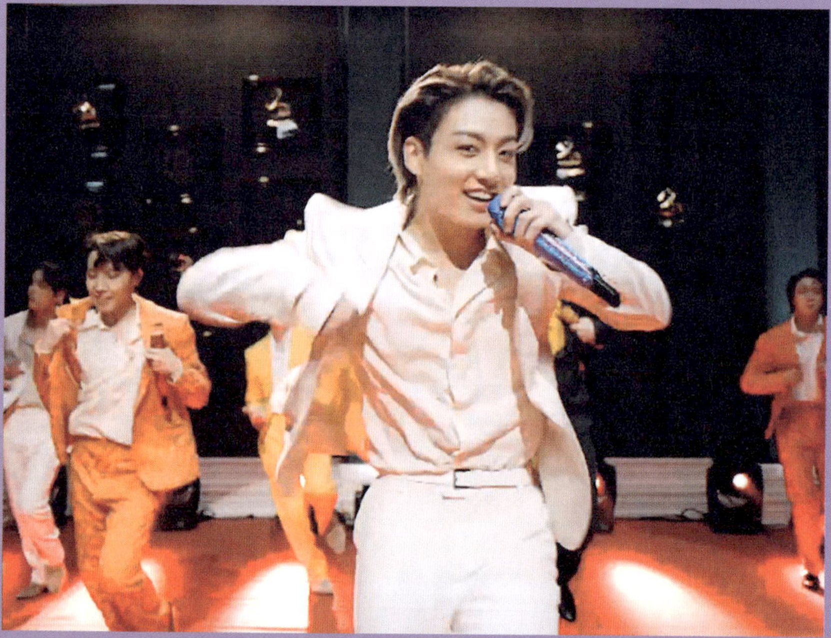

Jung Kook (front) and fellow BTS members at the 63rd Annual Grammy Awards in March 2021.

"We chose this song to cheer everyone up and comfort everyone..."

SUGA, ON "BUTTER", ZANE LOWE INTERVIEW, 2021

The BTS core fan base – known as ARMY, an abbreviation of "Adorable Representative M.C. for Youth" – usually show up in person, enthusiastically queuing (sometimes for days) for tickets and ensuring sold-out stadium concerts, as seen at the Rose Bowl Stadium in Pasadena, California, in Wembley Stadium in London and so on. They're also responsible for some of the hundreds of millions of dollars spent in annual sales on the band's merchandise, which includes the ARMY Bomb, the official light stick used by BTS fans.

That enthusiasm extends to the pre-owned sector: while K-pop-related products are the most popular category on globalbunjang.com, one of South Korea's largest second-hand trading platforms, the most searched for artist is BTS, according to an article in *The Korea Times*. The actual number of transactions of BTS items is also the highest – the highest-priced item traded on the platform in 2024 was Jimin's photo card, which sold for 3 million won (£1,600/$2,200) – highlighting ARMY's influence even during BTS's hiatus as a group.

Online, ARMY is one of the most active communities in existence. The band counts 45 million followers on X, 77 million on Instagram and 73 million on TikTok. Such is the vigour of BTS's fandom that, according to the BBC, in 2017 supporters cast an astounding 300 million online votes to ensure that the group won the *Billboard* award for Top Social Artist, beating internationally known names such as Justin Bieber (who, at the time, had more than 100 million followers on X) and Ariana Grande (at the time the third most followed account on Instagram).

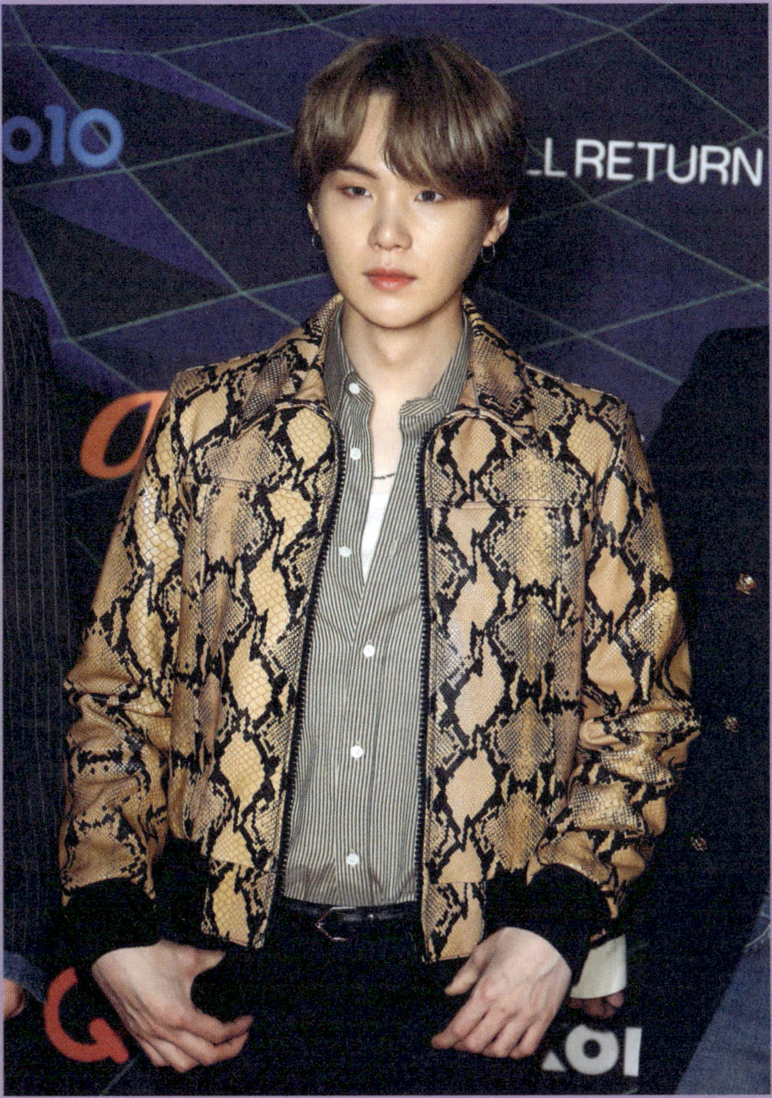

Suga in a snakeskin-patterned Celine bomber jacket at the 2019 Mnet Asian Music Awards in Nagoya, Japan in December 2019.

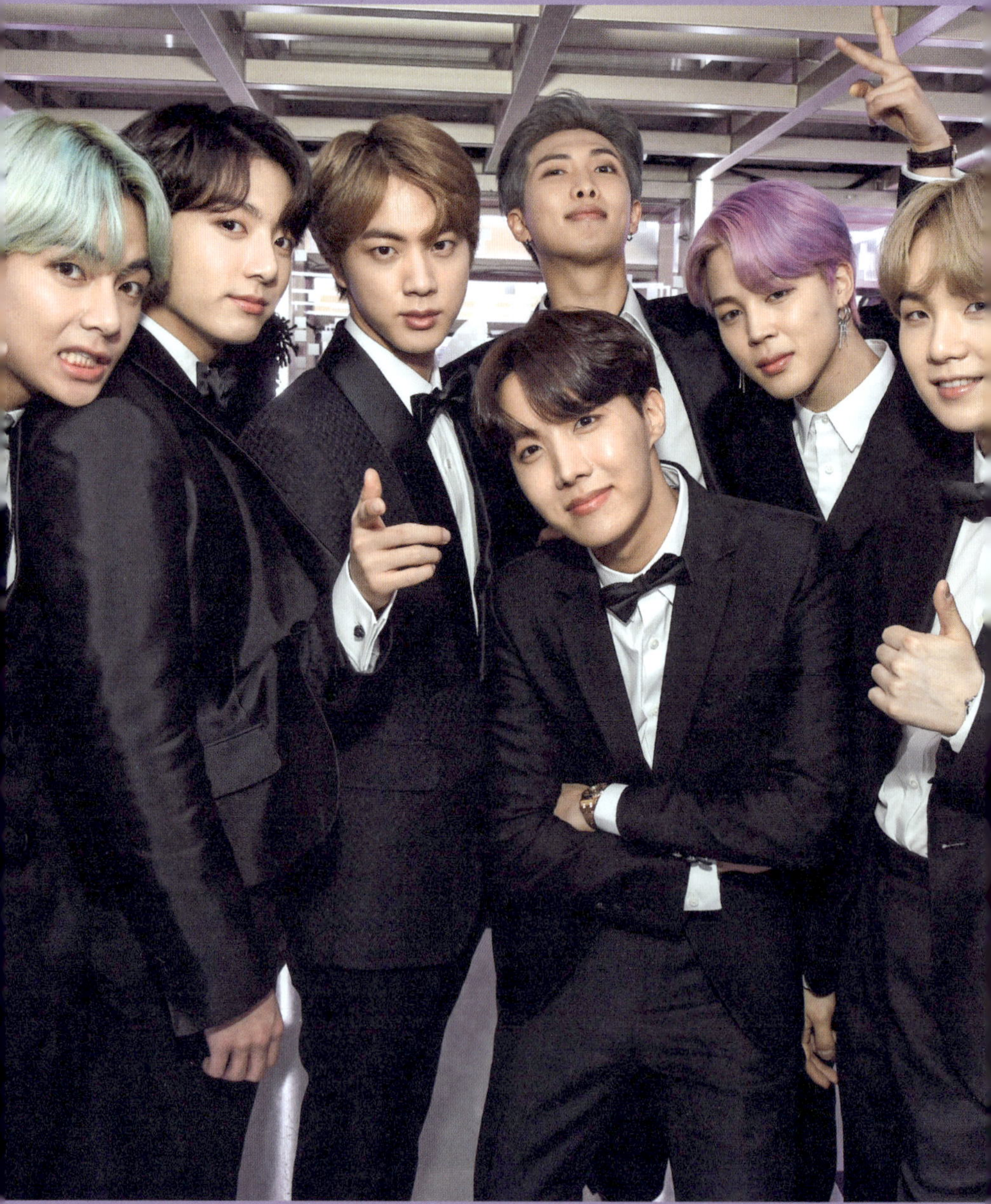

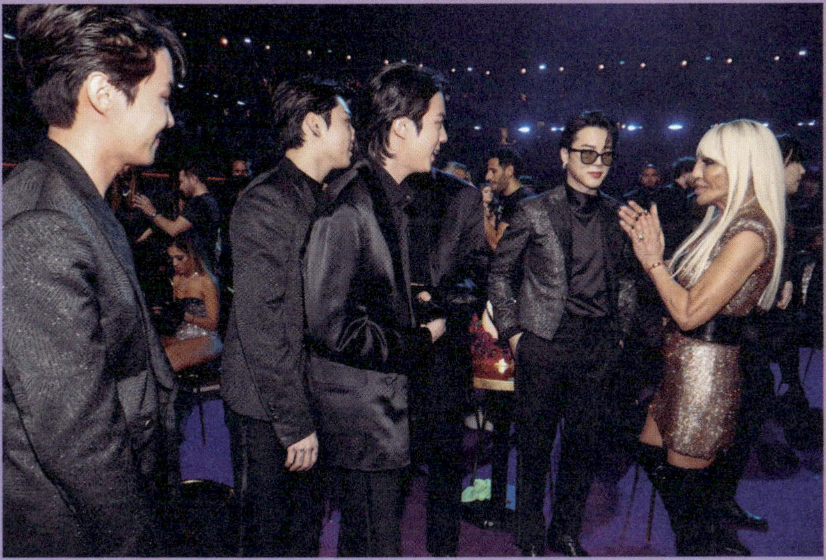

ABOVE J-Hope, Jung Kook, Jin, Jimin and Donatella Versace (right) at the 64th Annual Grammy Awards in April 2022.

OPPOSITE BTS backstage at the 61st Annual Grammy Awards in Los Angeles, California, 2019, wearing suits from JayBaek Couture and Kim Seo Ryong.

"I don't ever want to lose my principles. *I know it's impossible to always do the* right thing, *but for me, it's* very important *to act with honour."*

V, *GQ AUSTRALIA*, 2021

Black...: V on NBC's *The Today Show* in New York, in February 2020 in a Valentino white-collared coat.

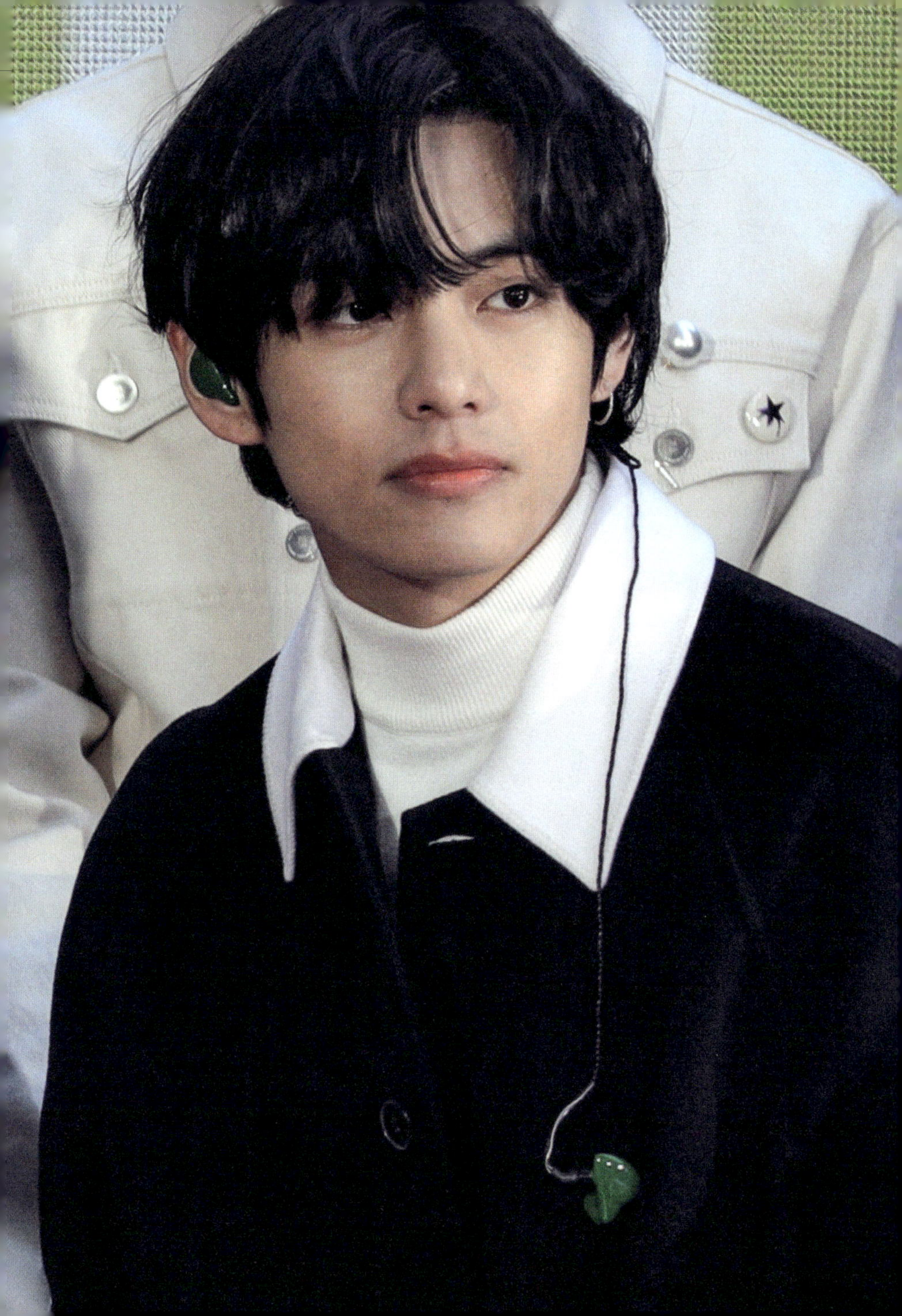

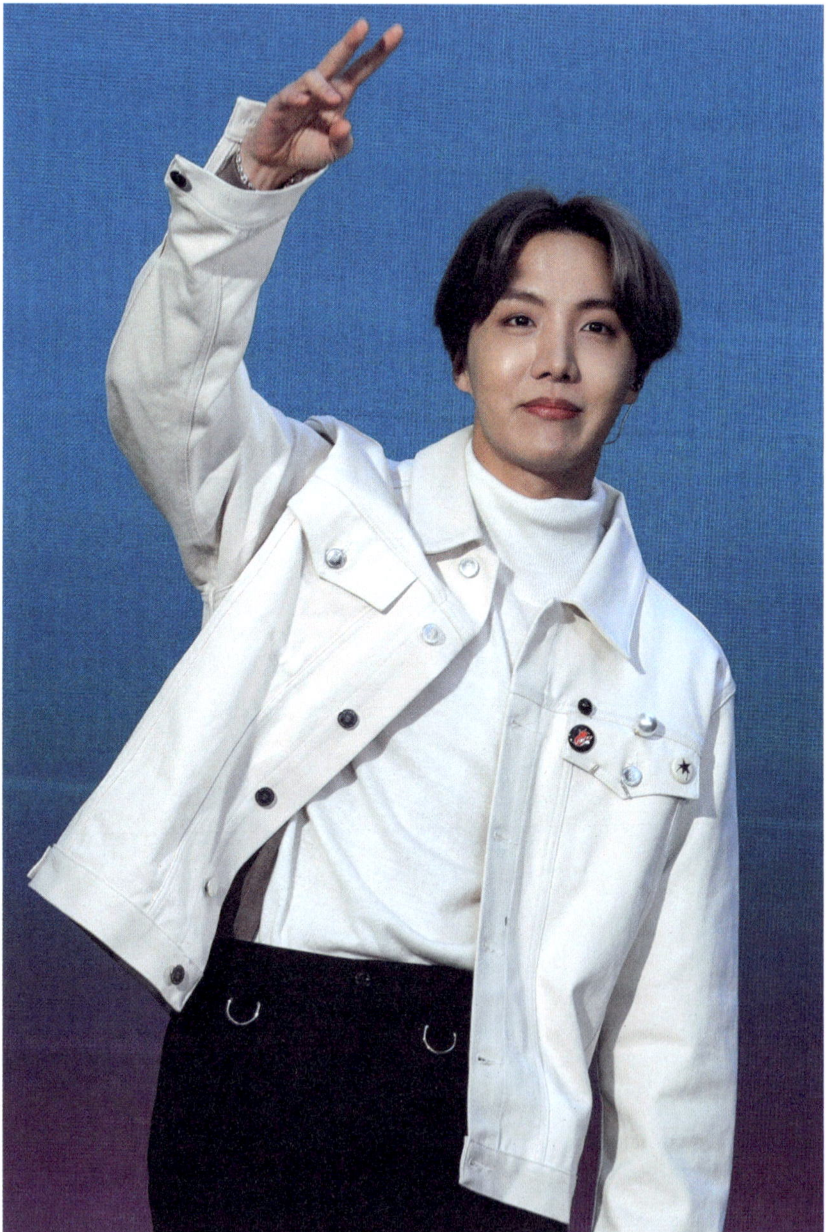

Grace Kao, the IBM Professor of Sociology and a Professor of Ethnicity, Race and Migration at Yale University, sees this reaction as a result of the band's commitment to their work and their fans. "These young people have trained for such a long time that, by the time they debut, they're professionals. So, I think that is really unique," she said in an original interview for this book. "They also have all kinds of live interactions with their fans, such as spending their birthdays with their followers online. Fans feel like they have a lot of interaction and can communicate or complain to the company about things they like and don't like. Those are some of the ways that they're very different to Western pop stars."

Recognizing the enthusiasm surrounding BTS, Suga told BBC Radio 1 in a 2020 interview: "I think we're so lucky to be born at the right time. Without social media, we wouldn't have been so successful."

OPPOSITE ... and white: J-Hope in a Raf Simons denim jacket on *The Today Show* in New York, in February 2020.

OVERLEAF Photos of J-Hope outside a cafe near Hybe Corporation (known as Big Hit Entertainment until 2021).

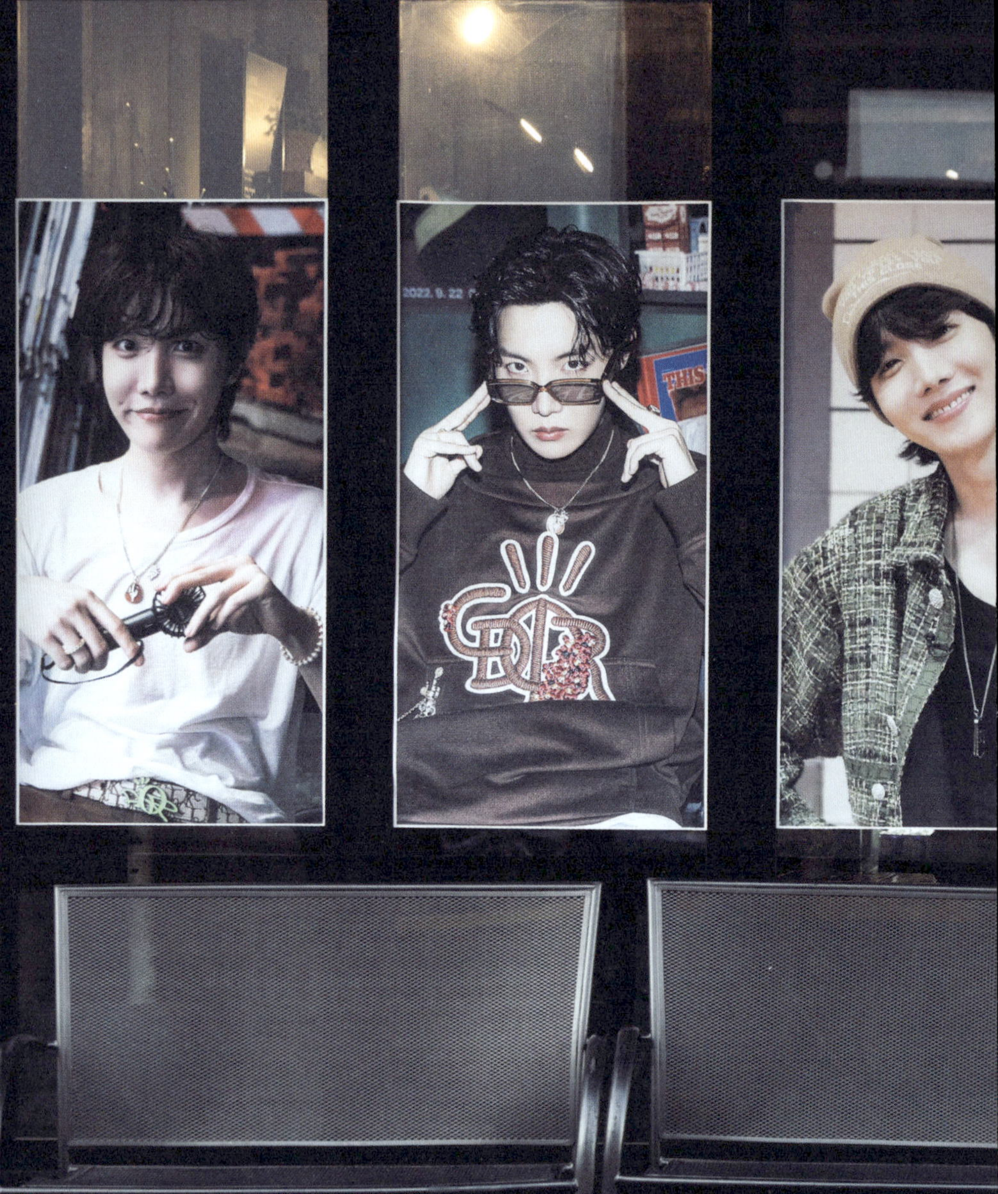

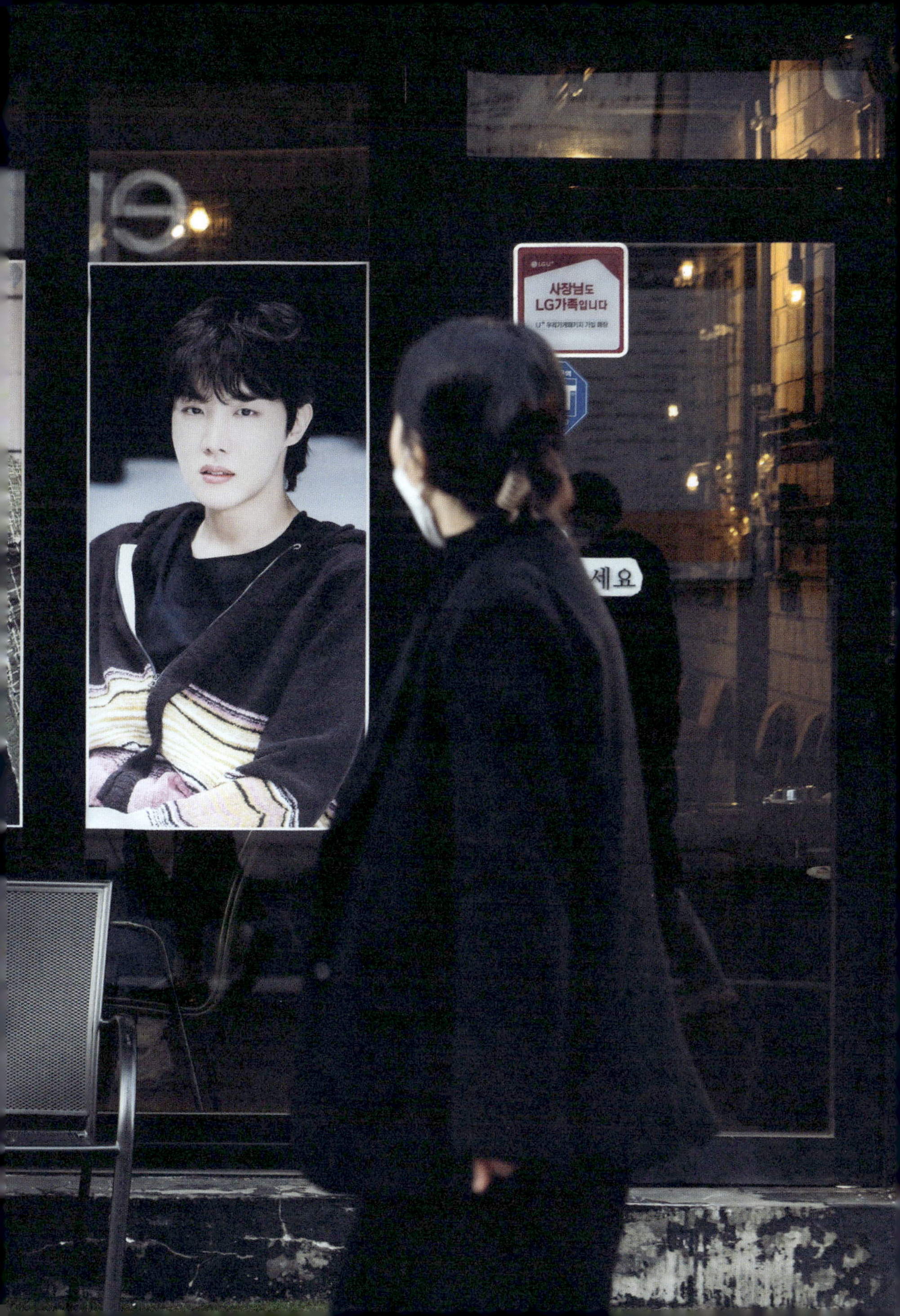
사장님도
LG가족입니다
세요

CHALLENGING

CHAPTER 3

STEREOTYPES

CHALLENGING STEREOTYPES

Broadening their repertoire from hip-hop, over the years the band have expanded their musical style to incorporate a wide variety of genres. The members co-write and co-produce much of their music, which has played a defining role in their success, especially as the material often includes a message around social issues for fans.

"The whole company's philosophy is to make music that matters," Asia pop culture journalist Tamar Herman said of BTS in a 2020 interview with *Business Insider*. Around the time BTS debuted, it was "pretty rare" that groups used their music for explicit social commentary, Herman said.

Indeed, while many K-pop songs tend to focus on relationships and love, BTS lyrics have addressed subjects that others may not, such as mental health, bullying, elitism and the pressure to conform. Some of these topics remain taboo in Korea and around the world.

The social and cultural commentary extends to their home country. One example is the song "Paldogangsan" from their second album *O!RUL8,2?*. It is a rap about Korean regional dialects, known as "satoori". The members also embrace local traditions: Suga's 2020 solo track "Daechwita", performed under the alias Agust D, begins with a powerful burst from a taepyeongso (a Korean wind instrument) and features the singer himself dressed in traditional Korean *hanbok* clothing. It's an approach that has resonated globally with audiences who appreciate the authenticity of BTS.

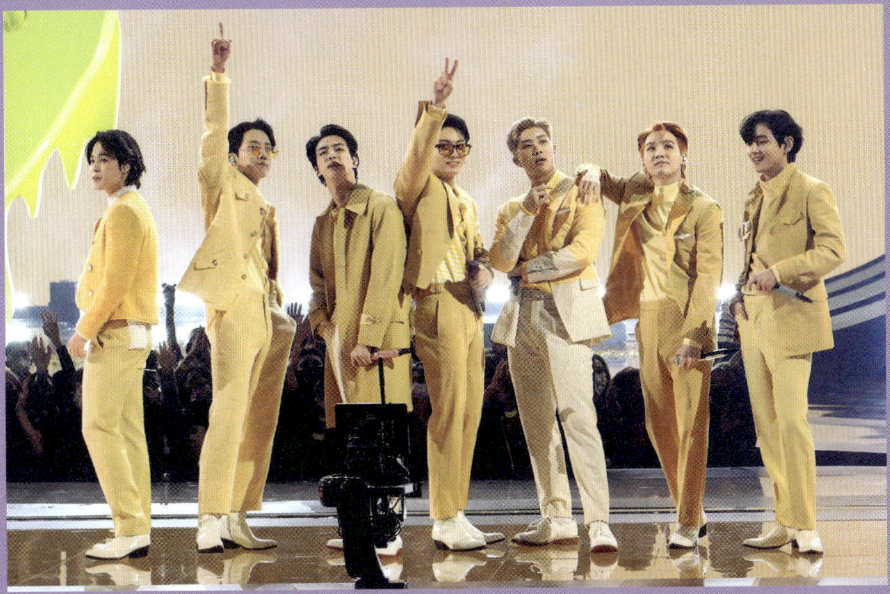

Jimin, J-Hope, Jin, Jung Kook, RM, Suga and V embrace head-to-toe yellow (in tailored suits by South Korean luxury menswear brand Tailorable) as they perform at the 2021 American Music Awards in Los Angeles, California.

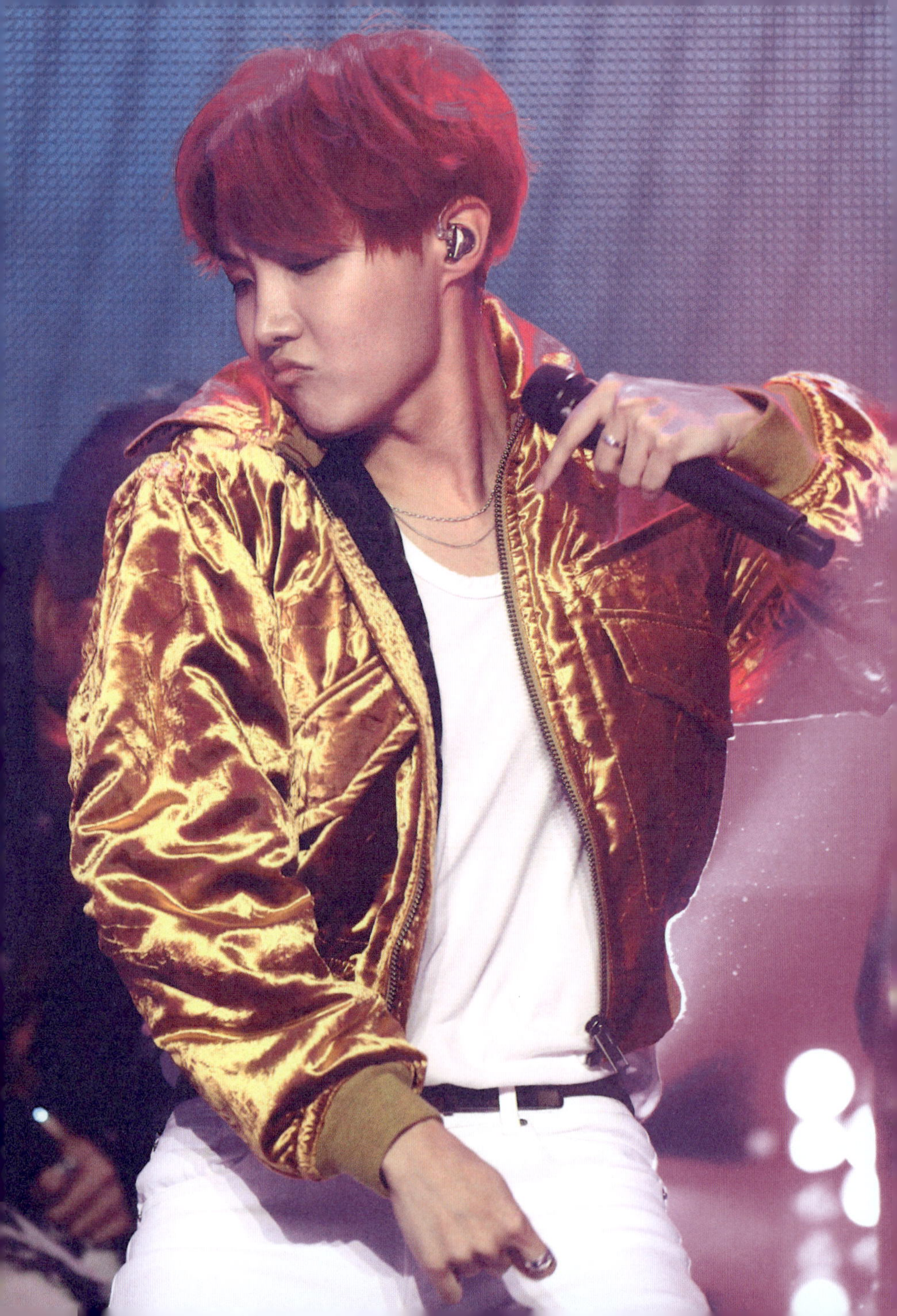

In 2020, BTS became one of the few groups since The Beatles to chart four US No. 1 albums in less than two years. Among their albums at the top of the US charts was *Love Yourself: Answer.* It was their second compilation album and it explored themes of self-love and acceptance. It prompted then South Korean president Moon Jae-in to take to social platform Twitter (now X) to congratulate the boys on their success. That same year, BTS's third Korean-language and sixth overall studio album, *Love Yourself: Tear*, became the first primarily foreign-language No. 1 album in the USA in over 12 years, according to *Billboard*.

Also in 2020, BTS broke the Guinness World Record for the most viewed concert live-streamed in the world. The virtual concert, titled *Bang Bang Con: The Live*, was a paid, ticketed performance that was held as part of the group's seventh anniversary celebrations. It was also organized to replace a world tour that was cancelled due to the COVID-19 pandemic. The concert was viewed by over 700,000 fans in more than 100 countries. In the following year, BTS became the first K-pop act to receive a Grammy nomination, with "Dynamite" earning one for Best Pop Duo/ Group Performance. (The group has received five Grammy nominations to date.)

J-Hope (along with his fellow BTS members) sported festive colours – and hair – as the group performed on *Dick Clark's New Year's Rockin' Eve with Ryan Seacrest* in December 2017.

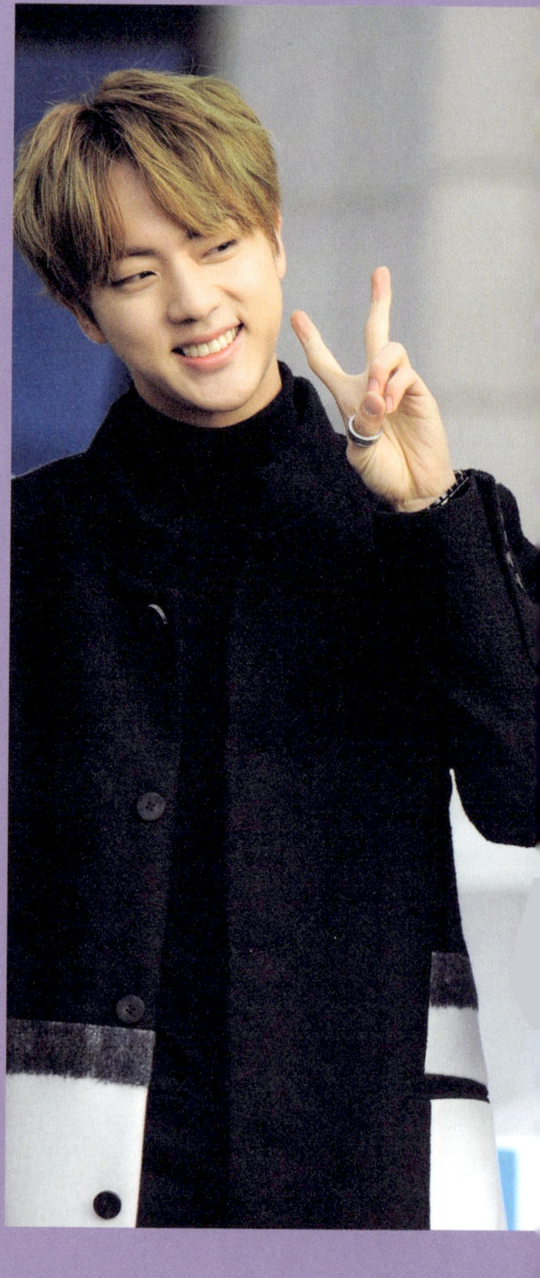

Jimin joined V and Jin by dyeing his hair a coppery shade in Seoul, December 2015.

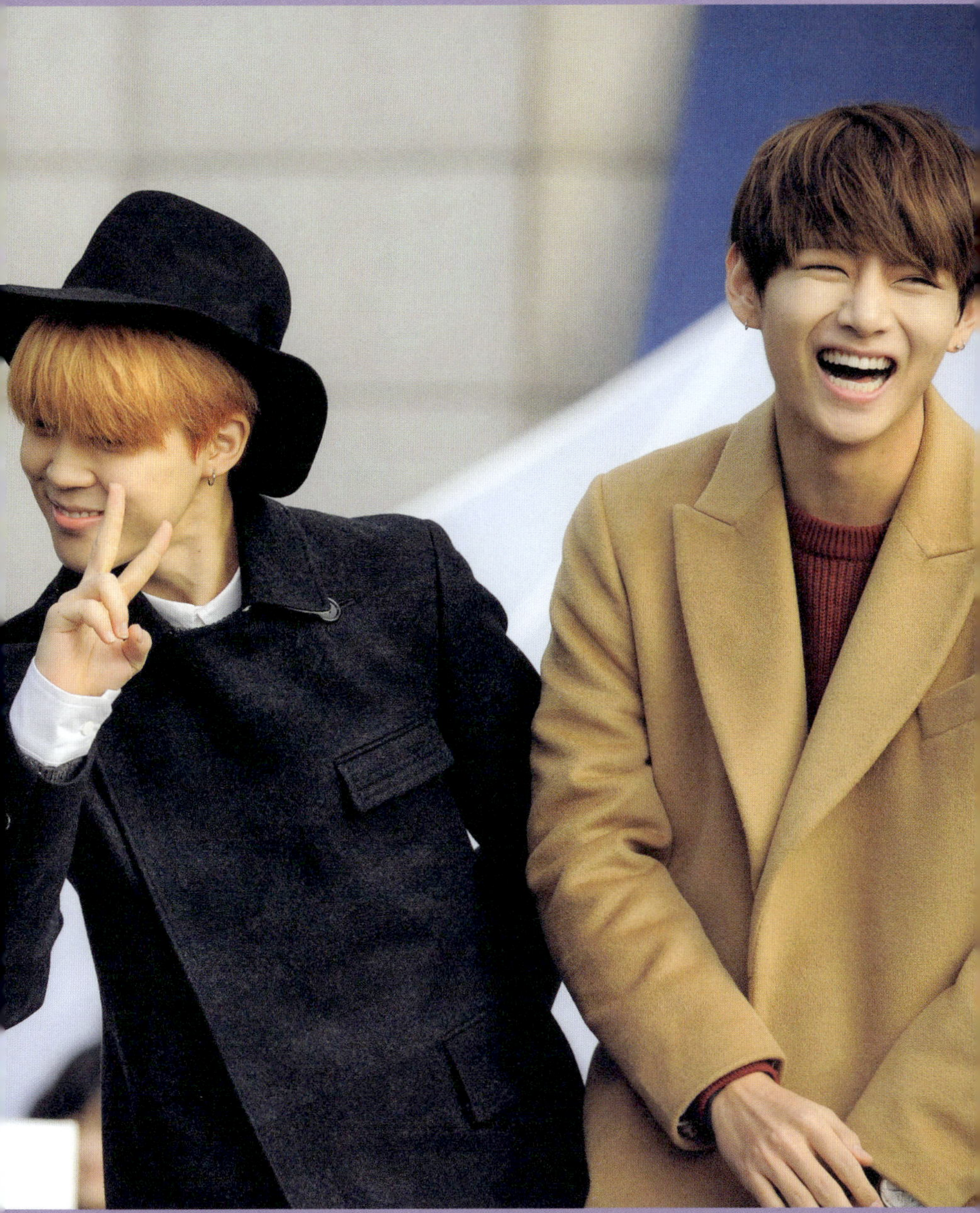

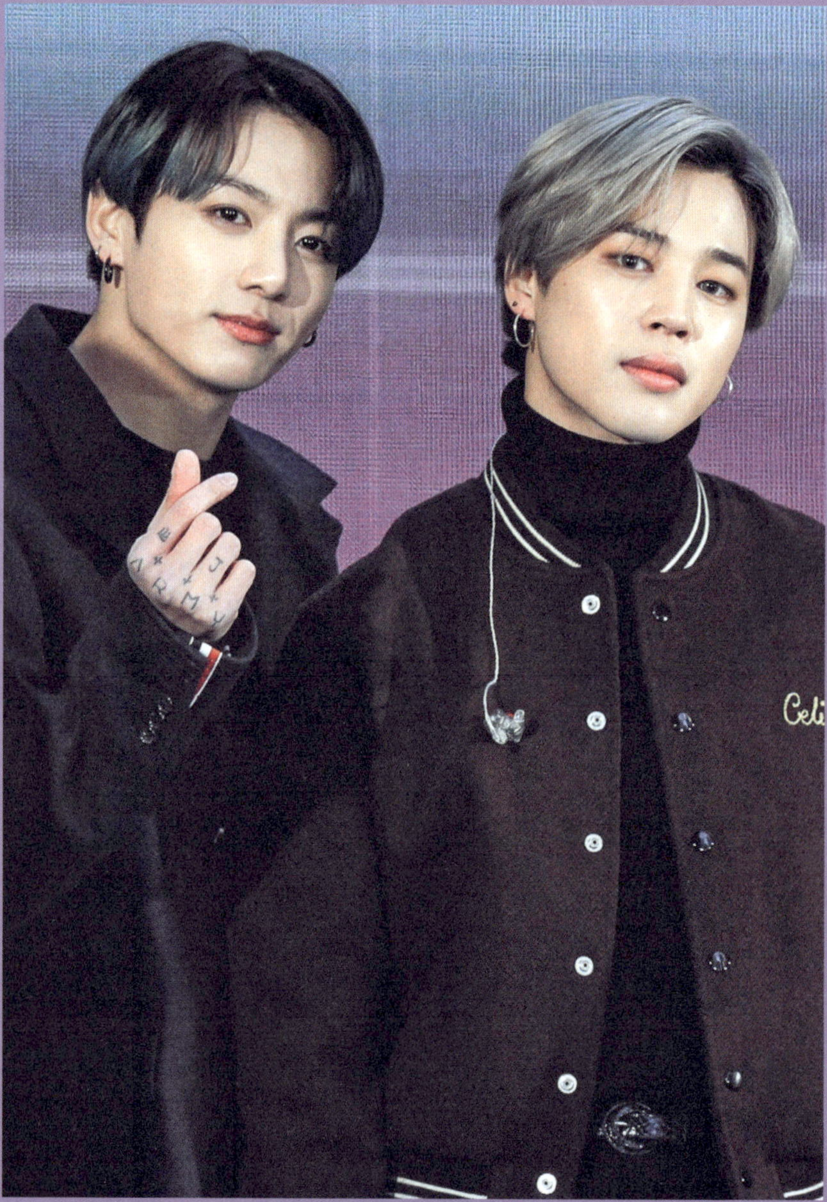

While BTS has significantly challenged traditional stereotypes in South Korea through their music, they've also broken down barriers by embracing vulnerability and defying gender norms when it comes to their appearance.

Traditional ideas of masculinity tend to be associated with power, dominance and aggression, while qualities such as submission, care and dependence are historically thought of as feminine. The expectations, then, are for men to possess masculine attributes, or else they'll be viewed as feminine, which is "weak" or "bad", as Rachael M. Joo and Stephen Epstein write in their 2012 research paper "Multiple Exposures: Korean Bodies and the Transnational Imagination", published in the *Asia-Pacific Journal*.

BTS, however, embody a mix of qualities associated with both genders. By adopting non-gender-specific clothing (each member embracing a style that is unique and personal to them) and androgynous make-up and promoting themes of kindness, self-love and vulnerability in their lyrics, they are seen as breaking from the traditional rigid standards of hegemonic masculinity and promoting a more inclusive and flexible understanding of what it means to be a man.

Jung Kook (in Valentino) and Jimin (in a Celine bomber) at the BTS live interview on *The Today Show* in New York in February 2020.

“There is this culture where masculinity *is defined by* certain emotions, characteristics. *I’m* not fond *of these* expressions... *What does being masculine mean?*

People's conditions vary day by day... Sometimes you're in a good condition; sometimes you aren't... Society should be more understanding."

SUGA, *ESQUIRE*, 2020.

As Milagros Wilson wrote in the influential youth culture magazine *Dazed* in 2018, "for young people everywhere, this fluidity in expression is momentous to see on display from an all-male group".

The concept of gender construction is something that BTS seems to be acutely aware of. Speaking with *Esquire* magazine in 2020, Suga voiced his disagreement towards restrictive labels: "There is this culture where masculinity is defined by certain emotions, characteristics. I'm not fond of these expressions", he said. "What does being masculine mean? People's conditions vary day by day."

RM shared a similar view in a 2021 interview with Brian Hiatt in *Rolling Stone*. "The labels of what being masculine is, is an outdated concept," said RM. "It is not our intention to break it down. But if we are making a positive impact, we are very thankful. We live in an age where we shouldn't have those labels or have those restrictions."

J-Hope, in full Dior, during the Times Square New Year's Eve celebrations in New York, December 2022.

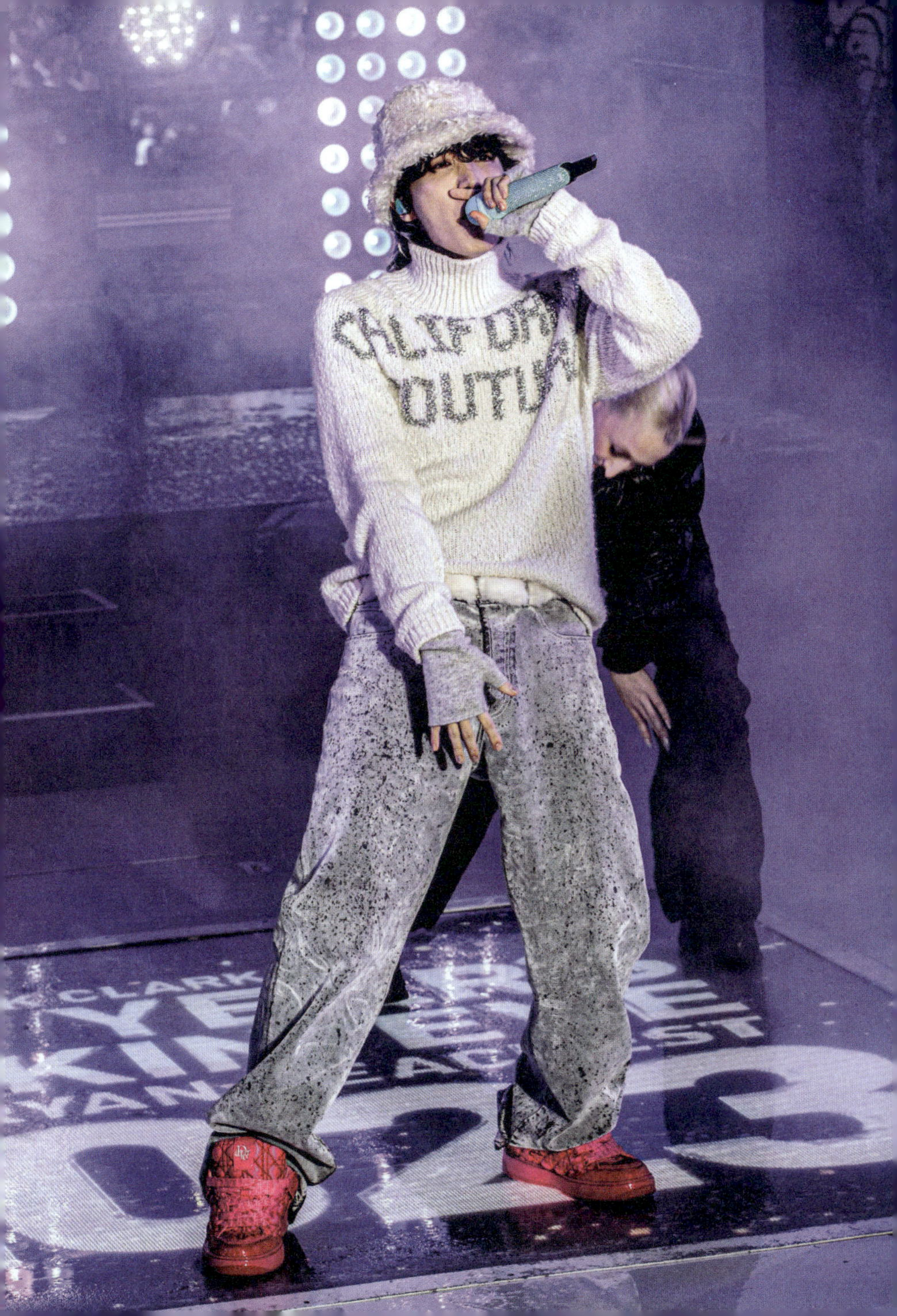

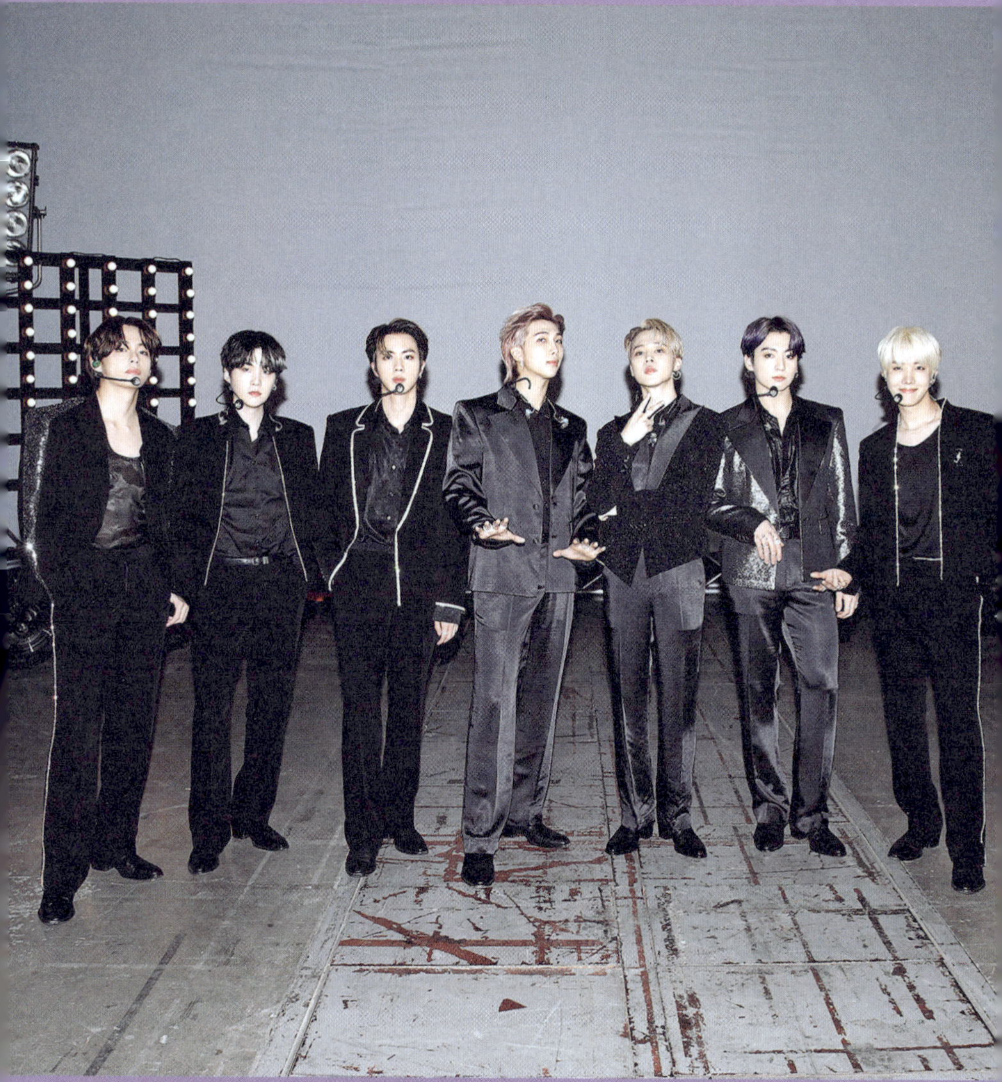

Androgynous or queer-friendly male style icons aren't an entirely new phenomenon. Musicians such as David Bowie, Prince and Kurt Cobain have long challenged gender stereotypes. There have also been key moments in men's fashion where women's trends entered the mainstream and fashion designers including Rick Owens, Jonathan Anderson and Martine Rose are known for subverting gender binaries with their interpretation of masculinity and femininity. But the notion of gender barriers – and how to overcome them – was given new focus following the rise of the #MeToo movement.

#MeToo was first established in 2006 as a social movement and awareness campaign against sexual assault and harassment, and a dedicated hashtag to draw attention to the magnitude of the problem spread virally on social media in 2017. In the years that followed, new representations of masculinity emerged on screen. Actor Timothée Chalamet and singer Harry Styles, who are known for challenging traditional masculinity and embracing more fluid expressions of gender and style, became the dominant heart-throbs of their generation. In this vein, the androgynous and fluid approach to fashion employed by BTS feels particularly pertinent.

OPPOSITE V, Suga, Jin, RM, Jimin, Jung Kook and J-Hope dressed sharply in black suits, demonstrating their take on evening wear, at the 2021 *Billboard* Music Awards in Los Angeles, California.

OVERLEAF The members of BTS showcased their individual personalities in the Gucci x NY Yankees outfits they wore to the 2018 Melon Music Awards in Seoul.

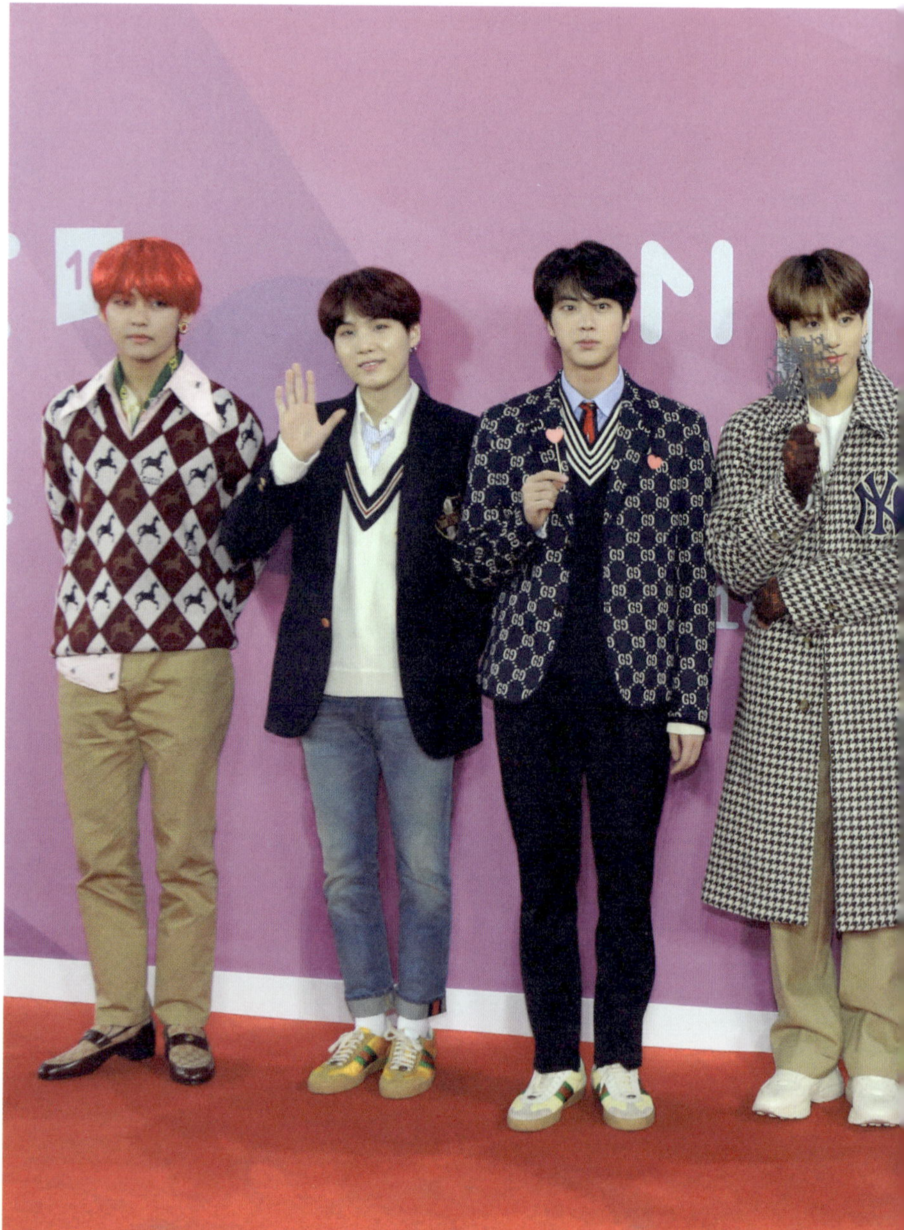

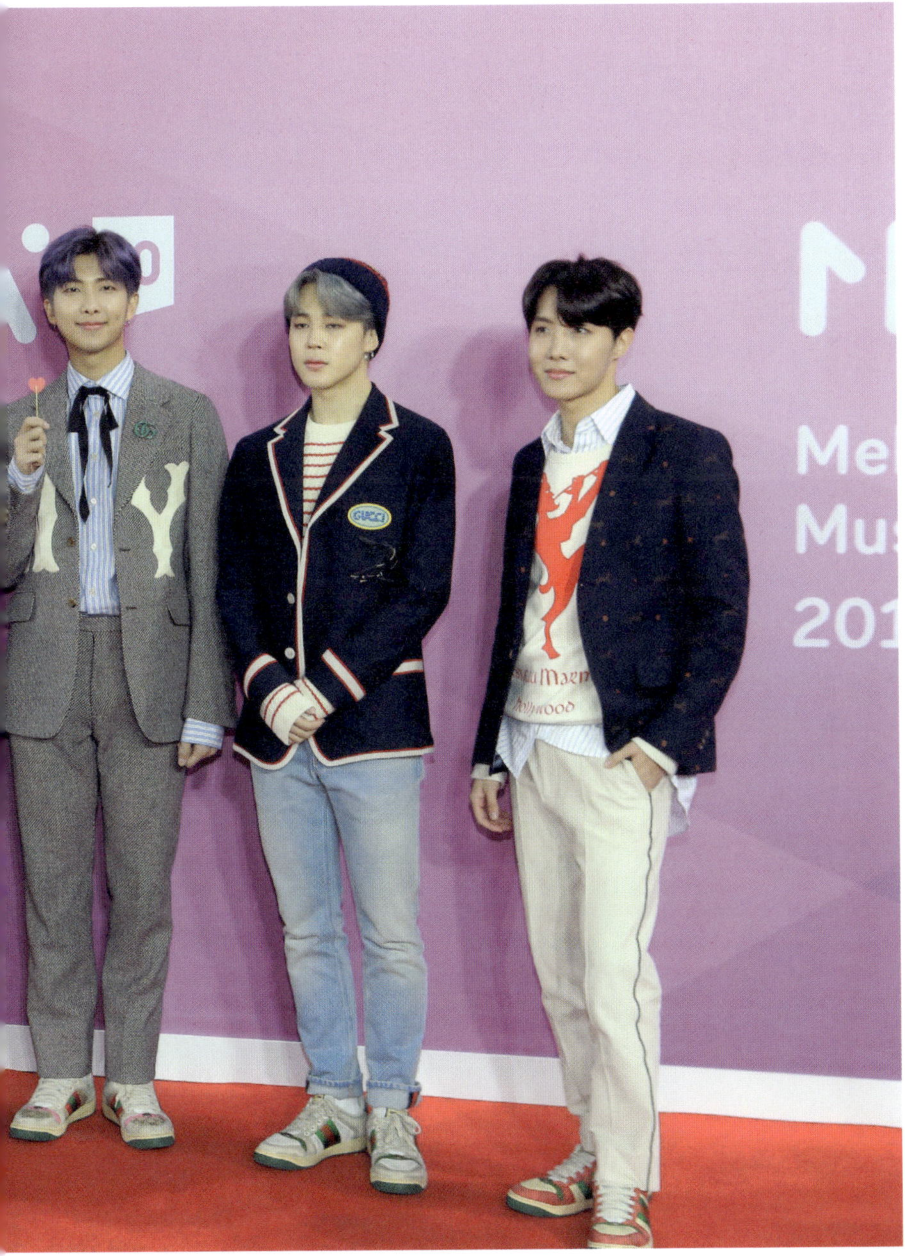

Seo Taiji and Boys, H.O.T. and many others from the first generation of K-pop bands had attainable style, as most of their members dressed casually and luxury brand styling had not yet come into play. The idols of that period largely embraced a natural look and generally did not dye their hair, keeping their make-up minimal. In contrast, the third generation, in tandem with Western counterparts, such as Backstreet Boys or NSYNC, BTS members often wore monochromatic and coordinated, nearly identical looks, though there were occasions in which the styling would become more theatrical. This was also the time when high school uniforms were first worn by performers – a trend that has appeared to transcend all K-pop generations.

By the second generation, K-pop was increasingly recognized as an important industry in the country and its marketing and entrepreneurial aspects became novelties of the time. It also marked a period when idols first showed up on television shows, with some having their own reality programmes while others starred in popular K-dramas. As the production quality of K-pop improved during this era, with music videos becoming more visually appealing and choreography more intricate, fashion and personal style also became an important ingredient for a successful group.

While some Korean stars during this time still looked to trends from the 1990s and other styles that were popular in America, a growing number were open to experimenting with different looks and did not necessarily stick to the "approachable" visuals that some of their predecessors had adopted. However, matching outfits remained common: if group members didn't all wear the exact same thing, there would be very minimal differences, such as a personalized colour or a small alteration to the design.

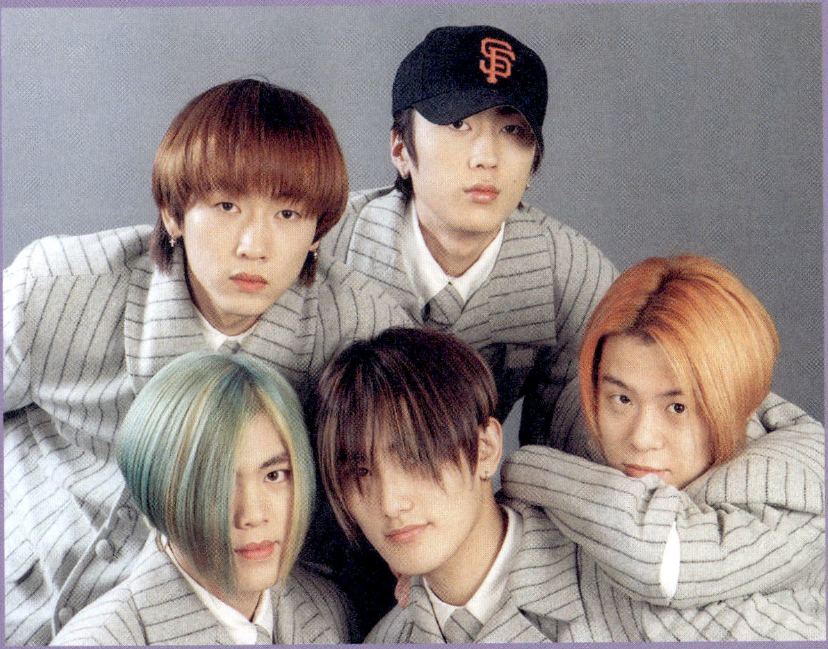

Influential South Korean boy band H.O.T.
pose for a photo in 1998.

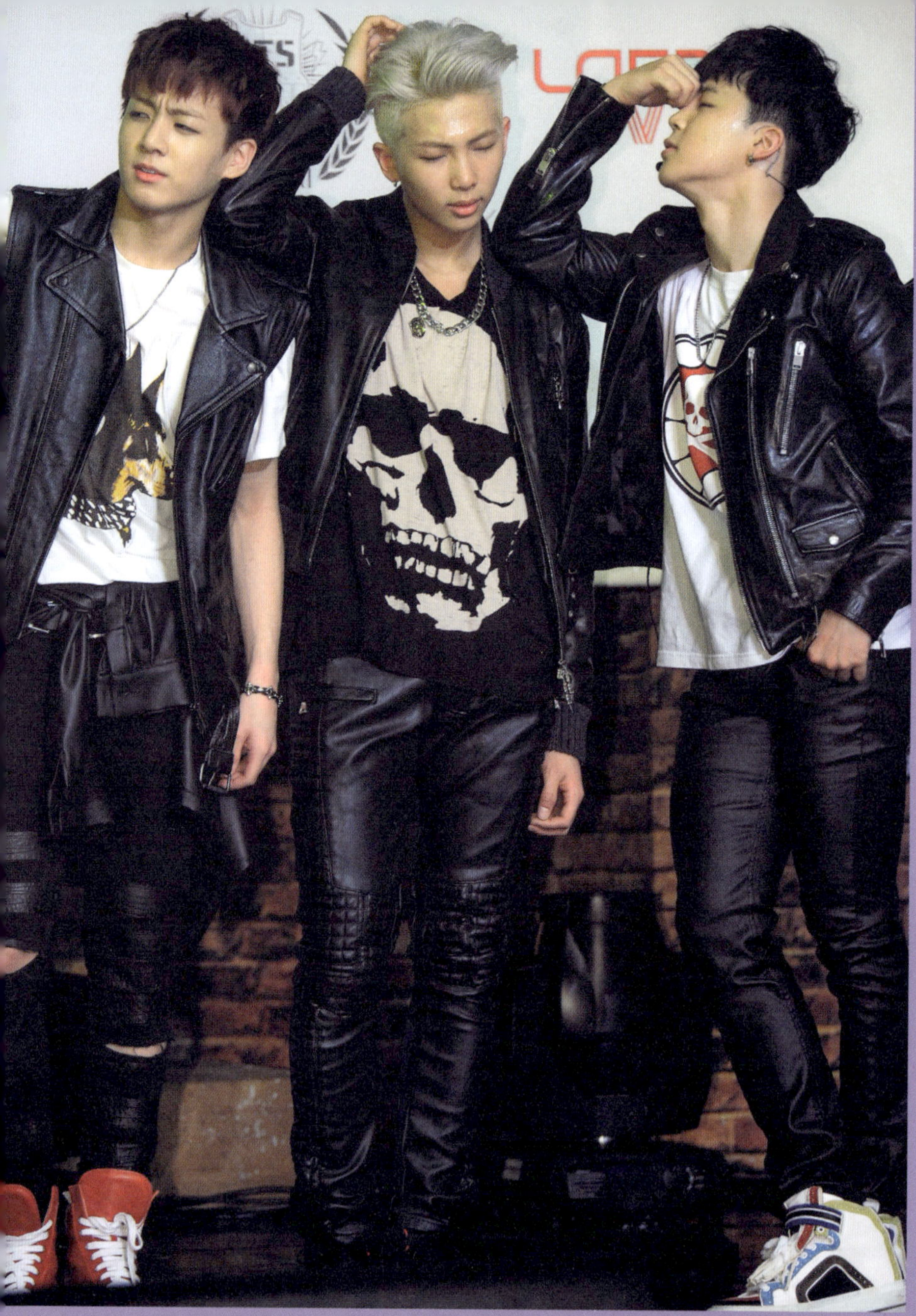

When BTS entered the music industry as part of the third generation, K-pop was becoming a global phenomenon. Not only did the popularity of social networks and streaming platforms contribute immensely to this expansion, so did international music festivals and global award shows that K-pop bands had started to perform in. As a result, there was more attention than ever on idol outfits, which became less coordinated across members and more about the individual personality of the artist or concept.

Following the hip-hop-inspired aesthetic seen during their debut, BTS began to experiment with a variety of styles. At a February 2014 event to promote their music at the Lotte Card Art Center in Seoul, BTS leaned towards a punk-rock style and members wore leather jackets and trousers, with RM, J-Hope and Suga accentuating their look with skull prints and crossbones. That same year, at the annual Kcon music event in Los Angeles, the group's members wore ties and decorative blazers with black trousers and trainers. For their "War of Hormone" music video, BTS played homage to 1990s grunge, with members wearing torn cable knit jumpers, pinstripes and brogues from various brands including Diesel and Kenzo.

BTS had a very punky look at the February 2014 event at the Lotte Card Art Center, Seoul.

"The way we think is that everything *that* we do, *and our* existence *itself, is* contributing

to the hope for leaving this xenophobia, *these negative things, behind.*"

RM, *ROLLING STONE*, 2021

As 2015 came around, BTS still kept their look smart and synchronized – they wore coordinated black suits for the 24th Seoul Music Awards in January and matching leather blazers and shorts for the Melon Music Awards in November, for example – but it marked the beginning of their wardrobe transformation and rise to mainstream stardom. The change could be felt in their music video "I Need U", which featured the group in Joe Gush bomber jackets, dark-washed Levi's jeans and Dr. Martens boots as they walked across a train track belting out lyrics about the pain and hardships of love.

By 2017, the members appeared to embrace their personal style more freely. That year, when BTS attended the American Music Awards (becoming the first K-pop group to perform at the event), they wore outfits by Gucci – some of them custom-made, according to *Teen Vogue* – and, for once, the looks were not near identical. J-Hope, for example, wore a red T-shirt that matched his newly dyed hair, while Jimin opted for a sparkly red, blue and green bomber jacket with a floral print. The only similarity was that all the BTS members wore distressed denim jeans – which, at the time, were all the rage among Western celebrities including Justin Bieber and Brad Pitt – albeit in different shades and fits.

Similarly, when BTS performed their song "Idol" on *The Tonight Show Starring Jimmy Fallon* in September 2018, they all wore glitzy, high-shine lamé suits, though in various colours and prints. Later that year, BTS became the first male pop group to collaborate with Dior and wore outfits from designer Kim Jones' pre-Fall 2019 collection at their Stade de France concert – the first of two sold-out Parisian shows, as part of their BTS World Tour: Love Yourself – which drew 80,000 attendees in one night. The look featured

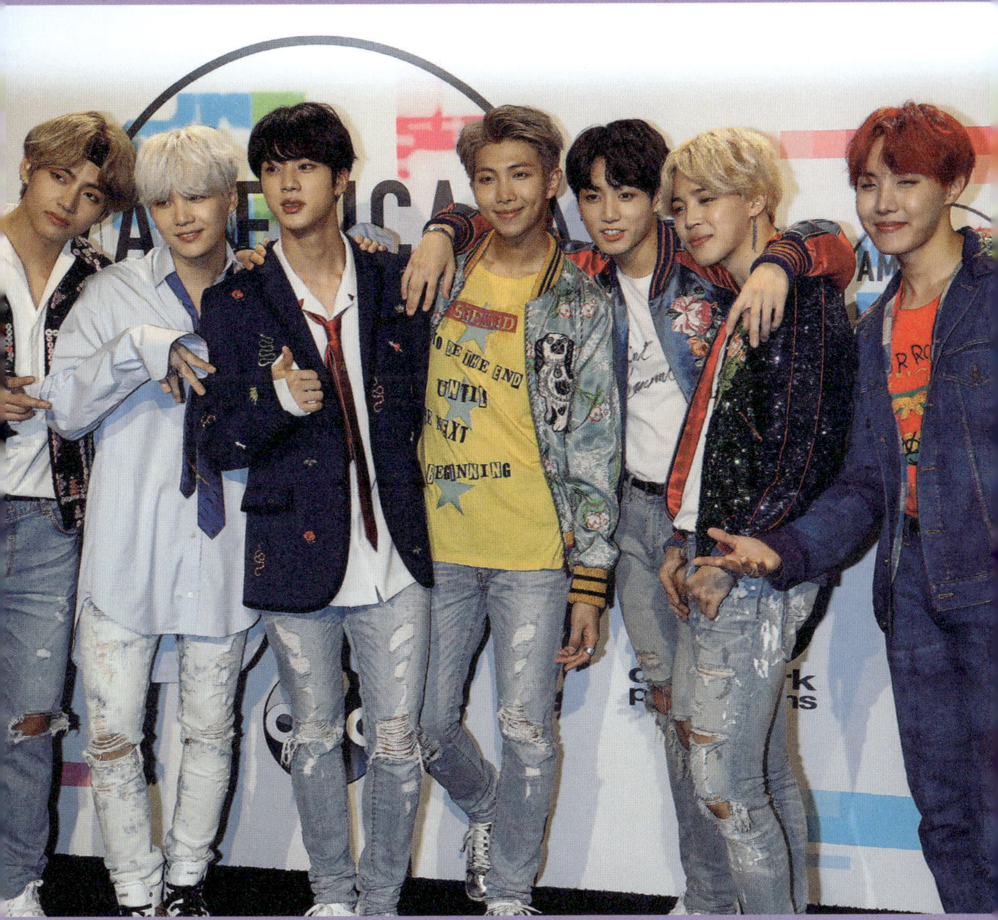

BTS took clothing cues from American preppy and hip-hop at the 2017 American Music Awards in Los Angeles.

cargo trousers, harnesses and bomber jackets, which were accessorized with industrial chains and brooches by the French luxury house's then-jewellery director Yoon Ahn. For Haesoon Jung, the Korean founder and director of Style Intelligence, an independent consultancy firm, it marked "the K-pop industry's most high-profile sponsorship ever".

By the 2019 Mnet Asian Music Awards, individuality had become an even bigger component of BTS style and each member had their own unique look – though the clothes worn to the event were all designed by the French luxury goods label Celine. From V and Jin's classic blazer and jeans combination to Jung Kook's long patterned coat and RM's wide-brimmed hat, each BTS member's appearance was distinctive. This marked a period when a growing number of K-pop stars – including BTS – worked closely with their stylists on their stage and red carpet looks, so that their personal tastes were properly represented.

Jung Kook, the youngest member of the group, making him the "Golden Maknae" (multitalented, most junior) of BTS, described in a 2018 interview with *Billboard* his approach to dressing as unfussy and "clean cut". His style is defined by a preference for utilitarian, practical garments, often imbued with elements of 1990s grunge and punk aesthetics. Sourced from labels such as Supreme, Nike and Balenciaga, typical pieces from Jung Kook's wardrobe include oversized boxy tees, baggy or wide-leg trousers, chunky shoes and often a bucket hat or beanie. He also favours a mainly dark colour palette, with black and dark greys being frequent choices.

In the same *Billboard* interview, RM and Suga agreed that music and fashion were two important forms of self-expression for them – and, in some respects, felt inseparable: "Music is not just about listening anymore", said Suga. "You can see it nowadays... The visuals are very important". However, as the clothing worn to red carpet events and in music videos need to be eye-catching, they are not always the easiest to wear, he suggested. It's why comfort is a

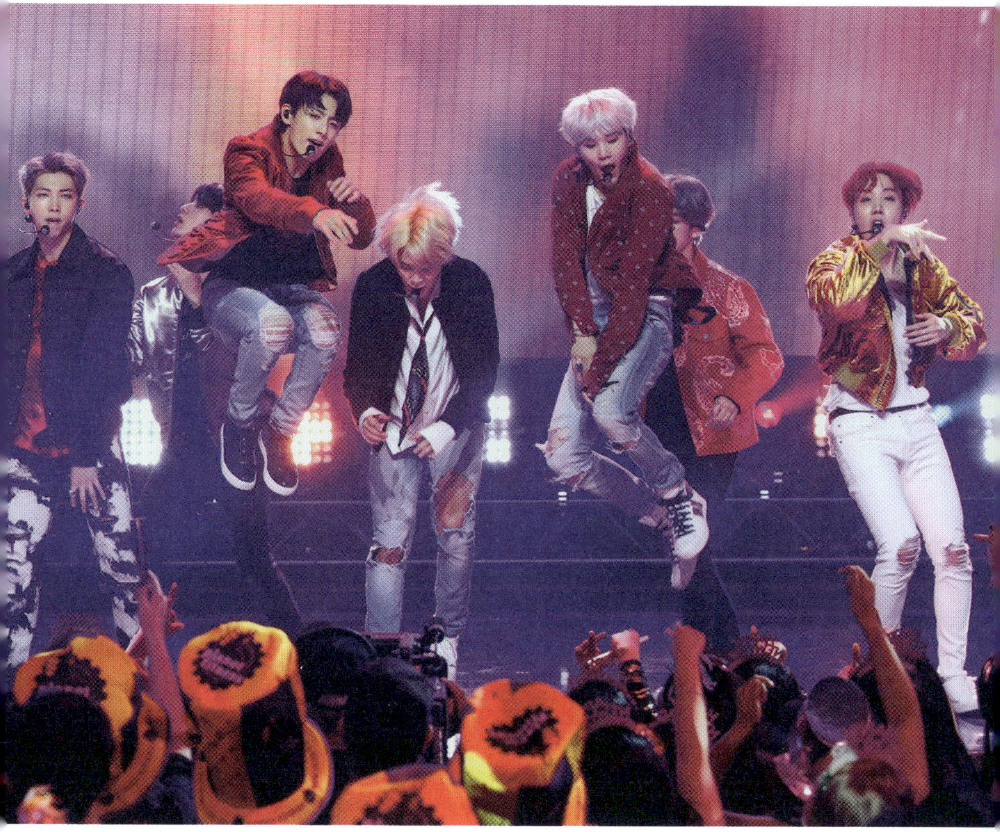

BTS in the holiday spirit for the annual television special, *Dick Clark's New Year's Rockin' Eve with Ryan Seacrest*, which aired on ABC.

"Since I watch a lot of old movies, shirts, ties and other accessories are the things I like."

V, *BILLBOARD*

priority when it comes to their off-duty style, which can be categorized by a mix of relaxed pieces such as baggy jeans and oversized jumpers. However, both RM and Suga have also been seen to adopt elegant, formal styles, demonstrating versatility in their fashion.

Fit is important, J-Hope agreed in the interview, noting that he was “always up to date on the latest trend” but also looked “for clothes that fit my body well”. Some fans have perceived his sense of fashion as cool, expressive and funky, in alignment with his bubbly personality. Think fun patterns like florals and colourful street fashion.

Jin also takes a playful approach to dressing and has shared enthusiasm for wearing T-shirts with animated characters, such as those from the BT21 merchandise collection. Fans were ecstatic when he was named as Gucci’s global brand ambassador in August 2024, with the Italian luxury house’s then-designer Sabato De Sarno describing Jin’s personality as “warm”, “kind” and “truly magnetic”, and saying that “his style is simply unique”.

While the concept of fashion became more important after his debut, Jimin has discussed how he wasn’t always confident in his stage presence and how it was more about proving himself and improving his skills rather than focusing on fashion choices. As a result Jimin has been more classic with his style choices, opting for tailored looks, timeless jackets and hardware accessories. Similarly, V, who takes style inspiration from older films, is known for his timeless yet modern dress sense. “Since I watch a lot of old movies, shirts, ties and other accessories are the things I like”, he told *Billboard*.

While BTS had already demonstrated a penchant for designer labels since their early days, their "Youth Trilogy" era (2015 to 2016) is distinct from their later collaborations with big brands, which they became more prominently associated with through subsequent projects and endorsements. And as their enthusiasm for high-end brands evolves over time, their preferences have grown beyond the streetwear pieces seen in their first music video.

For their 2020 appearance on *The Today Show*, the group wore outfits featuring sophisticated patterns and layering. RM is seen in a checked trench coat from the Italian brand Marni, while Jin is wearing a blazer by the American designer Thom Browne. Suga is in a Valentino coat, while J-Hope opted for a denim jacket by the Belgian designer Raf Simons. Meanwhile, Jimin sported a Celine varsity jacket, V a white-collared Valentino coat and Jung Kook his signature black, styled with a pair of chunky boots by Prada.

That same year at the Grammy Awards, the group wore smart neutral-hued looks by Bottega Veneta under former creative director Daniel Lee. Later, at the Golden Disc Awards – a major Korean music awards ceremony – the members were dressed by Givenchy, marking one of the final moments that clothing designed by the French luxury brand's then-designer Clare Waight Keller appeared on the red carpet.

On the whole it is open-minded attitudes to fashion that has set BTS apart from many of their counterparts and landed them on "Best Dressed" lists in titles such as *Vanity Fair* and GQ. Their playful and androgynous style – which is significant as luxury brands increasingly blend men's and women's collections on the runway – has included "cold shoulder" tops, feminine blouses and silky suits that resembled pyjamas, among other memorable outfits. Furthermore, BTS have also modelled for and collaborated with beauty and skincare brands, including Dior Beauty, Amorepacific, Laneige, Mediheal and VT Cosmetics, a position that is traditionally filled by female celebrities.

Avery Booker, the founding editor of *Jing Daily*, a website focused on luxury and cultural impact in China, told *Vogue Business* in 2021: "There isn't a similar pop group in the West as diverse and unisex".

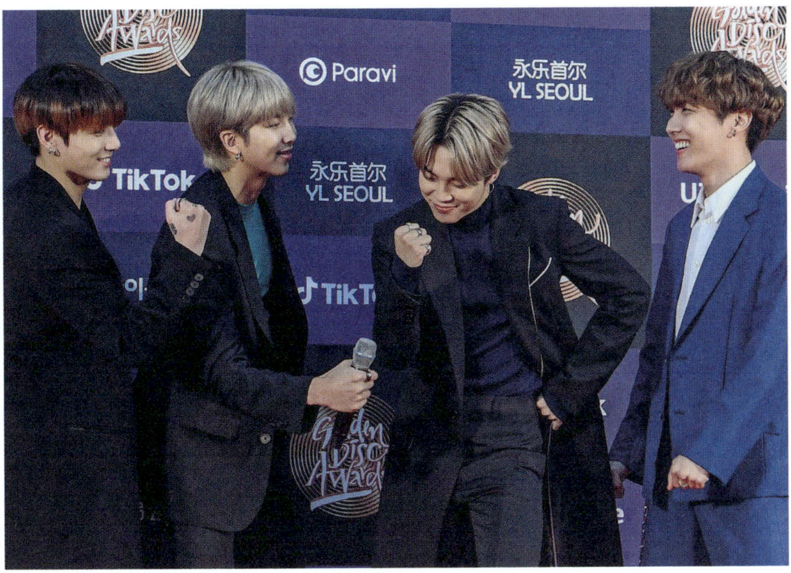

Jung Kook, RM, Jimin and J-Hope in Givenchy at the photo call for the 34th Golden Disc Awards in Seoul on 5 January 2020.

FASHIONABLE

CHAPTER 4

AMBASSADORS

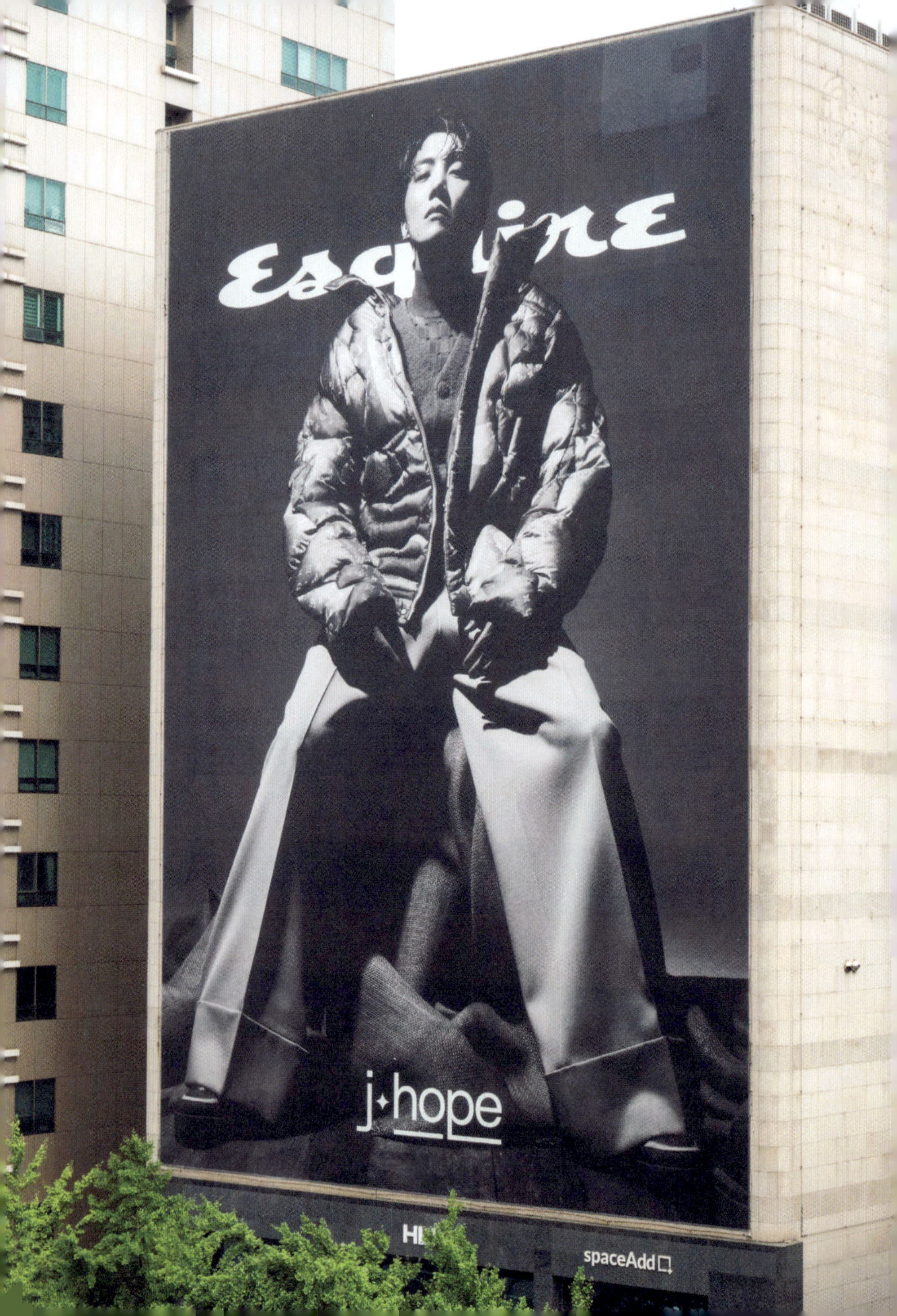
j·hope
spaceAdd

FASHIONABLE AMBASSADORS

Beyond print and billboard campaigns, brands have seen an opportunity for modern-day ambassadors to promote their wares across more diverse marketing channels – and it's across these new spaces traditional film stars don't always count for much. Jennifer Lawrence, Brad Pitt, Ryan Gosling, Emma Stone and Scarlett Johansson are among the A-listers that do not have a public Instagram account, for example. In that regard, the multifaceted and digitally savvy nature of BTS is attractive; the band is as likely to be seen sitting front row at a fashion show as much as they are being papped at the airport or directly engaging with their fans online.

"K-pop stars are all-round entertainers. They're the Swiss Army knife of marketing because they can reach audiences in so many countries on all these different platforms", said *Jing Daily*'s Avery Booker in 2021. "Brands want to work with more than just a face. It involves a little bit more thoughtfulness because the consumer is a bit harder to sell to right now. Maybe they want to shop, but they also want to be entertained. Giving them another photograph is not entertaining."

In February 2023, Louis Vuitton announced J-Hope as a house ambassador. He was on the cover of the August 2023 *Esquire Korea* magazine.

The intimacy of BTS's relationship with their followers is unique and unlike preceding K-pop stars. Typically, when a musical group launches in Korea, its members will go on television to promote their album and keep a low profile until the next release. Bang realized that the internet was a better way to reach young people – with BTS, he didn't bother with traditional avenues like TV appearances.

Instead, Bang sought "to figure out the most fandom-friendly thing to do and then take it to the extreme", he told *The New Yorker* in 2024. And so he established a YouTube channel for BTS well before their first single was released and used the platform to share behind-the-scenes footage. The group's members also ran their own account on Twitter (now X) – again, unusual for a K-pop act – and maintained a lively dialogue with their fans, live-posting about their days and even uploading seemingly candid photographs.

And the big companies came knocking. In April 2021, Louis Vuitton signed all the BTS members as its global ambassadors, marking the group's first sponsorship with a luxury house. Posts on Twitter (now X) and Instagram announcing Louis Vuitton's partnership with BTS topped half a million views within a few hours. That year, BTS wore Louis Vuitton designed by the brand's then-menswear designer Virgil Abloh to the Grammy Awards.

In January 2021, Louis Vuitton's best-performing post on its social channels featured BTS, according to analytics platform Launchmetrics. The fanfare continued through to July when BTS made their debut in a fashion film wearing looks from the Fall/Winter 2021 collection. The video has been watched over 7.2 million times on YouTube – and counting.

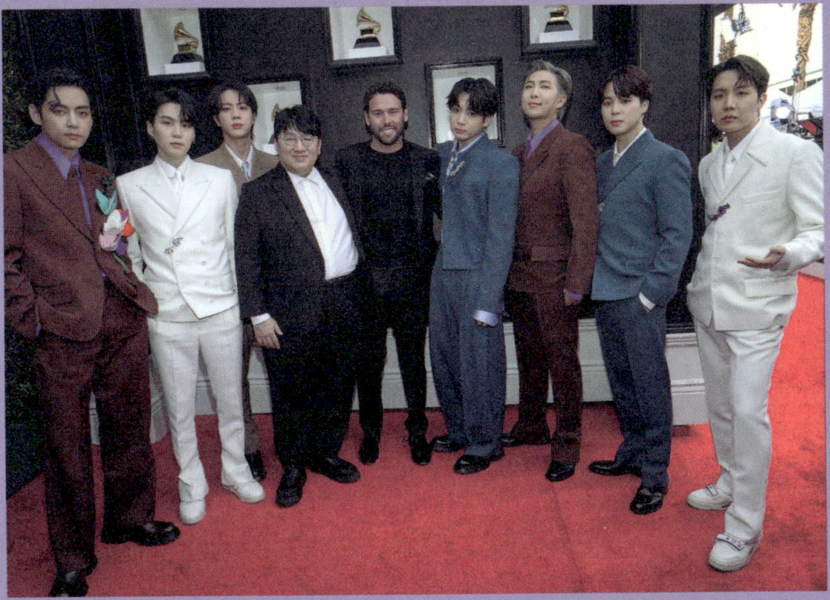

(Left to right) V, Suga, Jin, “Hitman” Bang Si-hyuk (Hybe Chairman), Scooter Braun, Jung Kook, RM, Jimin and J-Hope at the 64th Annual Grammy Awards in 2022. The band all wore custom-made Louis Vuitton suits.

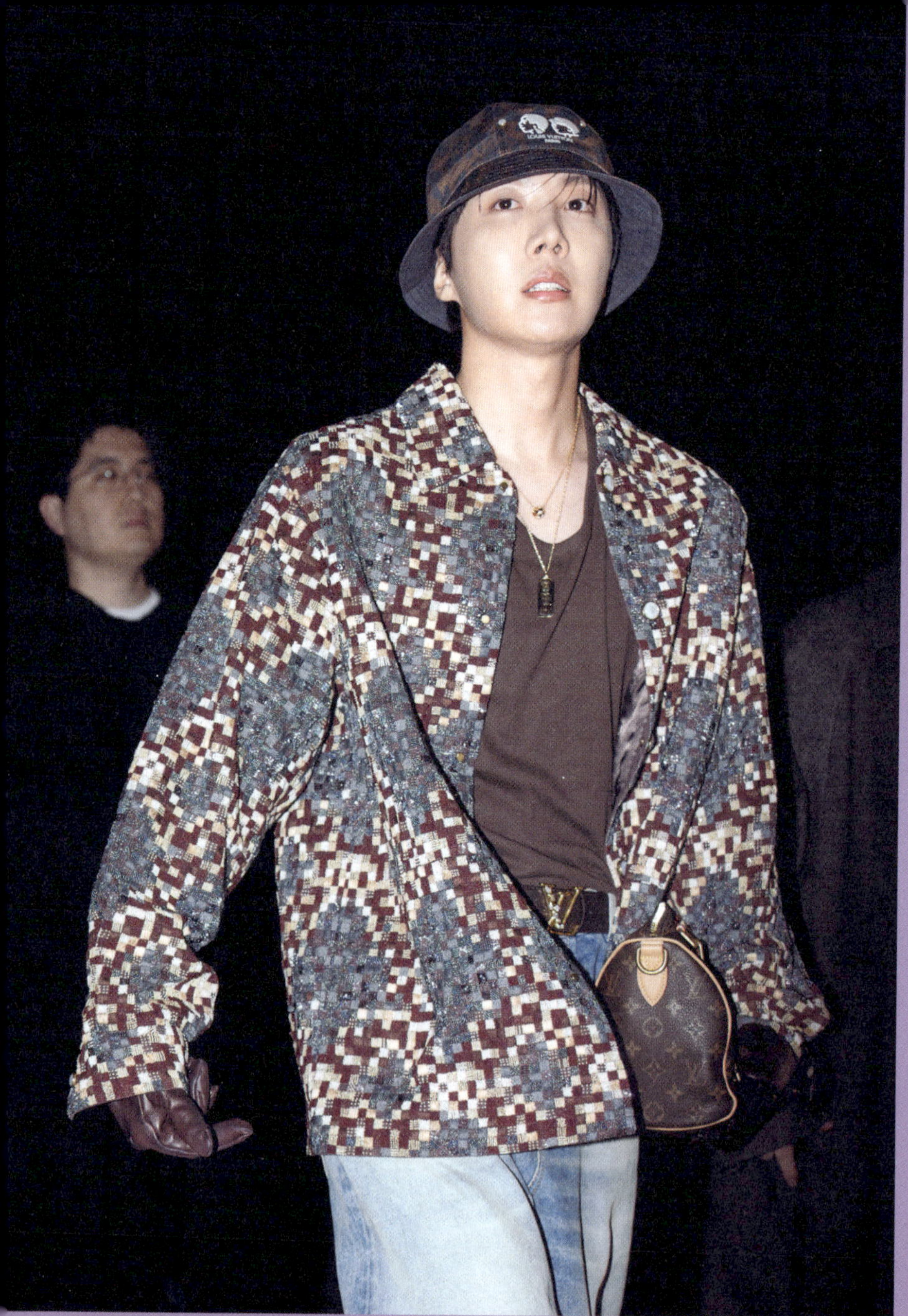

Louis Vuitton described the film as "a conversation between space, movement, and global connectivity", which Abloh believed was a vibe easily embodied by BTS. "They add their spin to the collection, make it their own and take it to new heights", said Abloh in *Women's Wear Daily*.

In the film, Jimin is the first from the group to appear, wearing a light grey marbled suit and salmon-coloured, gold-framed sunglasses. RM boasts the most accessories, wearing a wide brimmed hat with a stripe band that matches his shirt and tie, dark suit with aeroplane-shaped fastening and a silver briefcase. As the camera pans to Suga, he can be seen wearing a similar black suit, paired with green and white trainers that perfectly match the strap of his bag – from some angles it looks like a wide sash – that bears the writing of conceptual artist Lawrence Weiner. The suit worn by J-Hope encapsulates the travelling theme of the show, with a map of the world embroidered onto his jacket and tie. Jung Kook and V both stick to smart black coats and trousers, while Jin closes the video wearing a chequered black and crimson coat. The film was a good example of cohesion among the boy band members, whose outfits felt synchronized as they played the role of travelling businessmen, but still featured small details that expressed their personal identity.

J-Hope attended Louis Vuitton's men's Fall/Winter 2025 show at Paris Fashion Week in January 2025.

"I always wanted to become an artist *that can* provide comfort, *relief and* positive energy *to people."*

J-HOPE,
***TIME* MAGAZINE,**
2020

J-Hope at the Louis Vuitton menswear Spring/Summer 2026 show at Paris Fashion Week in June 2025.

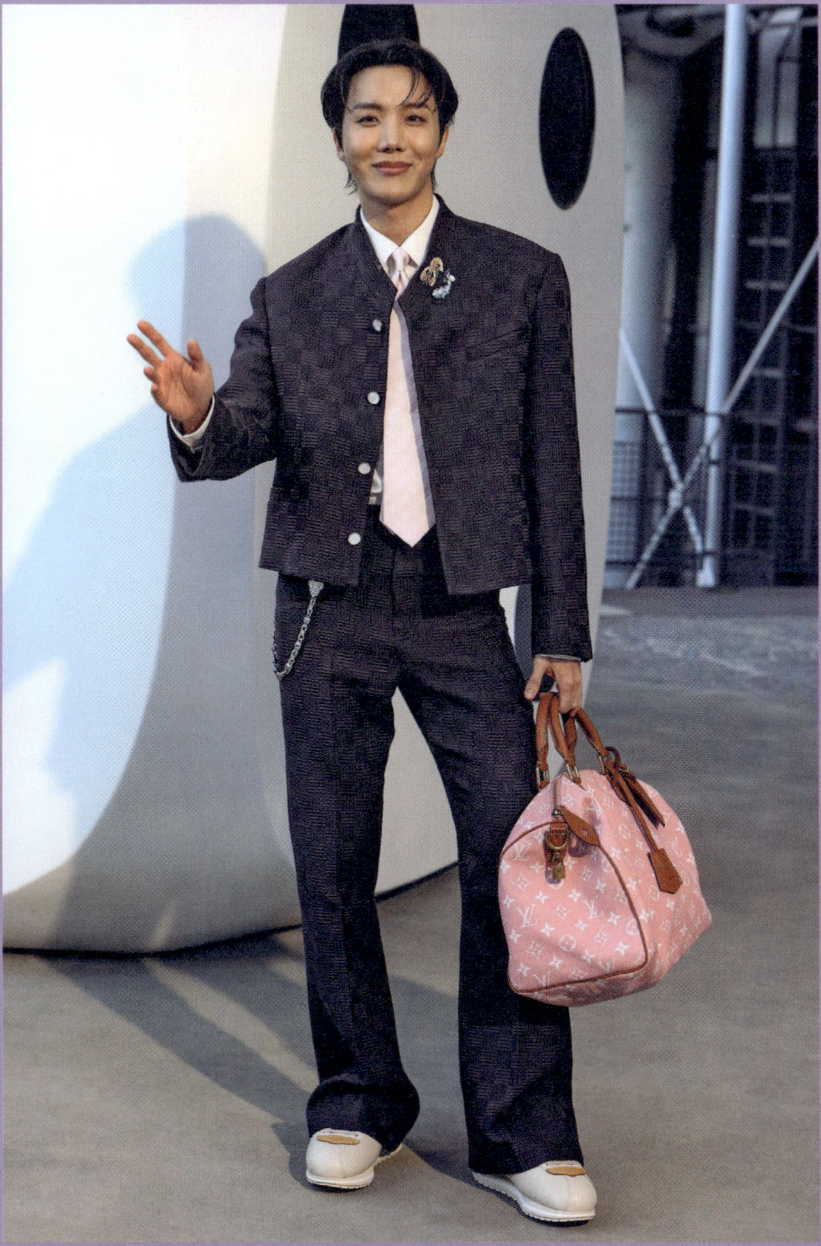

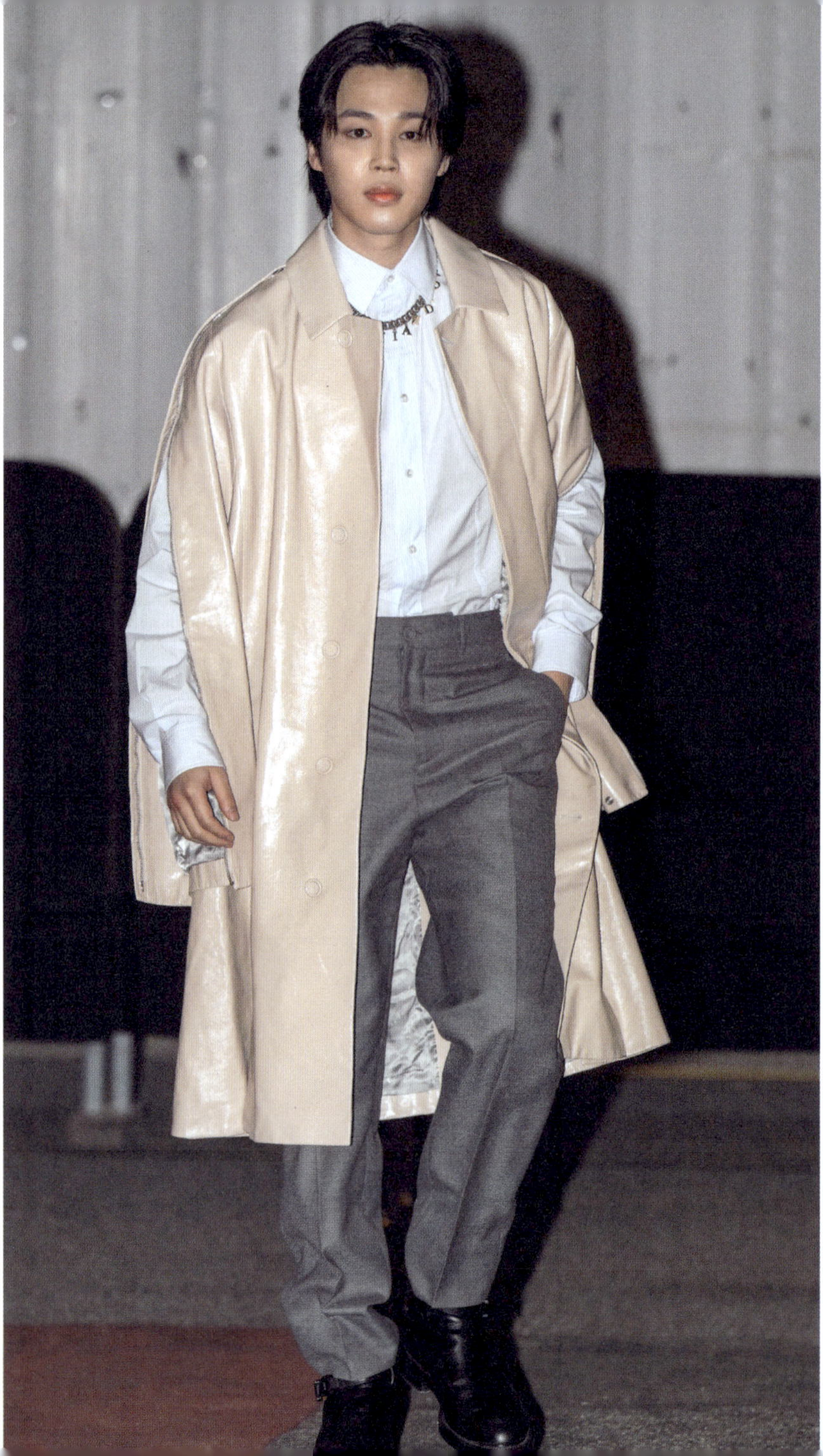

Individually, BTS members are also the faces of several companies. In January 2023, Dior named Jimin as its global brand ambassador, making him the first of the group to be appointed as the solo face of a luxury house. The announcement shared on Dior's official Instagram, alongside photos of Jimin in a series of looks from the French house's Spring/Summer 2023 collection, amassed more than four million likes. It was also widely covered by media around the world, including CNN, which noted that the appointment "signals South Korea's growing importance" to global brands.

Jimin has also since become the face of Tiffany & Co., which shares the same owner as Dior: LVMH. In March of that year, the jewellery company announced that Jimin would become an ambassador, joining stars on its roster such as Hailey Bieber and Blackpink's Rosé. Jimin's first campaigns for the brand launched later that spring, including "This is Tiffany", in which he featured alongside Zoë Kravitz and Gal Gadot.

Jimin, a global brand ambassador for the fashion house, attended the Lady Dior Celebration event in Seoul in September 2023.

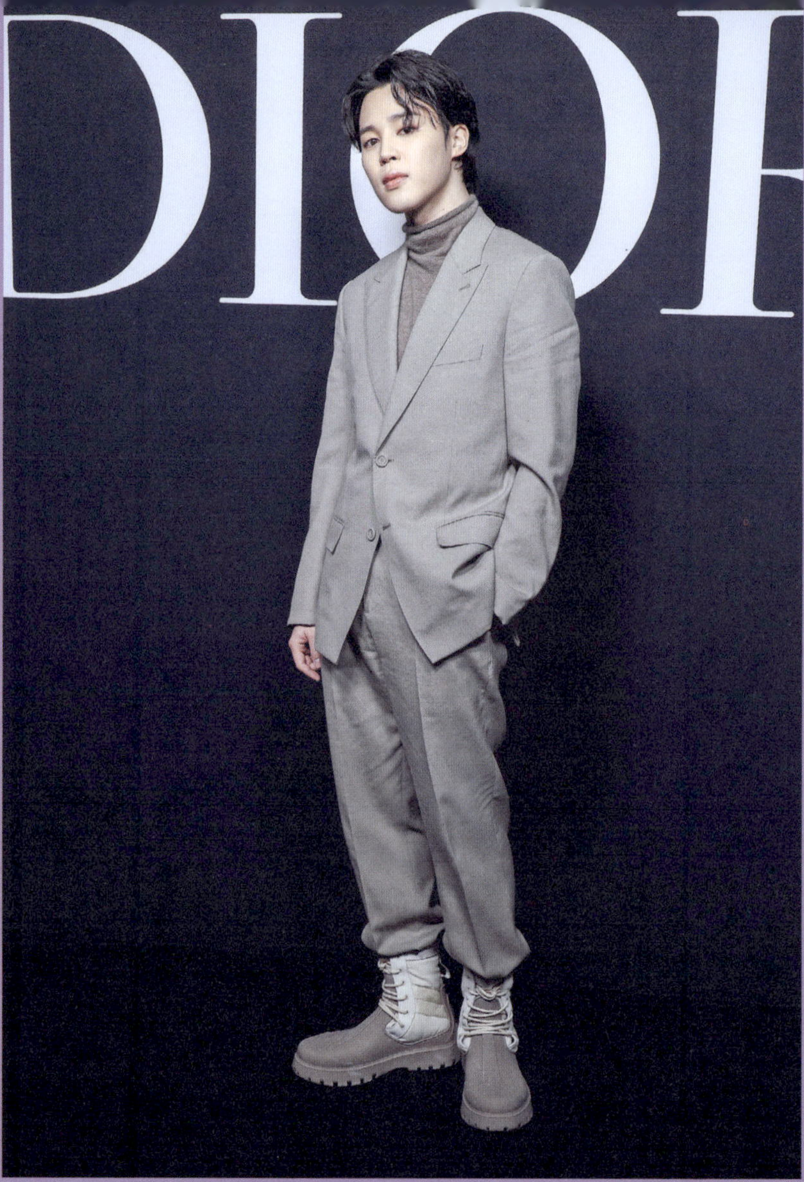

ABOVE Jimin, wearing Dior, at the Dior Homme Menswear show as part of Paris Fashion Week in January 2023.

OPPOSITE Jimin at the reopening of Tiffany's flagship store in New York City in 2023.

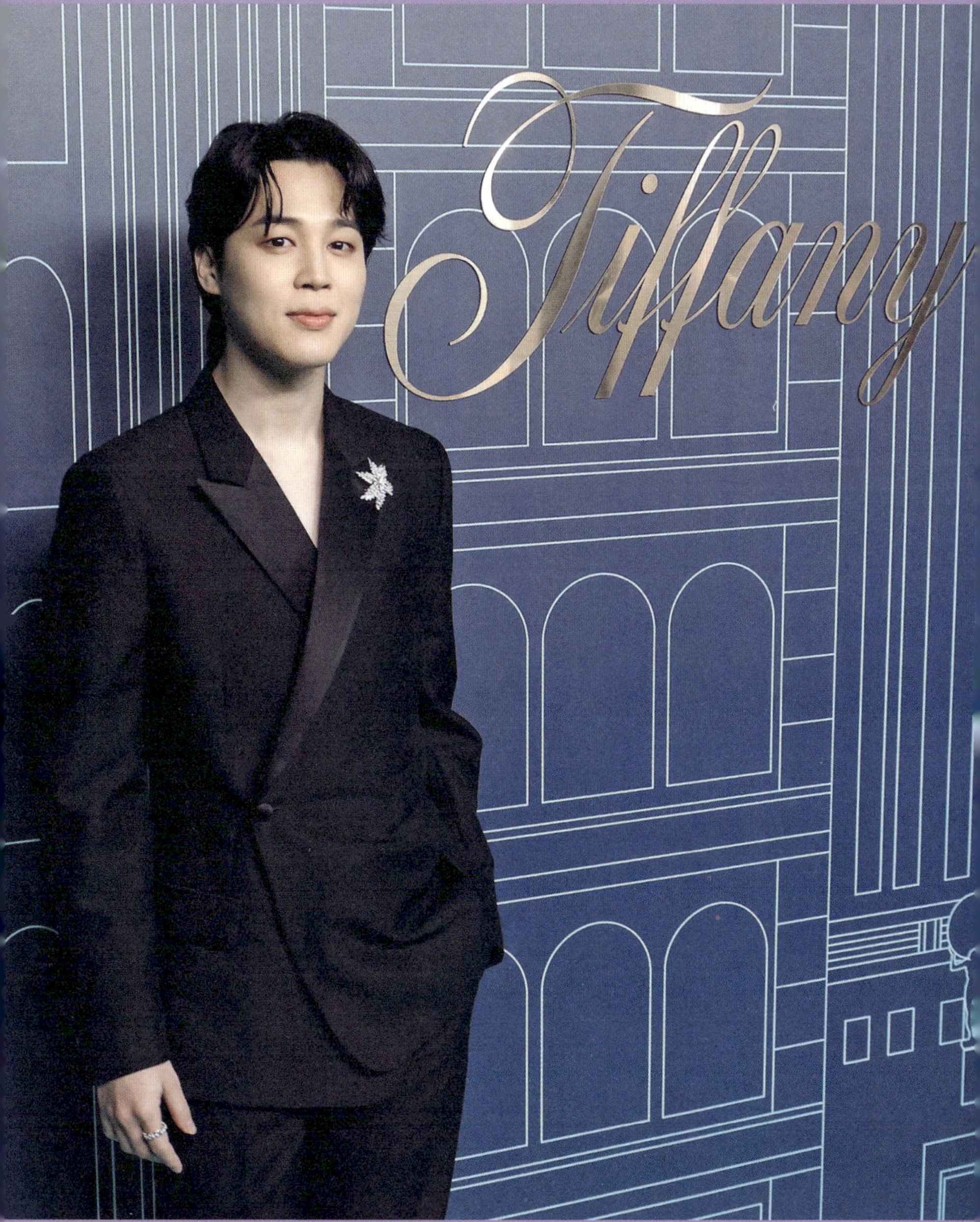
Tiffany

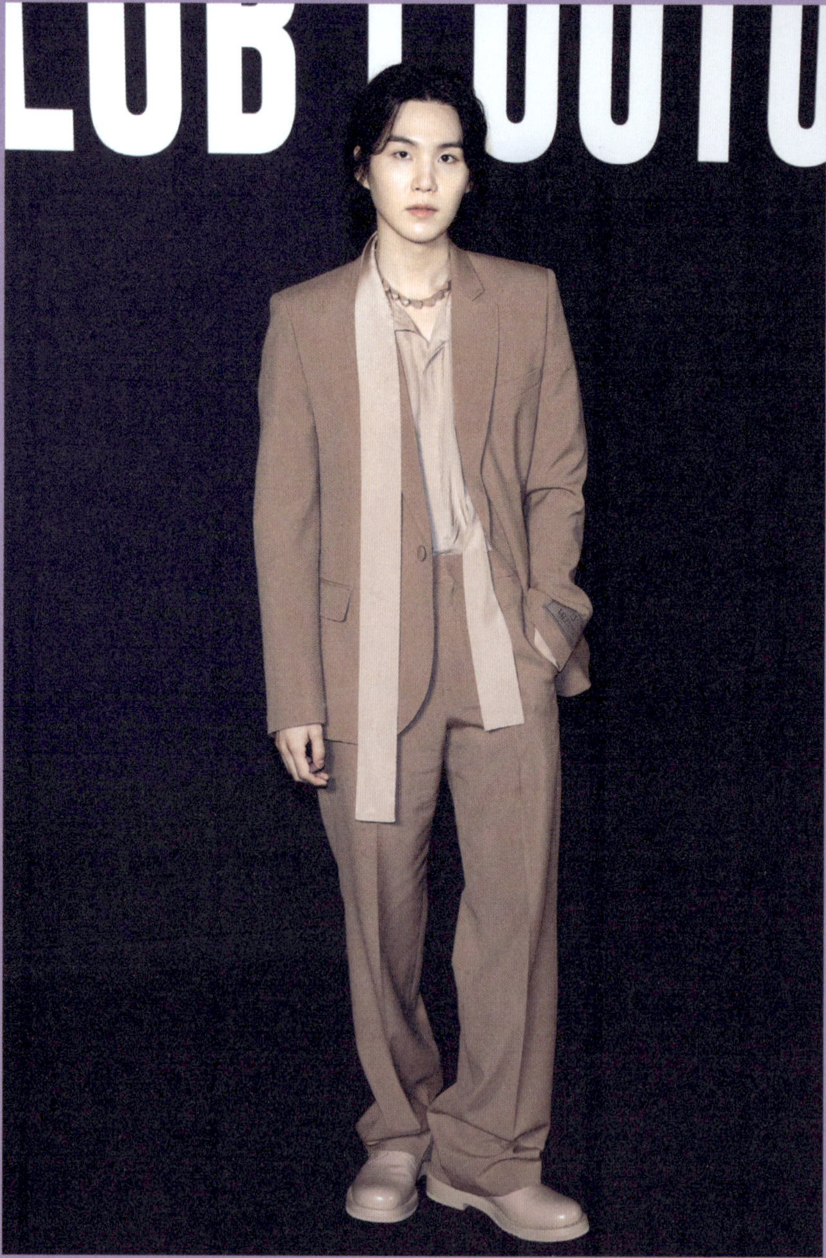

In January 2023, Valentino revealed that Suga would join its collective of ambassadors known as “Di.VAs”, an abbreviation of “Different Values”, which aims to bring together individuals who embody authenticity, diversity and creativity. Suga’s individuality and multifaceted artistic expression was cited as one of the key reasons for the Italian brand’s interest in him.

In February 2023, Louis Vuitton (also owned by LVMH) announced that J-Hope would be the sole BTS member to become its ambassador. He had already been photographed attending its runway show in January and continued to regularly wear the French luxury brand’s looks for his red carpet and public appearances. In August 2023, J-Hope was the cover star of *Esquire Korea*, photographed wearing selected Louis Vuitton pieces. He has appeared in Louis Vuitton’s advertising campaigns, including for its signature Keepall bag. He has also been spotted at Dior shows at Paris Fashion Week, though he is not currently a brand ambassador.

OPPOSITE Suga attended Valentino’s Haute Couture Spring/Summer 2023 show during Paris Fashion Week.

OVERLEAF Suga featured in Valentino’s “The Narratives” advertising campaign for the Spring/Summer 2024 collection. Shot by Theo Wenner, it aimed to capture Suga's personal style and his relationship with his fans, blending moments of fame with quiet introspection.

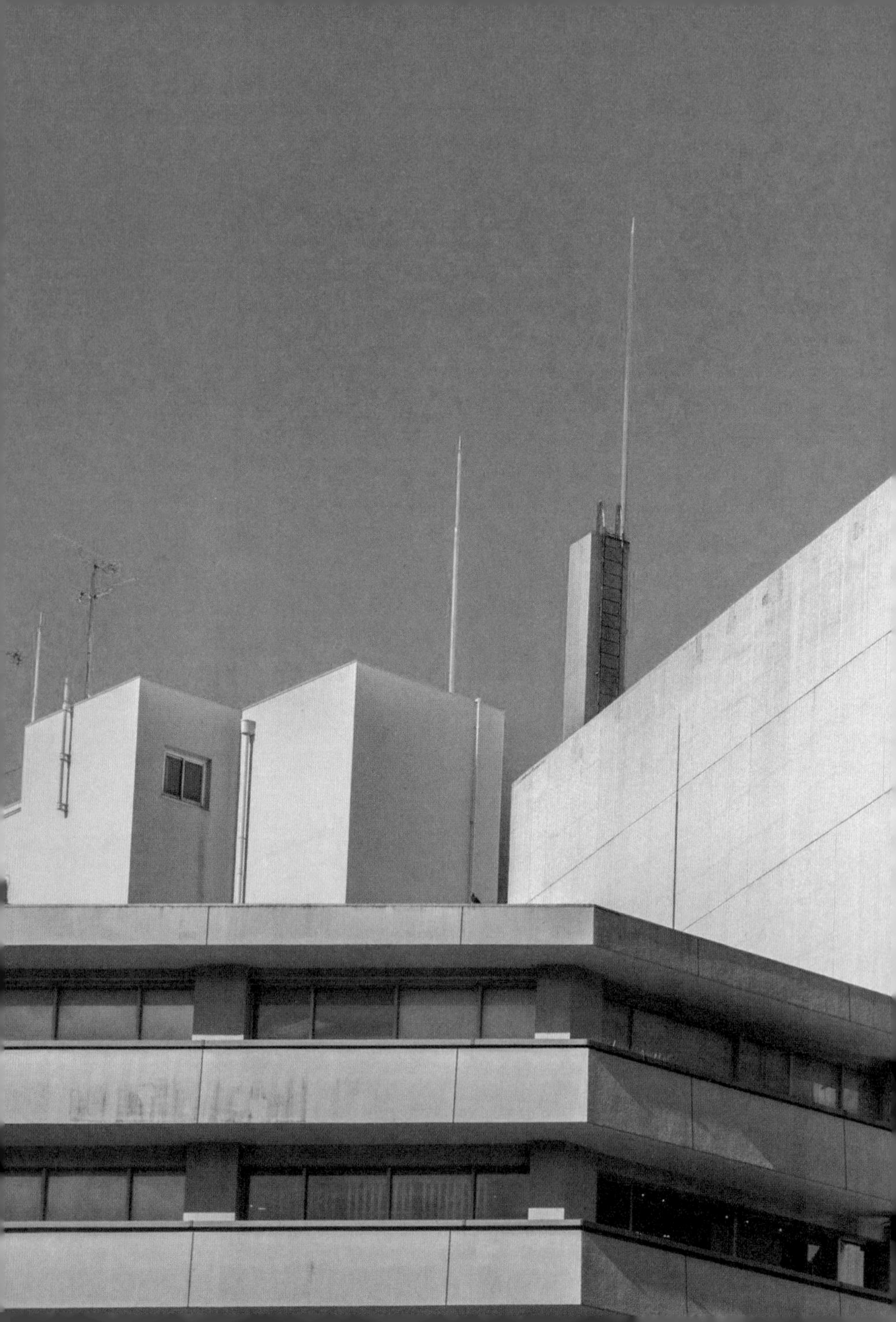

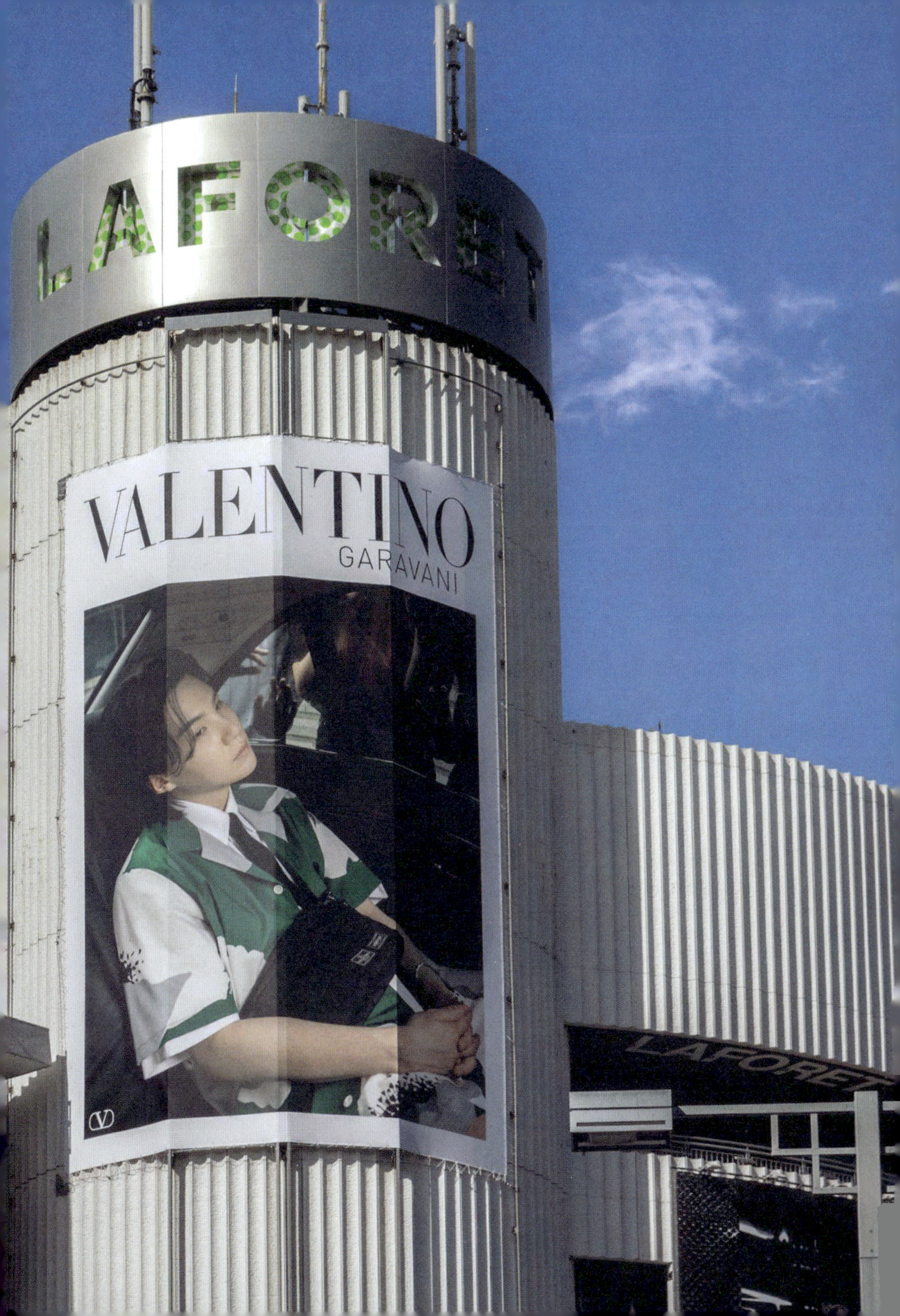
LAFORET
VALENTINO
GARAVANI
LAFORET

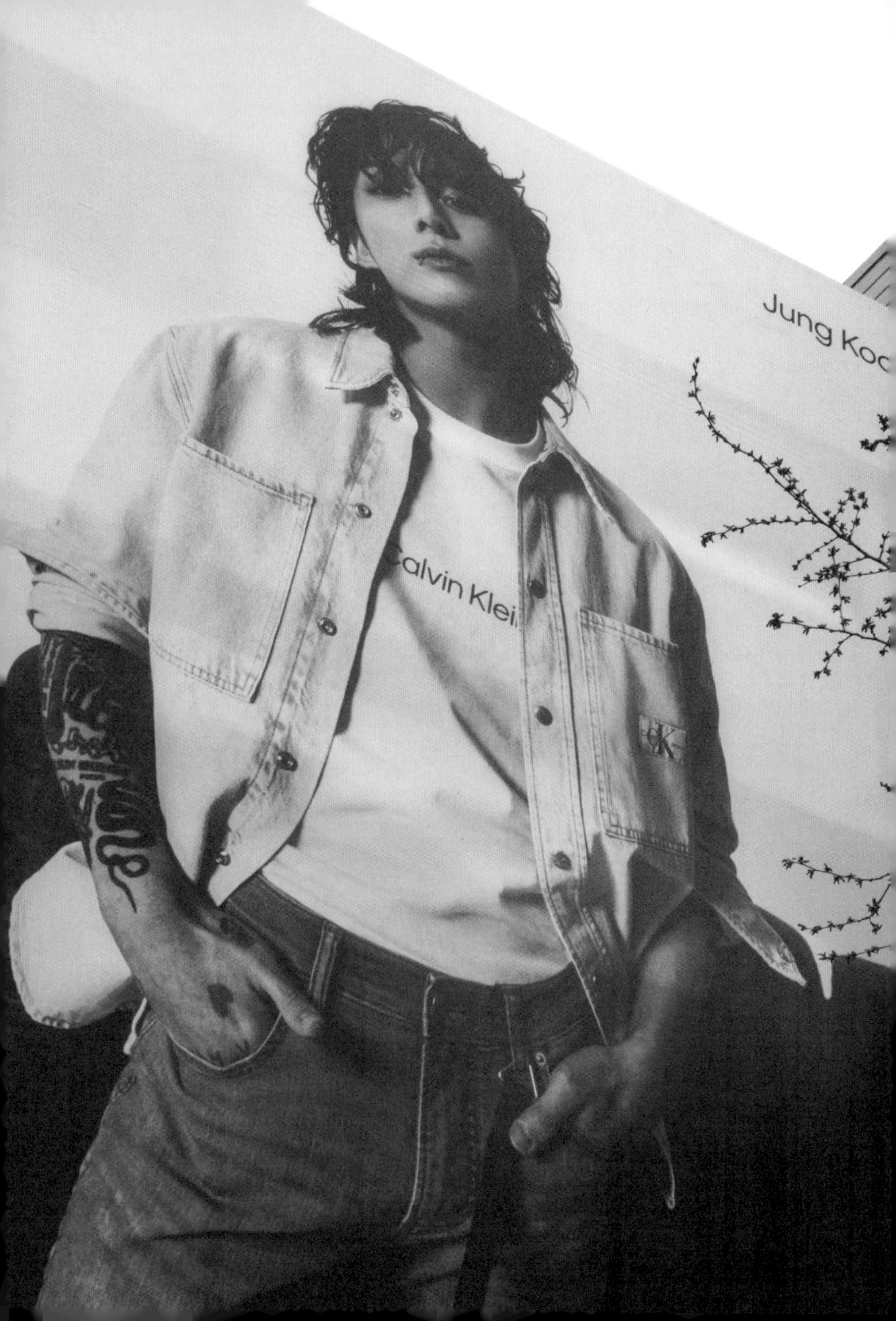
Jung Ko
Calvin Klei

Similarly, Jung Kook appears to be a fan of Versace, though no appointment has been made by the Italian luxury house to date. His decision to wear its glamorous ensembles on several high-profile occasions – including a crystal-embellished blazer in the "Butter" music video teaser in 2021 and a custom rhinestone bomber jacket at the 2022 FIFA World Cup opening ceremony – has prompted speculation that he could one day be the face of the label. Former designer Donatella Versace herself was charmed by Jung Kook's looks and has posted about them on her personal Instagram.

In February 2026, Jung Kook was named as a global brand ambassador for the Swiss luxury watchmaker Hublot. As of March 2023, he has also been a brand ambassador for Calvin Klein, featuring in the American label's advertising campaigns, including a series of photographs taken by the esteemed photographer Mert Alaş at Grand Central Station in New York City. He has also attended its fashion shows and other events. "I have been a fan of Calvin Klein for a long time", Jung Kook said in a statement. "My music is how I communicate with my fans around the world, and I see this partnership as an opportunity to connect with them in a new way".

In December 2025, he was named as a global beauty ambassador for Chanel. Thomas du Pré de Saint Maur, of Chanel Fragrances & Beauty, praised Jung Kook's "incredible talent, music career and distinctive commitment to self-expression, not to mention his bold creative choices," in a statement shared with *WWD*. "It perfectly embodies the essence of our house."

Calvin Klein announced Jung Kook as its brand ambassador in 2023.

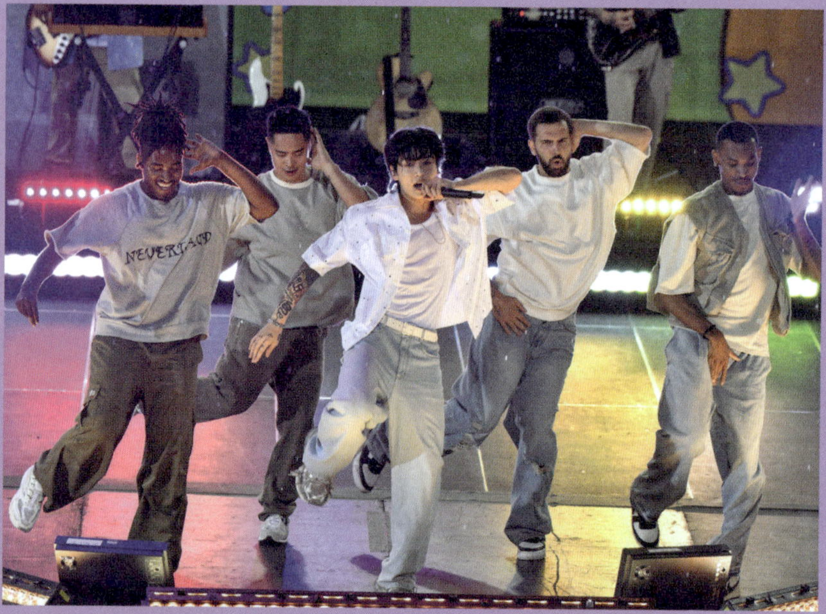

ABOVE While various BTS members were completing military service, Jung Kook took the opportunity to explore personal projects. He is pictured performing in New York City.

OPPOSITE RM (in a Bottega Veneta suit), J-Hope (in Louis Vuitton) and V (in Jaybaek Couture) at the 20th *W Magazine Korea* Breast Cancer Awareness Campaign "Love Your W" in October 2025.

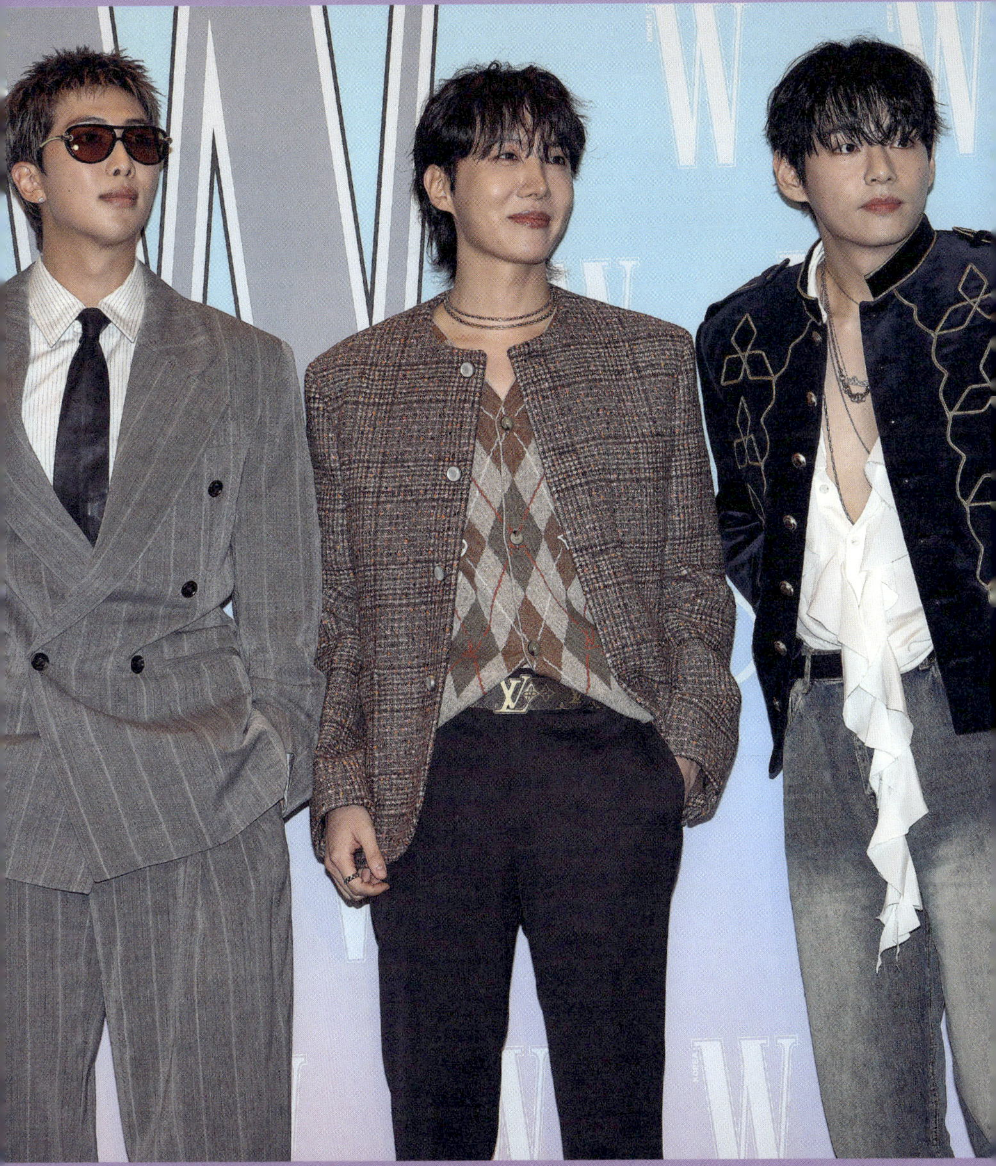

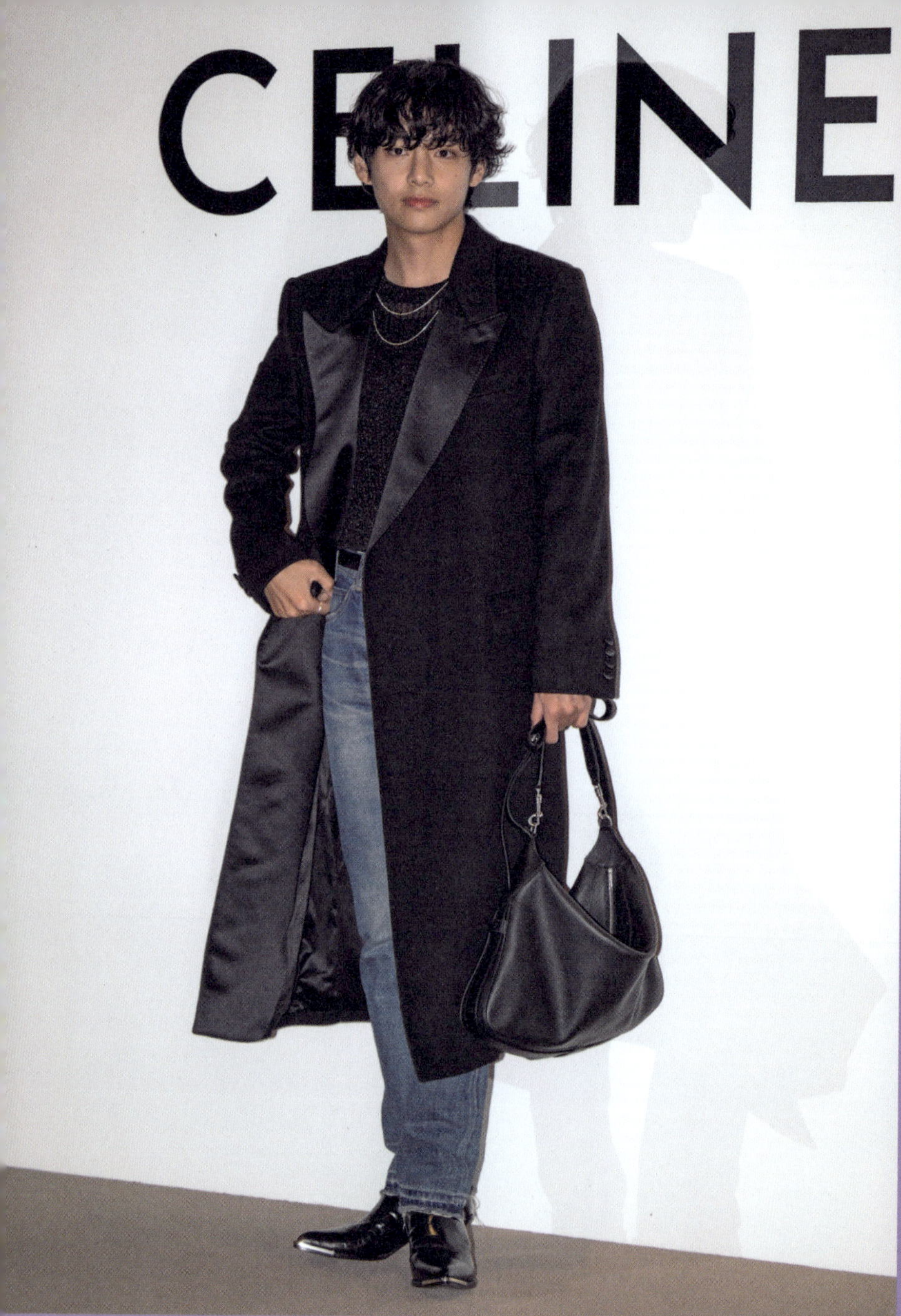
CELINE

Also in 2023, Celine confirmed that V would be its brand ambassador, following months of speculation from fans about the partnership. V had been seen attending Celine's events and, in the months prior, wore the French luxury label on the cover of *Elle Korea*, drawing support from online followers, who created nicknames for him such as "Celine prince" or "Celine boy". More recently V was the cover star of the September 2025 issue of *W Korea* magazine and wore looks from the Celine Spring 2026 collection.

V has also subsequently taken on ambassadorship roles for the Indonesian investment firm SimInvest, notably appearing in an advertisement alongside the Hong Kong martial artist and actor Jackie Chan in 2024. And he promoted the high-end jewellery brand Cartier's La Panthère de Cartier collection, embodying the spirit of the panther with his magnetic personality and unique style. In November 2025, he also became the first global brand ambassador for Tirtir, a K-beauty brand known for its cushion foundations.

V has been a longstanding ambassador of the LVMH-owned label Celine. He attended the brand's pop-up store opening at The Hyundai Yeouido in Seoul in March 2023.

“We do make sure that one person doesn’t stand out...

But then we are really unique. We all have our style, *so I think we all* stand out."

JUNG KOOK, *VOGUE*, 2018

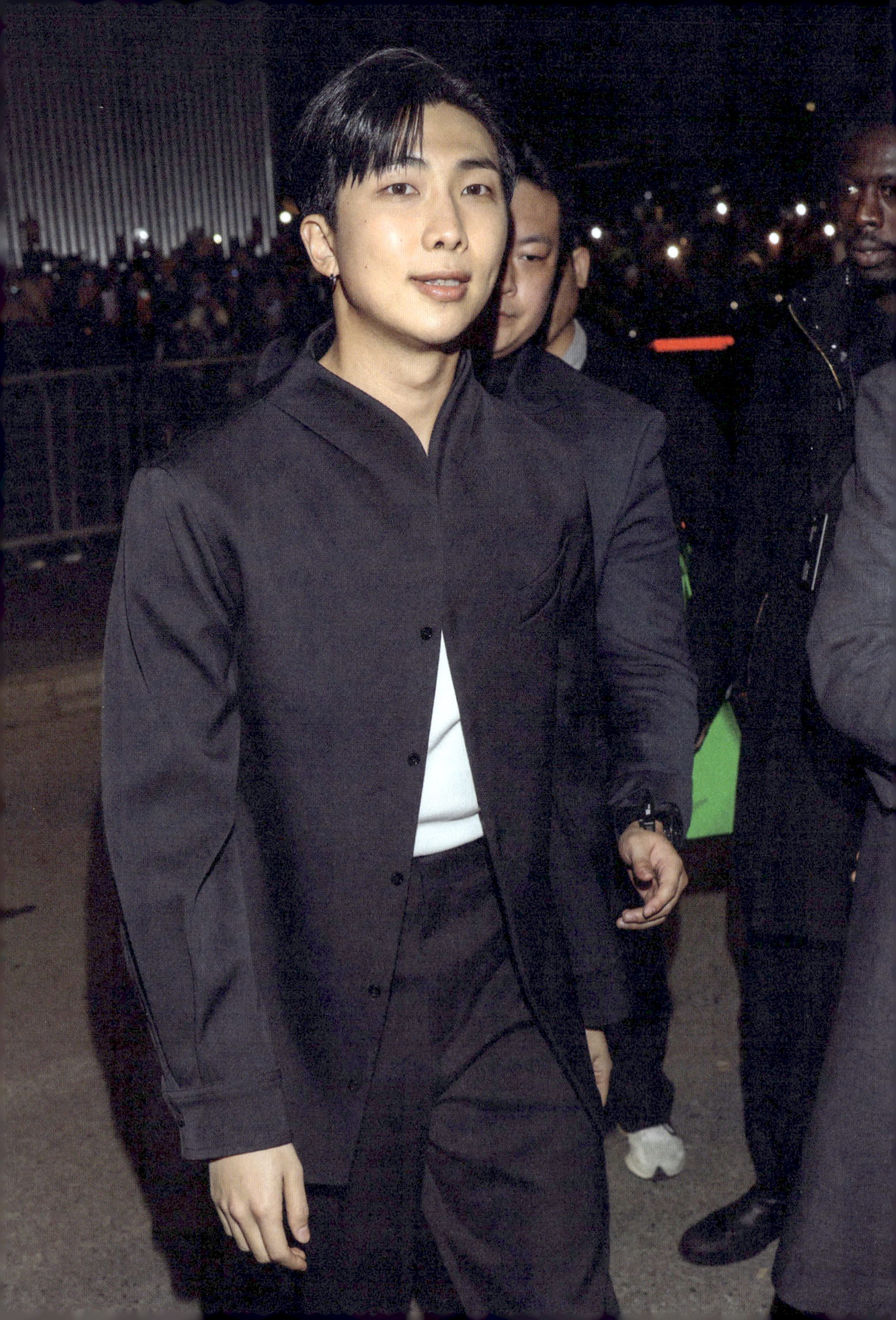

Given his mature and "quiet luxury" approach, RM made the apt choice to be the face of Bottega Veneta and featured in its Spring/Summer 2023 campaign, modelling the Andiamo bag. RM was seen at Bottega Veneta's runway show at Milan Fashion Week a month prior and had previously expressed his respect for the brand, noting its unique focus on craftsmanship and quality over logos.

On his personal Instagram account, Bottega Veneta's former designer Matthieu Blazy (now creative director at Chanel) welcomed RM for stepping into the role – a first for the Venetian luxury label, which until then had never appointed an ambassador. The announcement followed Bottega Veneta's exit from social media: in early 2021 the company deleted its accounts across Instagram, Facebook, Twitter (now X) and Chinese social network Weibo.

RM has been a brand ambassador for Bottega Veneta since 2023. He is pictured at the Italian label's show at Milan Fashion Week in February of that year.

“*Brands want to work with more than just a face. It involves a little bit more thoughtfulness because the consumer is a bit harder to sell to right now.*”

JING DAILY'S AVERY BOOKER, 2021

RM at Seoul's Incheon International Airport in February 2023 wearing a green trench coat and a black woven Bottega Veneta bag.

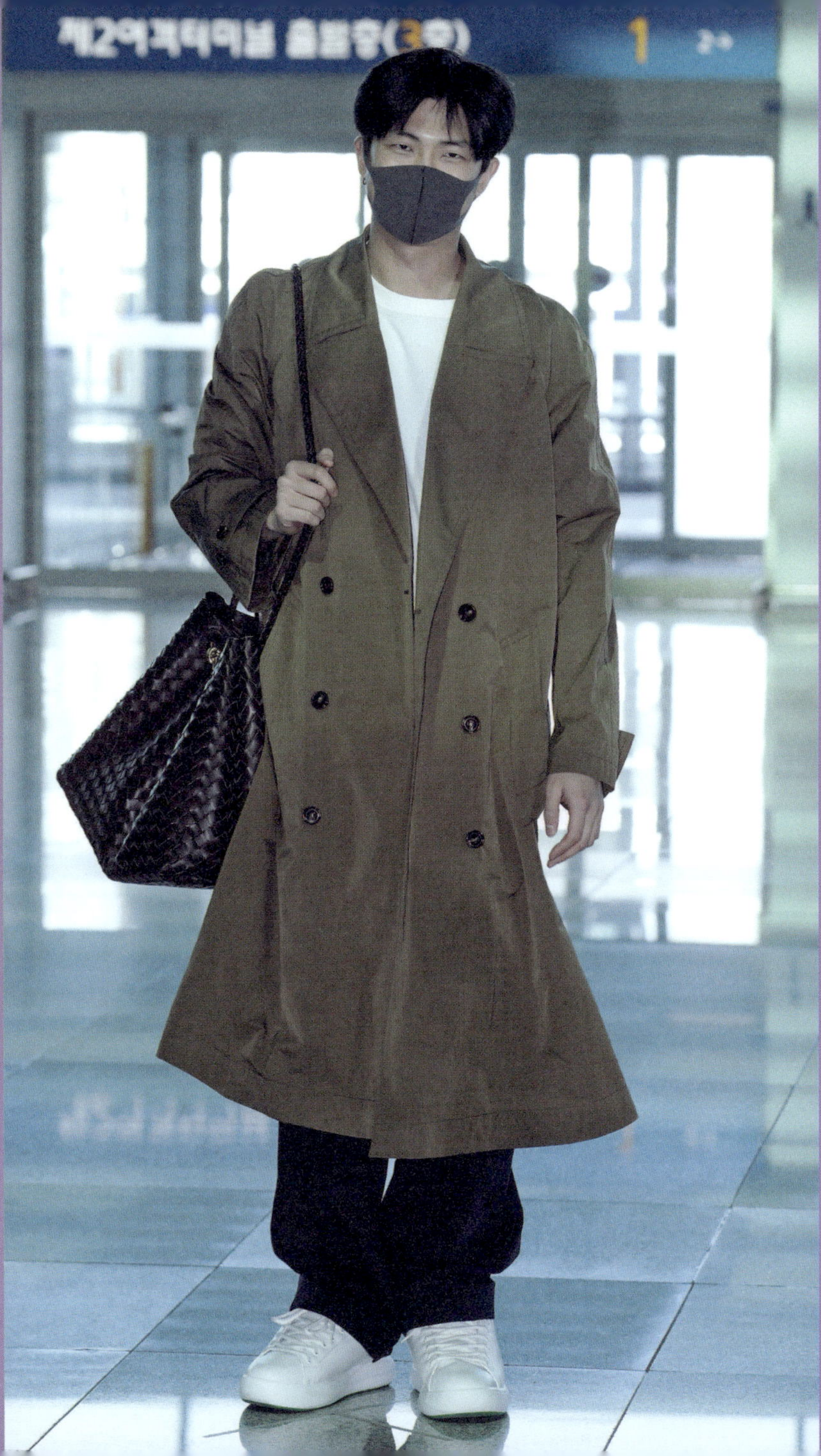
제2여객터미널 출발층(3층)
1

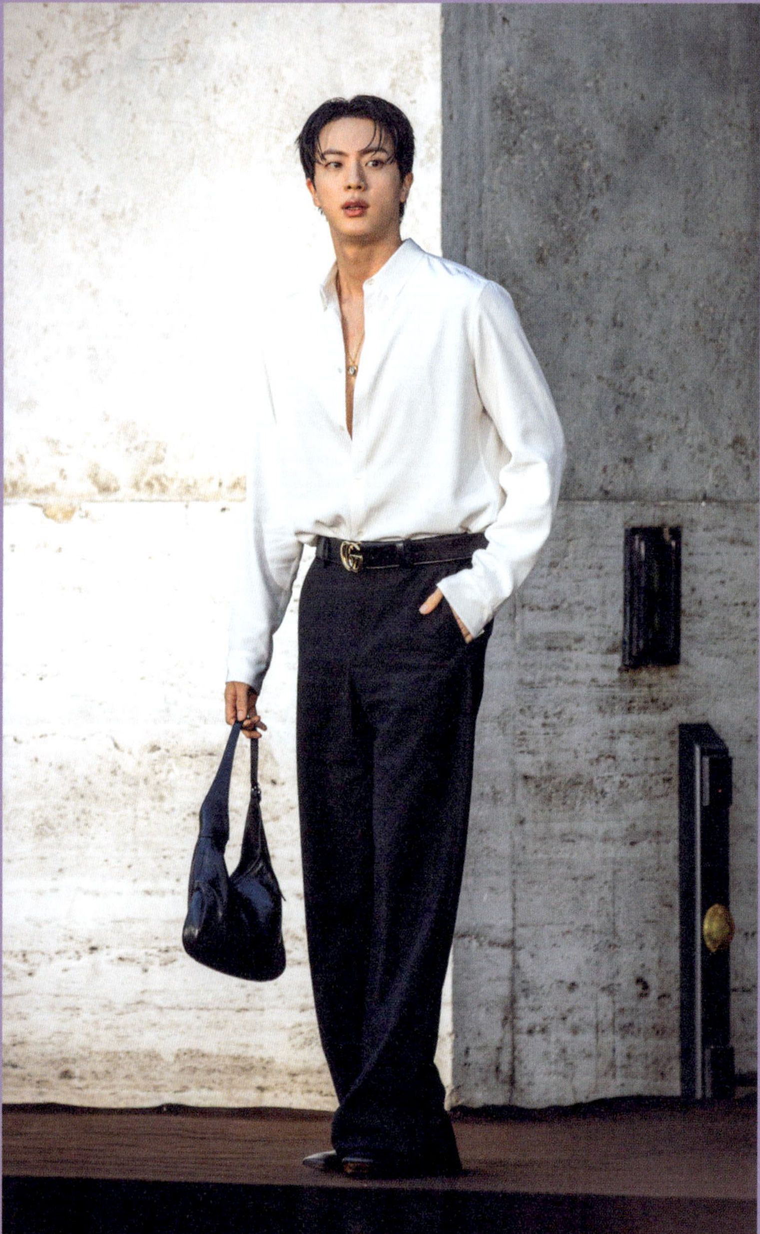

In August 2024, Gucci named Jin as its global brand ambassador. The announcement was made by Gucci's then-creative director Sabato De Sarno. Jin has since featured in Gucci's Spring/Summer 2025 campaign and attended the luxury brand's runway shows at Milan Fashion Week. The singer was also spotted wearing Gucci looks (including custom-made jackets) for his 2025 RunSeokjin Ep. Tour in Amsterdam and London.

Today, BTS members remain the most sought-after ambassadors in South Korea and across the world. Outside of luxury fashion, in April 2023, the NBA named Suga a brand ambassador as he is also an avid fan of basketball. BTS members have also been the face of several large companies, including Hyundai, LG Electronics, Puma and Coca-Cola, for which they represented South Korea at the 2018 World Cup – one of the biggest advertising stages in the world.

And their endorsements have directly led to sales increases. In 2020, the limited-edition Samsung Galaxy S20 Plus BTS edition (which came in purple and featured BTS-themed content) sold out quickly, especially in its initial pre-order phase in South Korea and neighbouring regions such as Singapore. Meanwhile, demand for Hyundai's new flagship SUV Palisade car skyrocketed in 2019 when orders reportedly nearly doubled the anticipated domestic volume after endorsement from BTS.

Jin, as a global ambassador for Gucci, at the premiere of the film *The Tiger* by Spike Jonze and Halina Reijn, presented by Gucci.

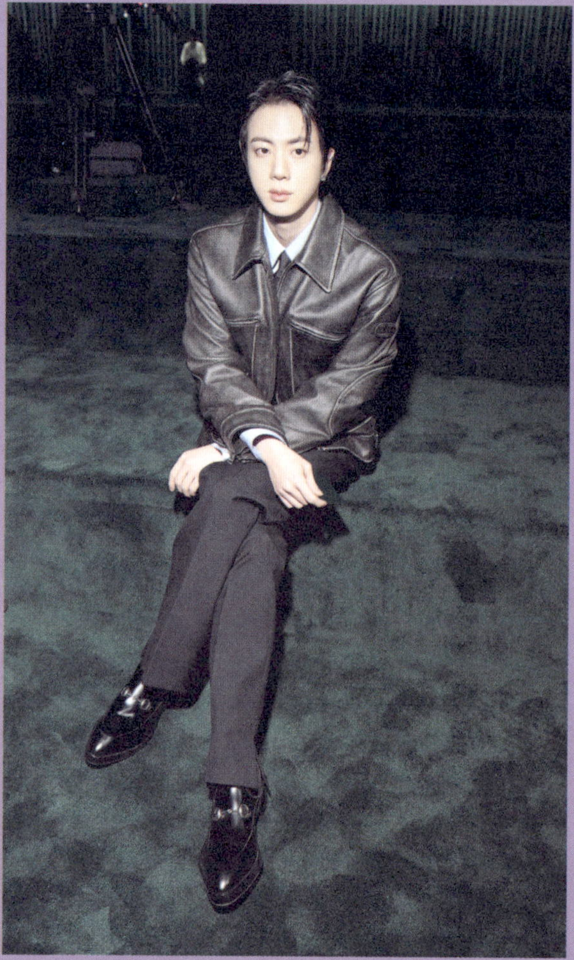

ABOVE In a bid to strengthen its presence in the South Korean market, Gucci named Jin as its global brand ambassador in August 2024. He is a regular at their shows, including the women's Fall/Winter 2025 at Milan Fashion Week in February 2025.

OPPOSITE Jin at the Gucci women's Spring/Summer 2025 show at Milan Fashion Week in September 2024.

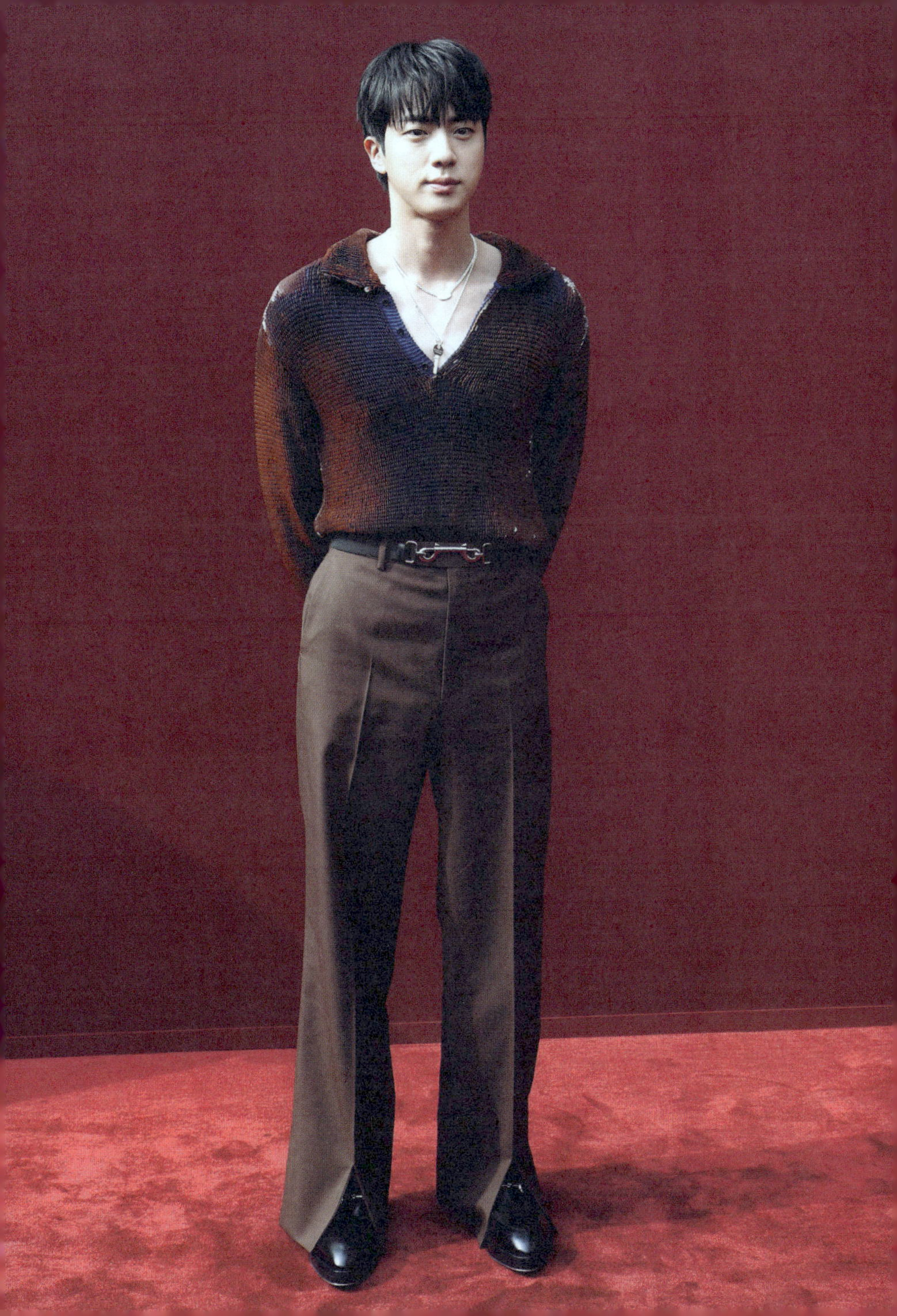

FROM IDOLS

CHAPTER 5

TO DIPLOMATS

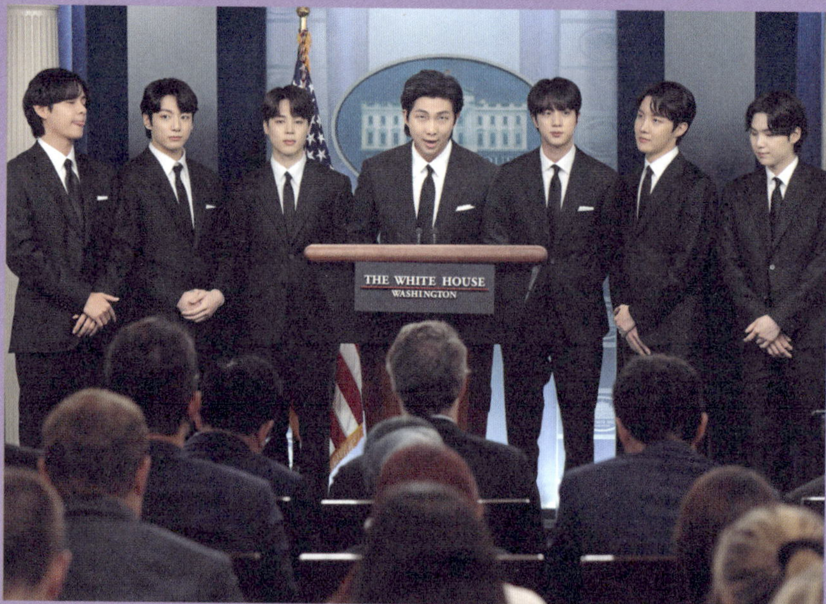

RM speaks for all seven members of BTS
at The White House, 31 May 2022.

FROM IDOLS TO DIPLOMATS

The influence of BTS stretches far beyond K-pop, music and fashion, and the group have increasingly been positioned as fearless activists and agents of change. While their advocacy for social causes initially emerged via their music's lyrical themes, the band has also used its global platform to champion and take more direct action in social movements, as evidenced in their partnerships, donations and public statements.

In September 2018, BTS became the first K-pop group to speak at the United Nations (UN) when the members delivered a historic address at the 73rd session of the UN General Assembly. The speech, which lasted three minutes, marked the launch of the "Generation Unlimited" campaign by UNICEF, the UN's humanitarian aid organization. In promoting education, employment and empowerment for young people globally, the goal of the initiative is for everyone aged between 10 and 24 to be in school, learning, training or employment by 2030.

Experts say the challenge for the UN is that many of its leaders are now elderly and there is also growing sentiment that younger generations need to take a more active role in achieving these goals since they represent the future and have the most to gain – or lose. As a senior diplomat told *CBS News* in 2018, "most heads of state coming to the General Assembly are 60-plus years old. We need the next generation to follow through." The hope is that a popular boy band, coupled with the right messaging on social media, could attract and influence the targeted demographic.

In a statement at the time, BTS, with their new title of UNICEF Global Supporters, declared: "We think the mutual support from youth to each other is the first step to show love." When BTS spoke at the General Assembly, the high-spirited band swapped out their usual playful attire (such as the colourful patterned suits worn for their performance on *The Tonight Show Starring Jimmy Fallon* that same year) for a more formal ceremonial look – white collared shirts and smart black suits, some styled with a dark tie – proving their ability to be versatile and adapt to varying situations.

This wasn't the first time BTS had partnered with the UN. Their involvement began with the "Love Myself" campaign, launched in 2017 to raise awareness and funds to end violence against children. The group has also subsequently returned for appearances in 2020 and 2021, speaking on topics such as the COVID-19 pandemic, climate change and the importance of vaccines.

"After releasing the *Love Yourself* albums and launching the 'Love Myself' campaign, we started to hear remarkable stories from our fans all over the world, how our message helped them overcome their hardships in life and start loving themselves", said RM in a UN press statement. "These stories constantly remind us of our responsibility".

During his 2018 UN address, RM recalled how he had a happy childhood after being born in Ilsan, a city near Seoul. But when he was about nine or ten years old he started to become more self-conscious and worried about what other people thought of him. “I had one sanctuary, and that was music”, he said. “There was a small voice in me that said, ‘Wake up, man, and listen to yourself!’ But it took me a long time to hear music calling my name.”

“Tell me your story. I want to hear your voice, and I want to hear your conviction”, he added. “No matter who you are, where you’re from, your skin colour, gender identity: speak yourself.”

RM made another impassioned speech at the United Nations, this time as part of the General Assembly 76th session General Debate on 20 September 2021.

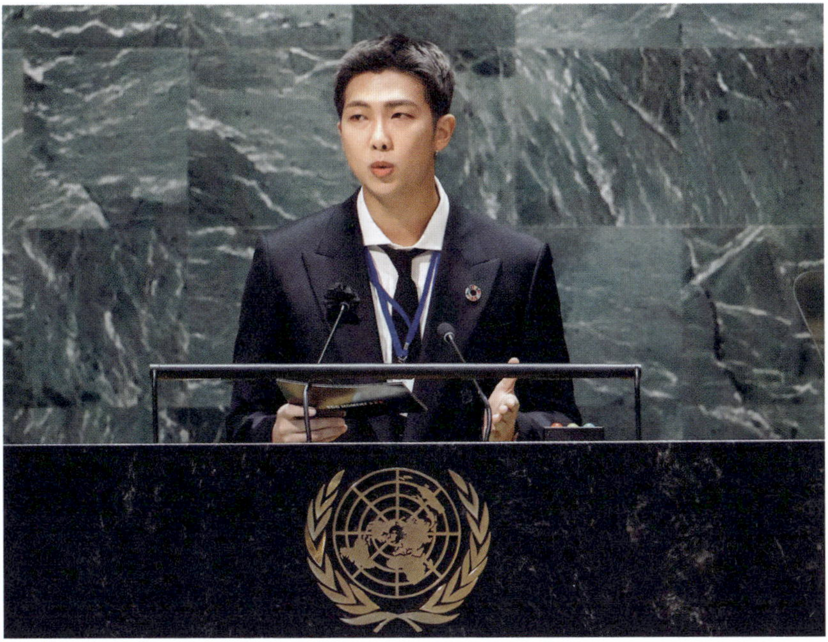

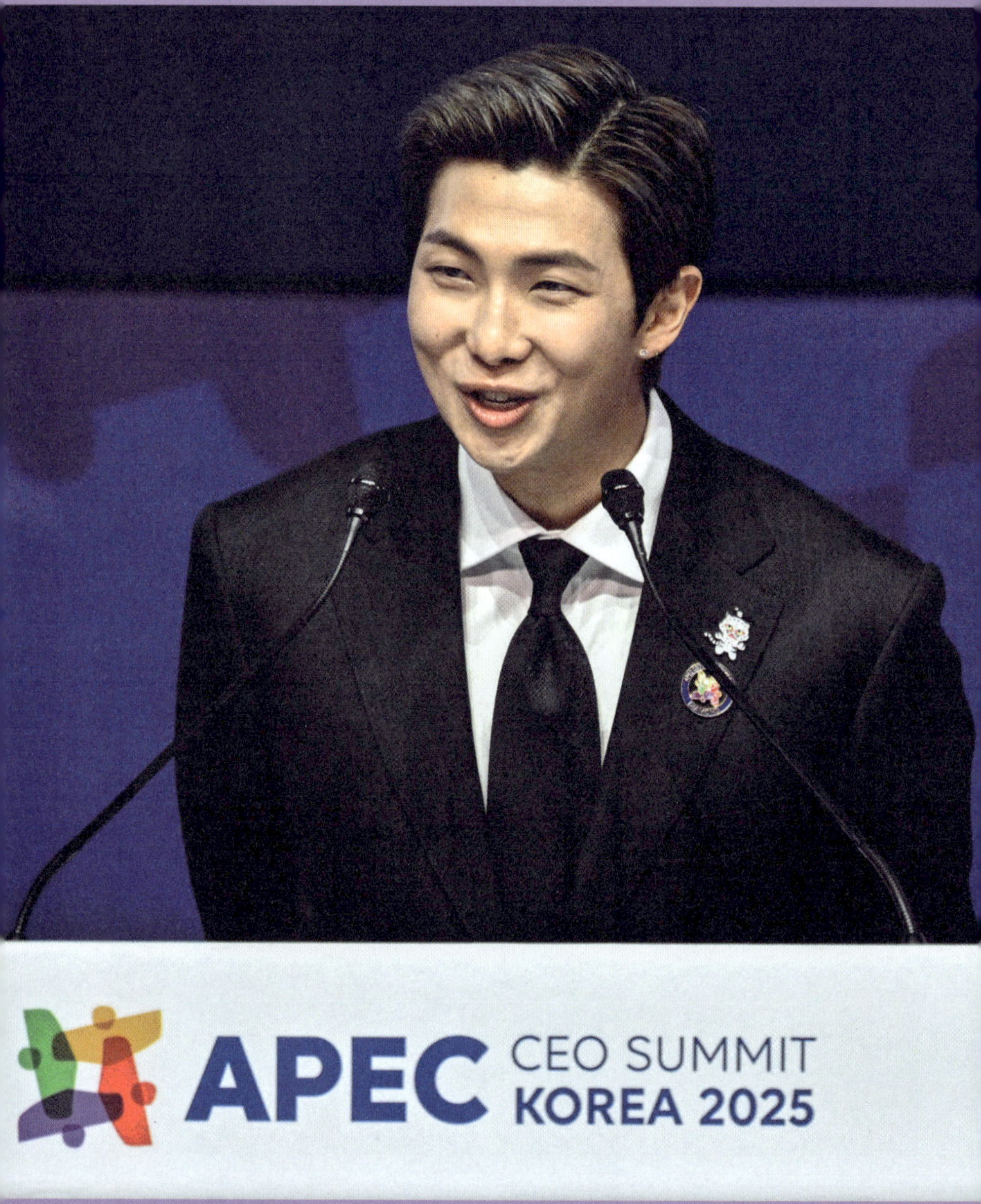
APEC
CEO SUMMIT
KOREA 2025

The BTS dedicated ARMY fan base has also received national attention for the organization, mobilization and subsequent impact of their digital activism. They often match the band's charitable donations, participate in campaigns for causes the members care about and even make personal donations on band member's birthdays. The OIAA group, short for "One In An ARMY", collaborates with non-profit organizations around the world and encourages donations. Its first campaign, launched in April 2018 in partnership with the non-profit Medical Teams International, helped to bring medical care to Syria.

In June 2020, BTS shared their solidarity with Black Lives Matter by donating $1m to the organization while also sharing their support on Twitter (now X), writing: "We stand against racial discrimination. We condemn violence. You, I and we all have the right to be respected. We will stand together." It was reposted over 852,000 times.

This prompted Kailee Scales, managing director for Black Lives Matter, to share a statement with *Variety*, which first reported the news of the BTS donation. "We are moved by the generosity of BTS and allies all over the world who stand in solidarity in the fight for Black lives", she said.

RM was the first K-pop artist to deliver a keynote speech at the APEC CEO Summit 2025 in Gyeongju, South Korea.

"We and our ARMY are always charging each other's batteries. When we feel exhausted, when we hear the news all over the world,

the tutoring programs, and donations, and every good thing, we feel *responsible for all of this...*"

RM, *ESQUIRE*, 2020

Inspired by the group's actions, BTS ARMY set a #MatchAMillion goal that saw the fan base match – and ultimately surpass – the group's $1m donation to the Black Lives Matter movement. The impressive figure raised is just one of several displays of solidarity from the BTS ARMY, several of whom also banded together on social media to form an intense resistance movement against police brutality that same year.

Some experts have observed that The Black Lives Matter movement may have been of particular interest to K-pop fans given the artists' debt to hip-hop culture and Black music, with BTS (among other groups) having been accused in the past of cultural appropriation or insensitivity. In 2018, a photograph of Jimin wearing a shirt depicting the US atomic bombing of Japan and a Korean liberation slogan drew much ire, prompting Big Hit Entertainment to apologize on the band's behalf. Just a week prior, RM was criticized by the Simon Wiesenthal Center, a leading Jewish human rights organization, for wearing headgear that featured a Nazi-style symbol. Big Hit subsequently defended the singer, noting that a stylist had given him the hat during a magazine photo shoot in 2014, according to *CNN*, but also stressed in a lengthy Facebook post that it "does not support any organizations or groups oriented towards political extremism and totalitarian beliefs including Nazism" and that the band were "in no way responsible for any of the issues outlined".

J-Hope and RM pose at the annual *W Magazine* Korea Breast Cancer Awareness Campaign "Love Your W" in October 2022 in Seoul.

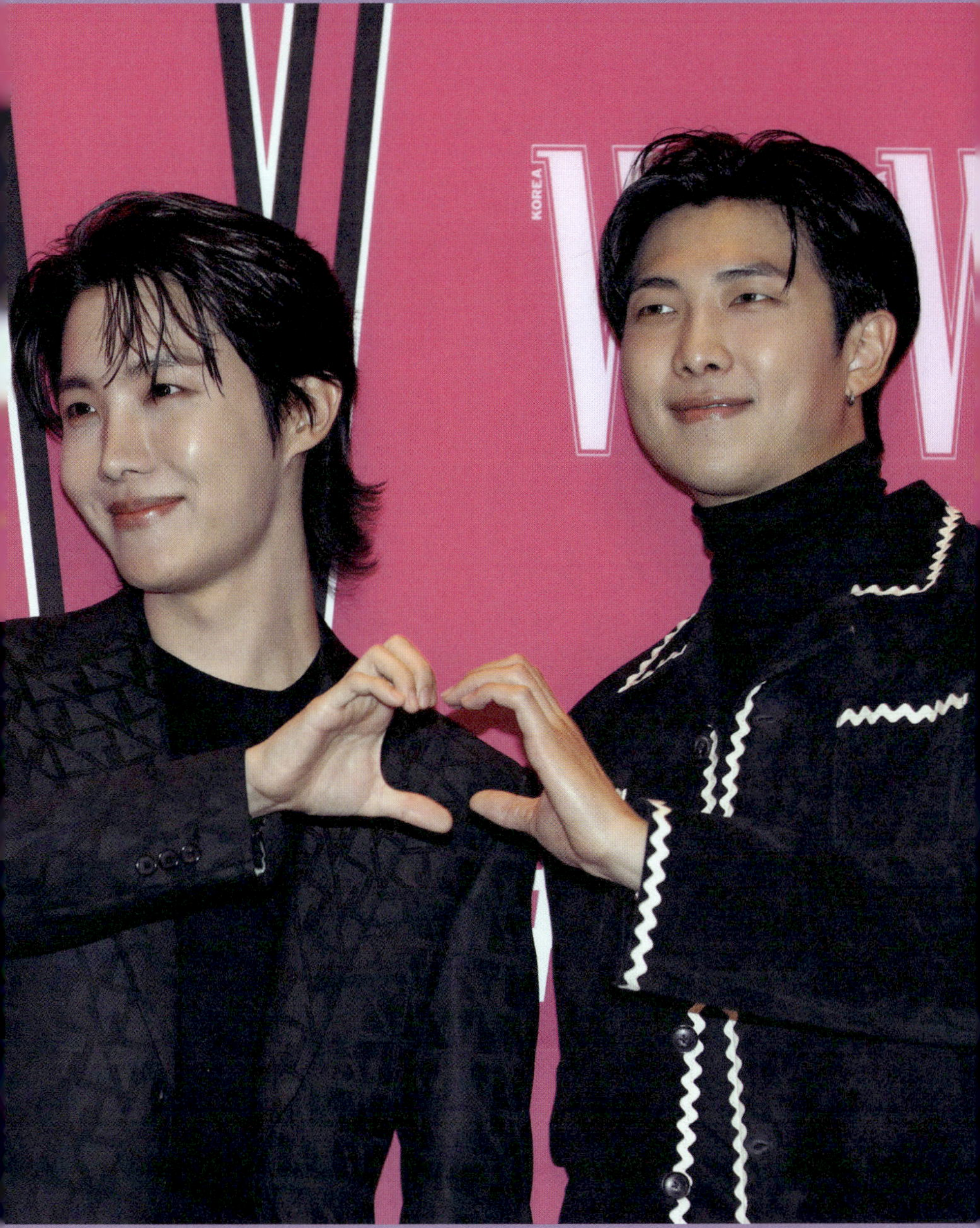
KOREA

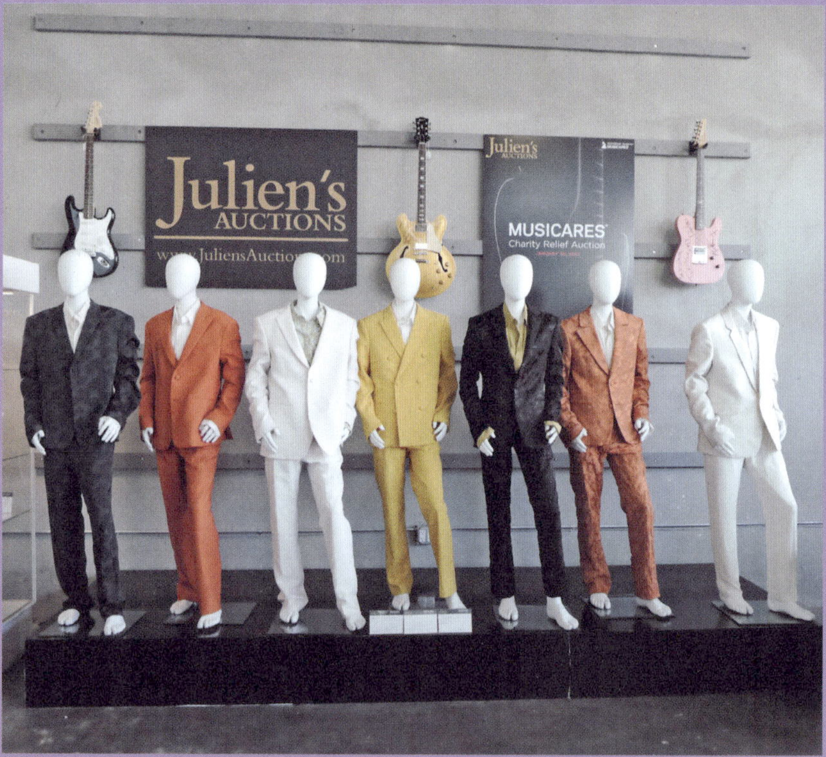
Julien's
AUCTIONS
Julien's
AUCTIONS
MUSICARES
Charity Relief Auction

As fans push their idols to be socially progressive, K-pop groups have consequently reached across cultural boundaries to find new inspiration. BTS, for example, was praised for their 2018 song "Idol", which was infused with Afrobeats and Korean folk rhythms. An accompanying music video shows the group's members clad in jackets inspired by *hanbok*, Korean traditional clothing.

As part of their charitable efforts, BTS donates many of their outfits – often from popular performances or music videos – to auctions that support causes such as MusiCares, a non-profit that provides health and welfare support to musicians, and the Grammy Museum Foundation, which is dedicated to celebrating and preserving music's history and cultural significance. Previously auctioned BTS items have included the pastel outfits from the music video for their chart-topping 2020 song "Dynamite". According to BBC Newsround in 2021, the seven sets of clothing were sold by Julien's Auctions in Beverly Hills to the Japanese art collector Yusaku Maezawa and YouTuber Hikakin for a final bid of $162,500 (£125,000) – significantly more than the estimated $20,000 to $40,000 (£15,000 to £30,000). Other pieces that have also been sold at auction are the band members' custom Louis Vuitton suits from the 2021 Grammy Awards and multiple outfits from their 2020 "Life Goes On" music video.

The colorful suits worn by BTS in their "Dynamite" music video were sold by Julien's Auctions for charity at an auction in January 2022.

In March 2021, BTS members made their voices heard again, as they (and other high-profile celebrities) publicly denounced anti-Asian attacks by sharing their personal experiences of discrimination and condemning the rise of anti-Asian hate crimes through social media. Their reactions came in response to the deadly mass shootings in Asian-owned spas in Atlanta, Georgia, where four of the eight victims were of Korean descent. The incident came during a spike in the deliberate targeting of Asian individuals as some people blamed China for the global pandemic.

A statement at the time from BTS – published in Korean and English – recounted discriminatory experiences that made them feel "powerless". The group expressed "grief and anger" over the violence, particularly the Atlanta spa shootings, and called for greater respect and understanding for all people.

"We cannot put into words the pain of becoming the subject of hatred and violence for such a reason", the BTS statement read. "Our own experiences are inconsequential compared to the events that have occurred over the past few weeks. But these experiences were enough to make us feel powerless and chip away at our self-esteem".

OPPOSITE A Seoul Tourism Organization campaign featuring BTS. It was aimed to console and uplift those in the city during the Covid-19 pandemic.

OVERLEAF One of the group's final performances before various members started their mandatory military service: the 64th annual Grammy Awards, in 2022.

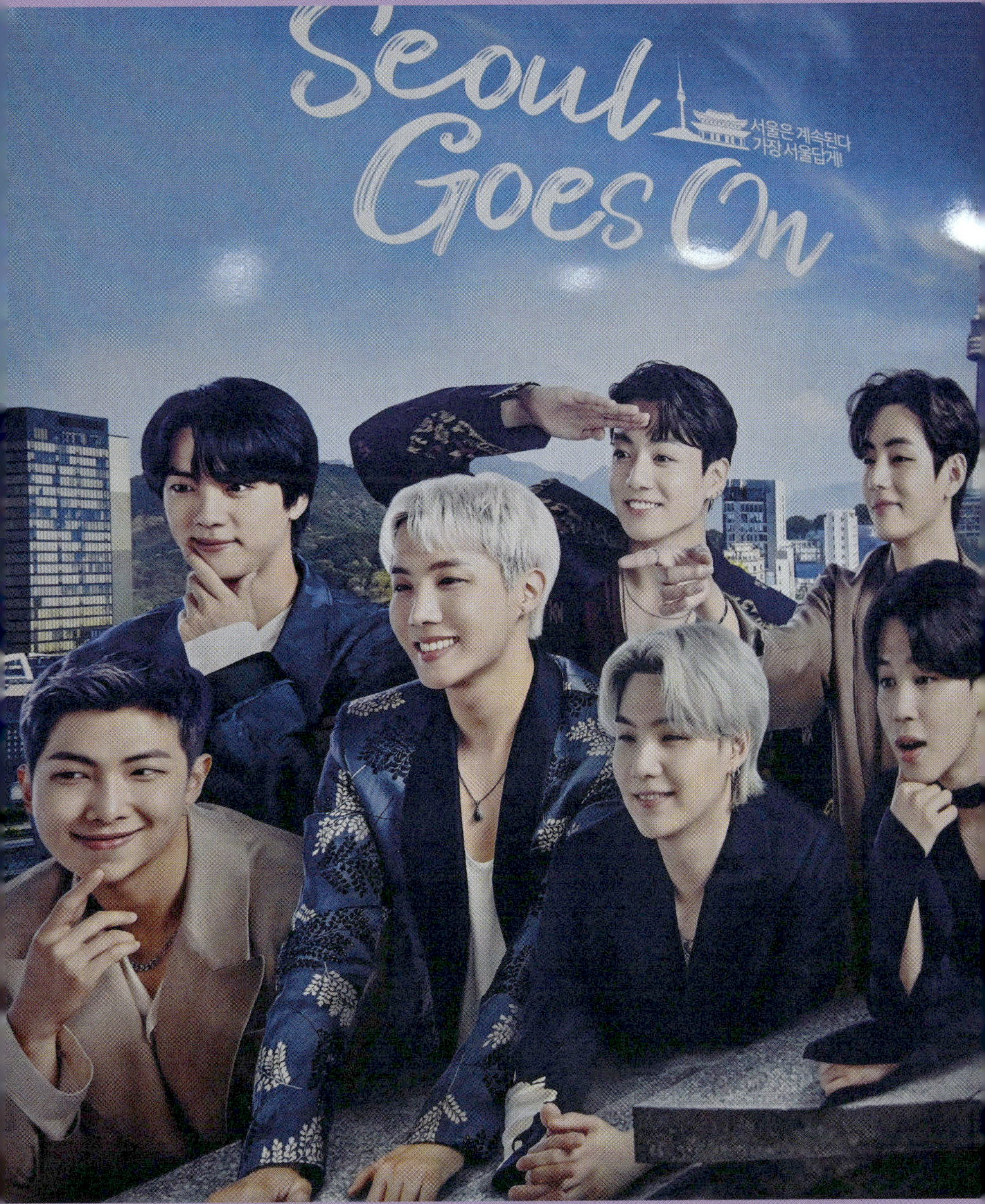
Seoul Goes On
서울은 계속된다
가장 서울답게!

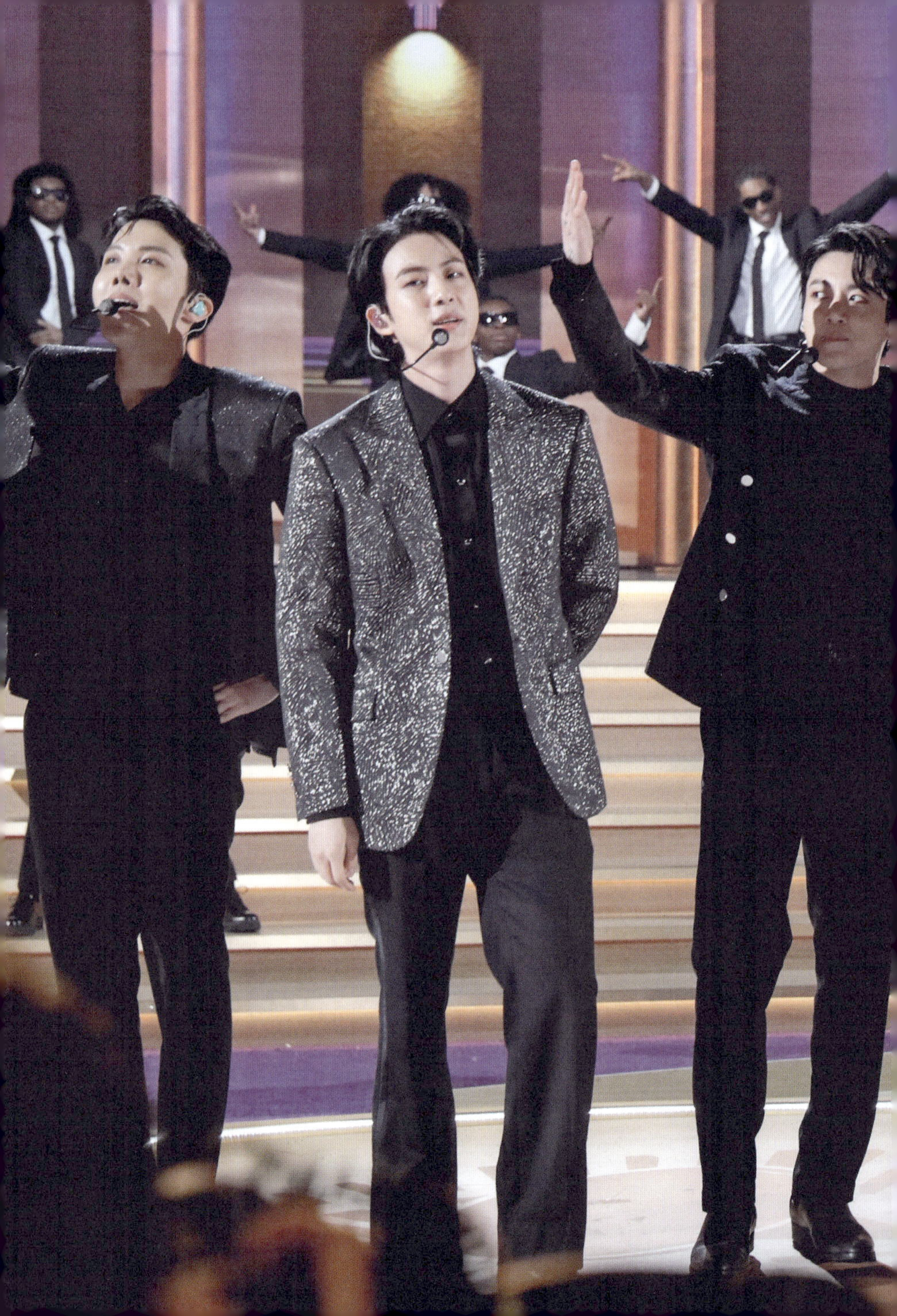

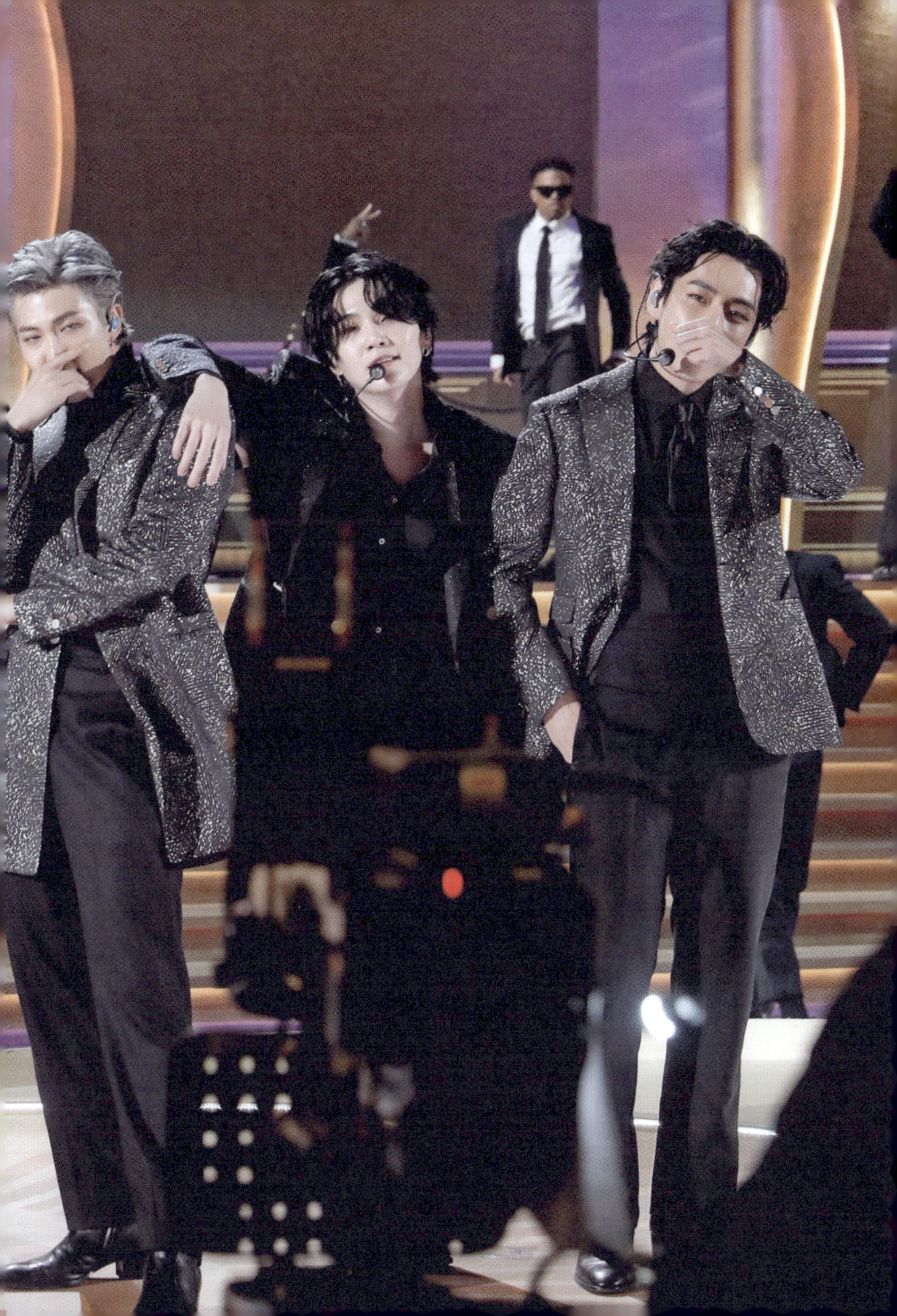

In September 2021, BTS members were officially sworn in by then-South Korean president Moon Jae-in as special presidential envoys for future generations and culture. In a ceremony, each member was given a diplomatic passport, certificate of appointment and a custom fountain pen in return for representing South Korea and raising awareness for global issues such as sustainable development and climate change among younger generations.

Former US president Joe Biden acknowledged BTS in May 2022, when the group made an official visit to the White House to discuss the rise in anti-Asian hate crimes, along with Asian inclusion and diversity. The band, wearing matching black suits for the occasion, thanked Biden for signing the COVID-19 Hate Crimes Act into law. It marked the first conversation at the Oval Office to occur between Korean artists and a US president.

RM spoke first and introduced the group in English, calling their invitation to Washington, D.C. a "great honour". On the new federal law, he said: "We want to say thank you, sincerely, for your decision. We just want to be a little help and we truly appreciate the White House and the government's trying to find solutions."

Suga added: "It's not wrong to be different, and equality begins when we open up and embrace all of our differences", while V said: "Everyone has their own history. We hope today is one step forward to respecting and understanding each and everyone as a valuable person."

"Let's all take one more step... No matter who you are, where you're from, your skin colour, your gender identity, just speak yourself. Find your name and find your voice by speaking yourself."

RM AT THE UNITED NATIONS, 2018

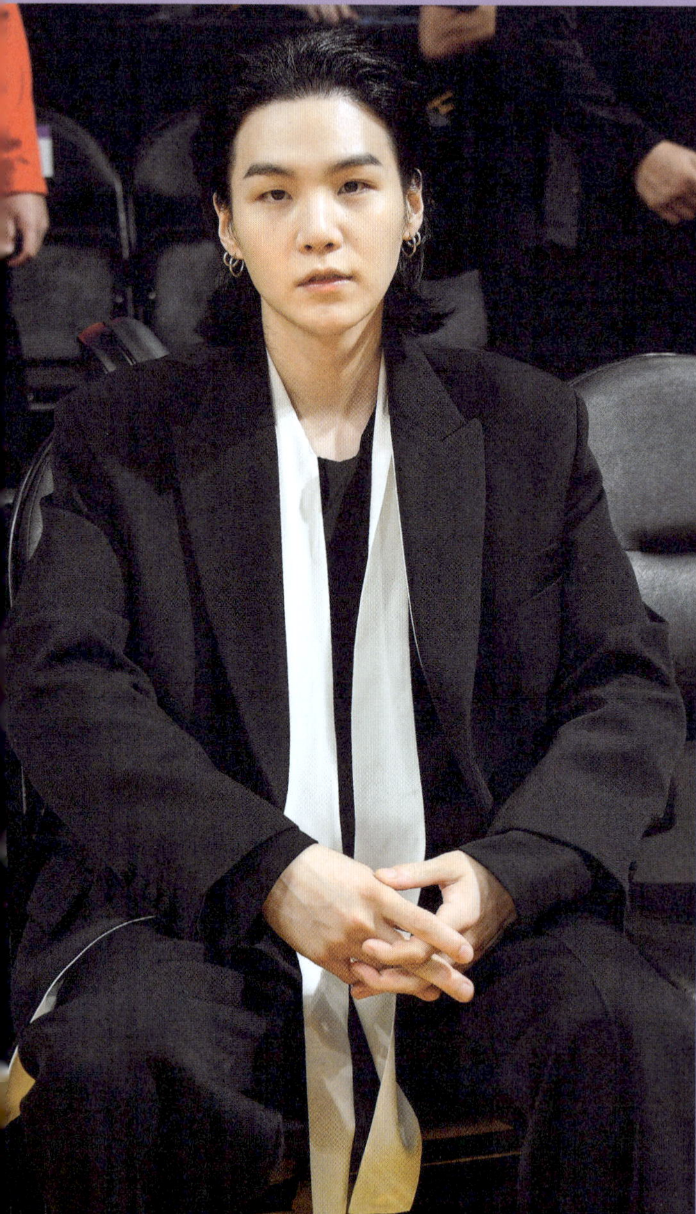

In June 2022, at the height of the band's fame, their agency Big Hit Music (previously Big Hit Entertainment), owned by Hybe, confirmed that BTS would have a break from group musical activities as all seven members had to undertake military service – and to also allow the members time to pursue solo projects.

Military service is mandatory in South Korea and all able-bodied South Korean men between the ages of 18 and 28 are required to serve for 18 months. In 2020, the country's parliament had passed a bill that allowed pop stars – namely those who "excel in popular culture and art" – to defer their service until the age of 30.

Even so, the news surprised some fans, who argued that as South Korea's most famous cultural export, BTS had already served their country by earning it billions of dollars and raising awareness on a global scale. (Shorter military service term is a perk that has been granted to Olympic and Asian Games medallists and some classical musicians with international achievements.)

Suga is a basketball enthusiast and NBA ambassador, and attended the game between the LA Lakers and the Dallas Mavericks in January 2023 in Los Angeles, California.

Jin, the oldest member of the band (he turned 30 in 2022), was the first to start the process and enrol. By 2023, all the rest of the band had also enlisted. J-Hope in April, Suga (as a social service agent – an alternative to military service, due to an injury he sustained in a past accident) in September and then RM, Jimin, V and Jung Kook in December. In the run up to their service, gone was the signature floppy hair the singers were so famous for. In its place were buzz cuts, a requirement of South Korean soldiers.

For many within the BTS ARMY, the absence of their beloved icons felt bittersweet and on the week of their departure fans wrote emotional tributes in languages ranging from Vietnamese to Spanish, highlighting just how widespread the BTS fan base had become. Many pledged their loyalty and commitment to the band's members – a reaction that the BBC compared to those of the Second World War wives sending their sweethearts off to the war.

And with that, BTS were gone, leaving behind hopeful fans counting down to their 2025 discharge, eager to see them reunite and perform as a group once more.

Dressed in a Louis Vuitton tracksuit, J-Hope was at the basketball game between the LA Lakers and the Golden State Warriors in Los Angeles in April 2025.

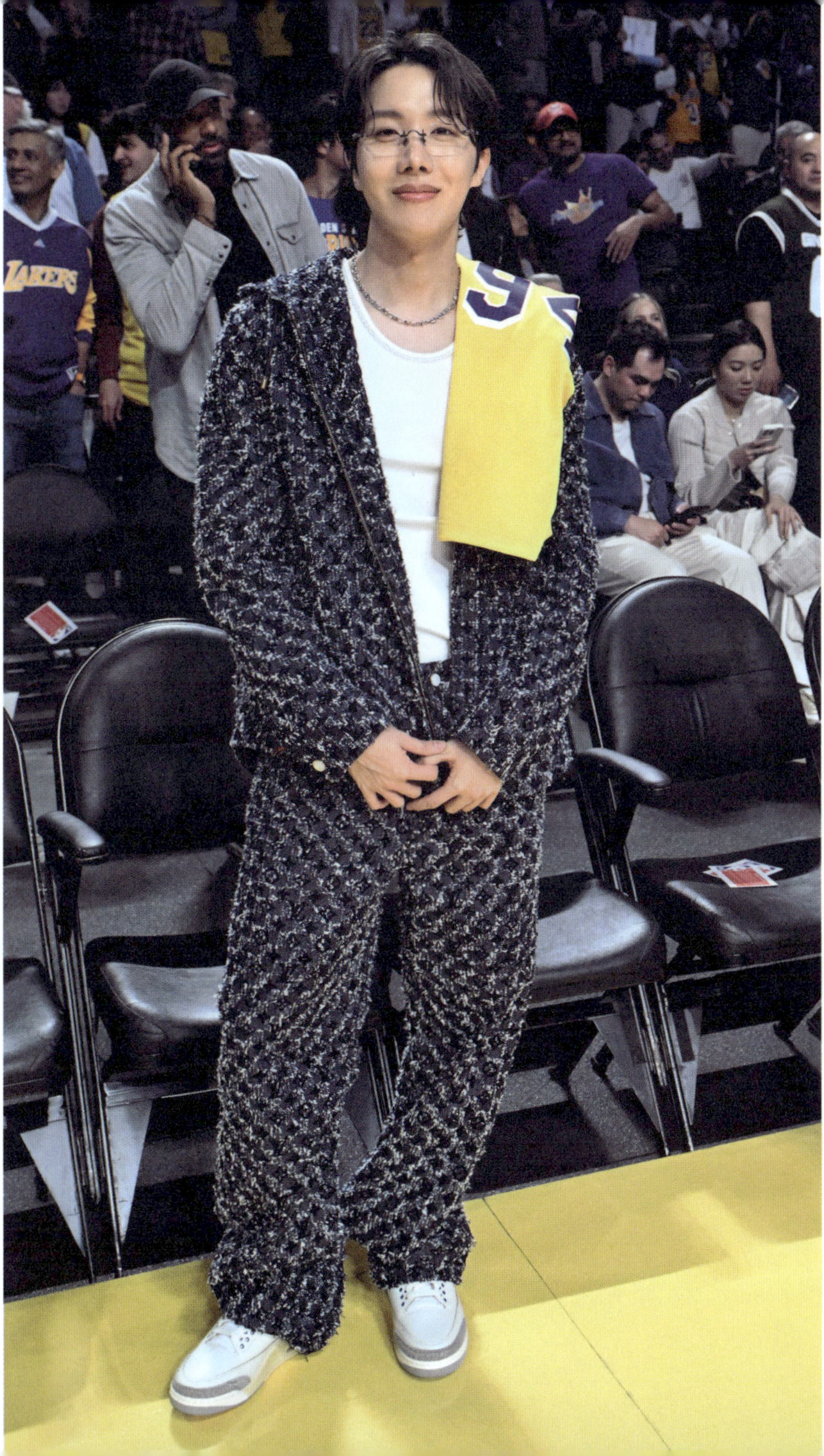
LAKERS

RETURN TO

CHAPTER 6

THE STAGE

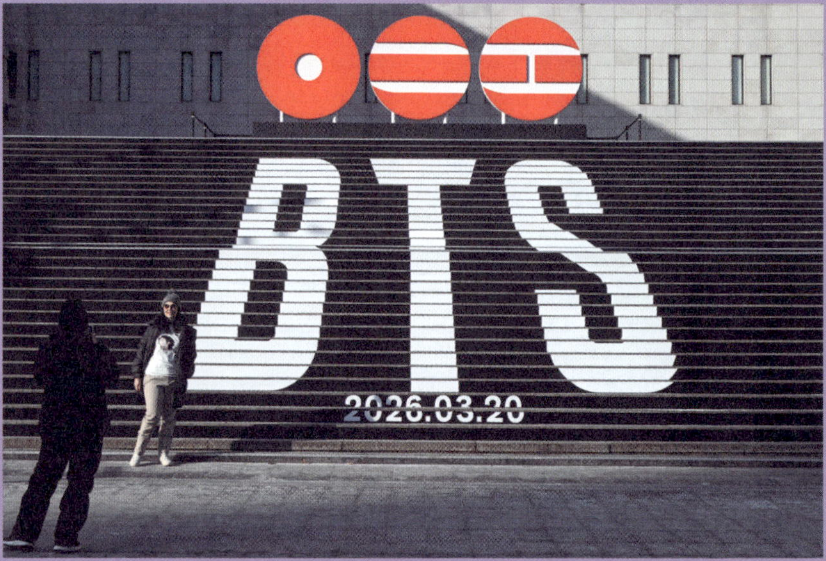

The logo of the new BTS album, *Arirang*, and the release date painted on stairs in Gwanghwamun Square, Seoul in January 2026.

RETURN TO THE STAGE

In May 2025, fans gathered in the Goyang district, north-west of Seoul, for the BTS Festa – a major event held every year on the BTS anniversary.

By then Jin and J-Hope had been discharged from the military, while RM, V, Jung Kook and Suga were due to be released throughout June. At the time of BTS Festa, there were no plans for all seven members to appear together but that didn't stop the ARMY from gathering early and forming long queues that stretched from the subway station before the event's doors opened.

Some fans had travelled from as far as Greece, the USA and the Netherlands. Chatter could be heard in many languages, including Korean, but also English, Chinese, Japanese and Spanish, which threw off local passers-by, even prompting one to ask: "Why are there so many foreigners here?" according to a BBC report.

Inside the Korea International Exhibition Center, where the event was held, there were more queues as people lined up to enter the "voice zone", where they could listen to voice notes from BTS members. Other interactive fan experiences included photo zones, game areas and DIY stations. When BTS music blared through the speakers, the attendees cheered as if they were at a concert.

To coincide with the annual BTS Festa, the group typically releases a family-style portrait for their fans, along with other new content. These photos often feature the members in creative or themed outfits and are highly anticipated each year leading up to their anniversary. In 2023, for their tenth year, BTS wore matching pastel-coloured clothes that created a clean and cohesive feel. They also complemented the vibrancy of the furnishings and background, which came in various shades of purple – the band's official colour.

However, in 2024 and 2025, a family portrait was not released due to BTS being on hiatus. Instead, they released a "2013–2023 photo collection", showcasing their journey over their first decade as a group. The images show their preference for monochromatic streetwear in their debut days, and the transition to more formal and sometimes colourful attire as the members grow up. (In 2025, all the members were in their late 20s or early 30s.) As part of the package, a solo song by Jung Kook, "Never Let Go", was also released.

Then in July 2025 came the announcement that the ARMY had fervently been waiting for: BTS were ready to resume their K-pop careers. During a live-stream on the online fan platform Weverse, all seven members appeared in their first broadcast together since September 2022 to reveal that they were returning in spring 2026 with a new album, *Arirang*, and a world tour. The band also teased a cryptic image, depicting three red circles. CNN reported theories ranging from "hello" to the symbols on the South Korean flag.

Merchandise from a BTS pop-up store in April 2024.

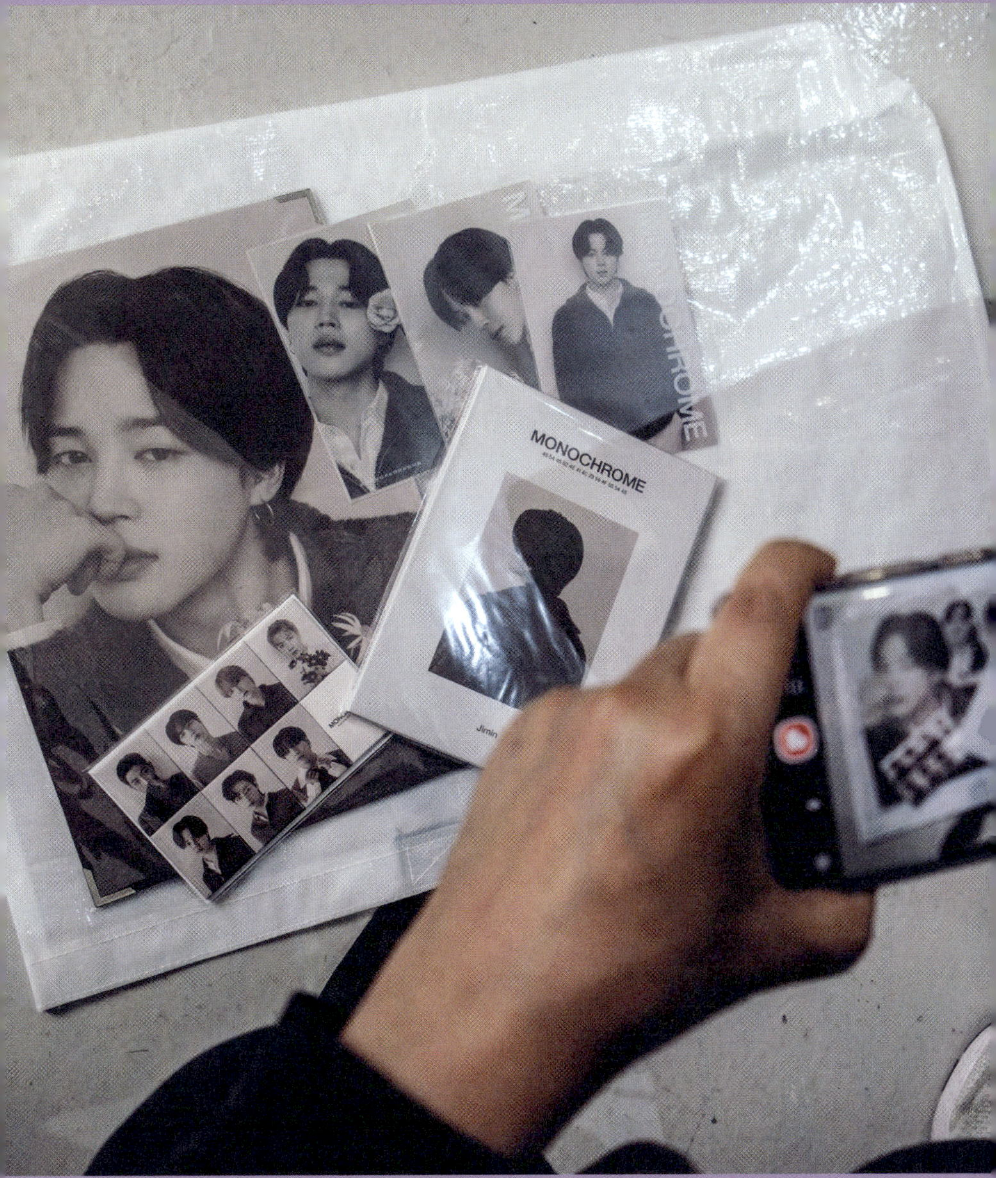
MONOCHROME
Jimin

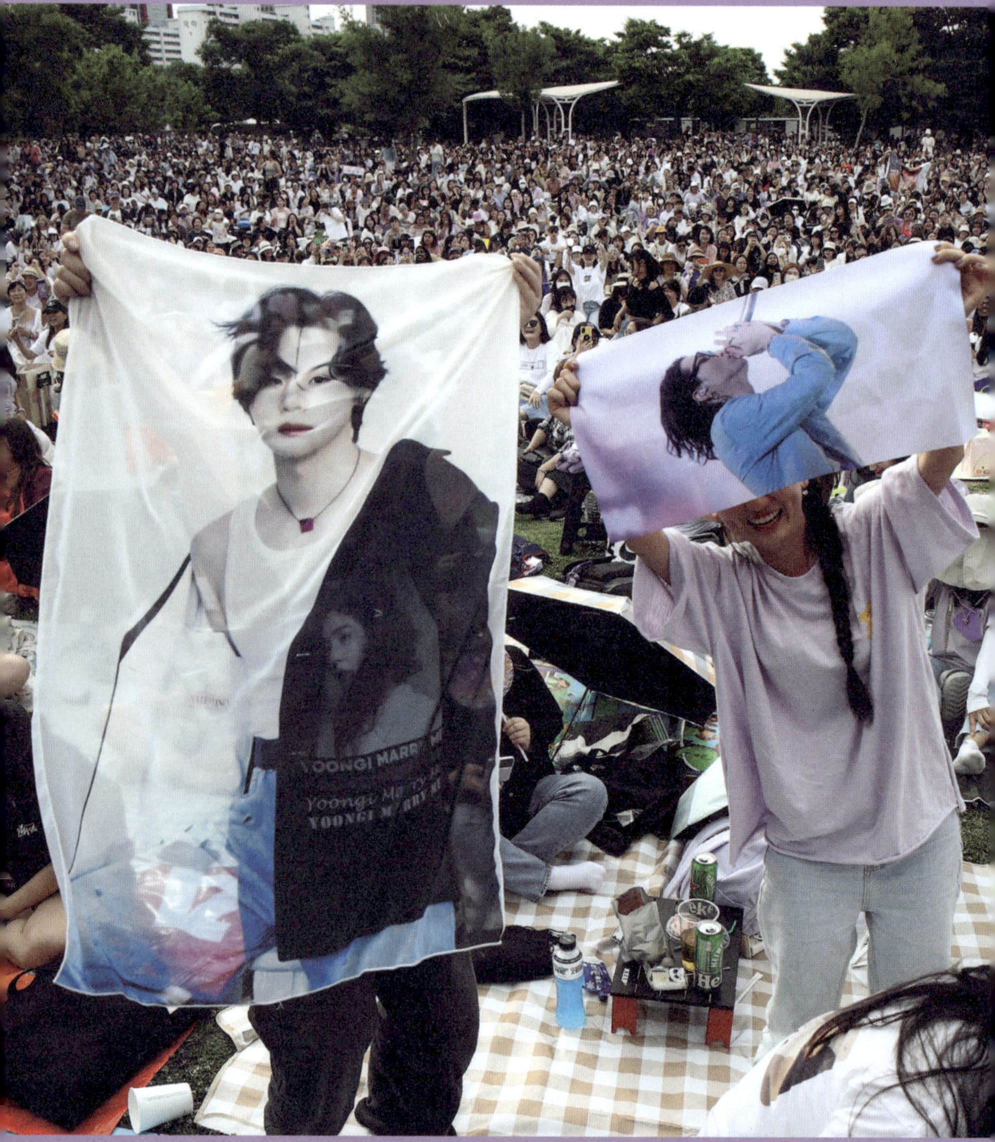
YOONGI MARR
Yoongi
YOONGI

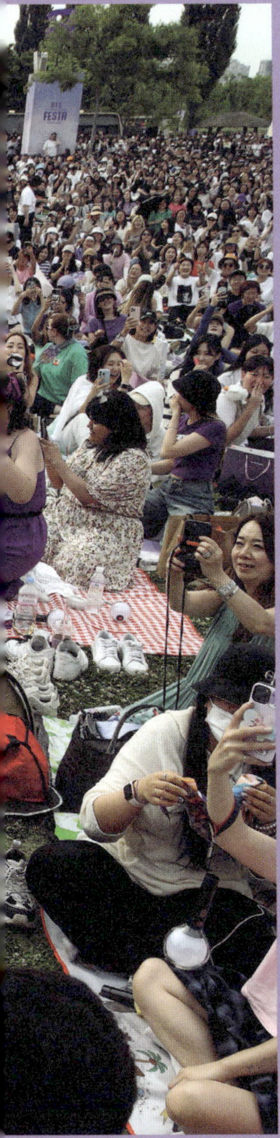

"We're approaching the album with the same mindset we had when we first started."

BTS BAND STATEMENT, 2026

Fans of BTS gathered for the BTS Festa in Seoul in June 2023, to celebrate ten years of the group. At the time, BTS was on hiatus as band members completed their compulsory military service.

"Since it will be a group album, it will reflect each member's thoughts and ideas", the BTS statement read. "We're approaching the album with the same mindset we had when we first started." The band added that they would stay in the USA as they worked on their new music. The 2026 album was their first since 2022's anthology *Proof*, the 2021 Japanese compilation album *BTS, the Best* and their last studio album, *Be*, released in 2020. The world tour was their first full tour in nearly seven years, starting in April 2026 with concerts in South Korea and Japan, before traveling across Asia, North America, Europe, South America and Australia.

Many experts consider BTS and Blackpink as the leaders of K-pop's third generation. Amid their absence, however, K-pop has become more diverse than ever and newer acts classed as the fourth and fifth generations have brought fresh style to the genre. Several bands, including Le Sserafim and Stray Kids, have made it onto Western mainstream charts.

The news of the BTS comeback came at a crucial time for the K-pop industry. While revenue from concerts remains strong, global album sales for Korean music – a key market metric – have been declining since its peak in 2023, according to a report in the *Financial Times*. The slump matched a time when BTS and Blackpink did not release albums. (Blackpink, the other major K-pop sensation, opted instead for solo releases. However, in July 2025, the group unveiled a new single, "Jump", and a third mini-album, *Deadline*, in 2026.)

Fans of BTS queued up for the annual BTS Festa, celebrating the group's debut anniversary – and completion of military service – in Goyang in 2025.

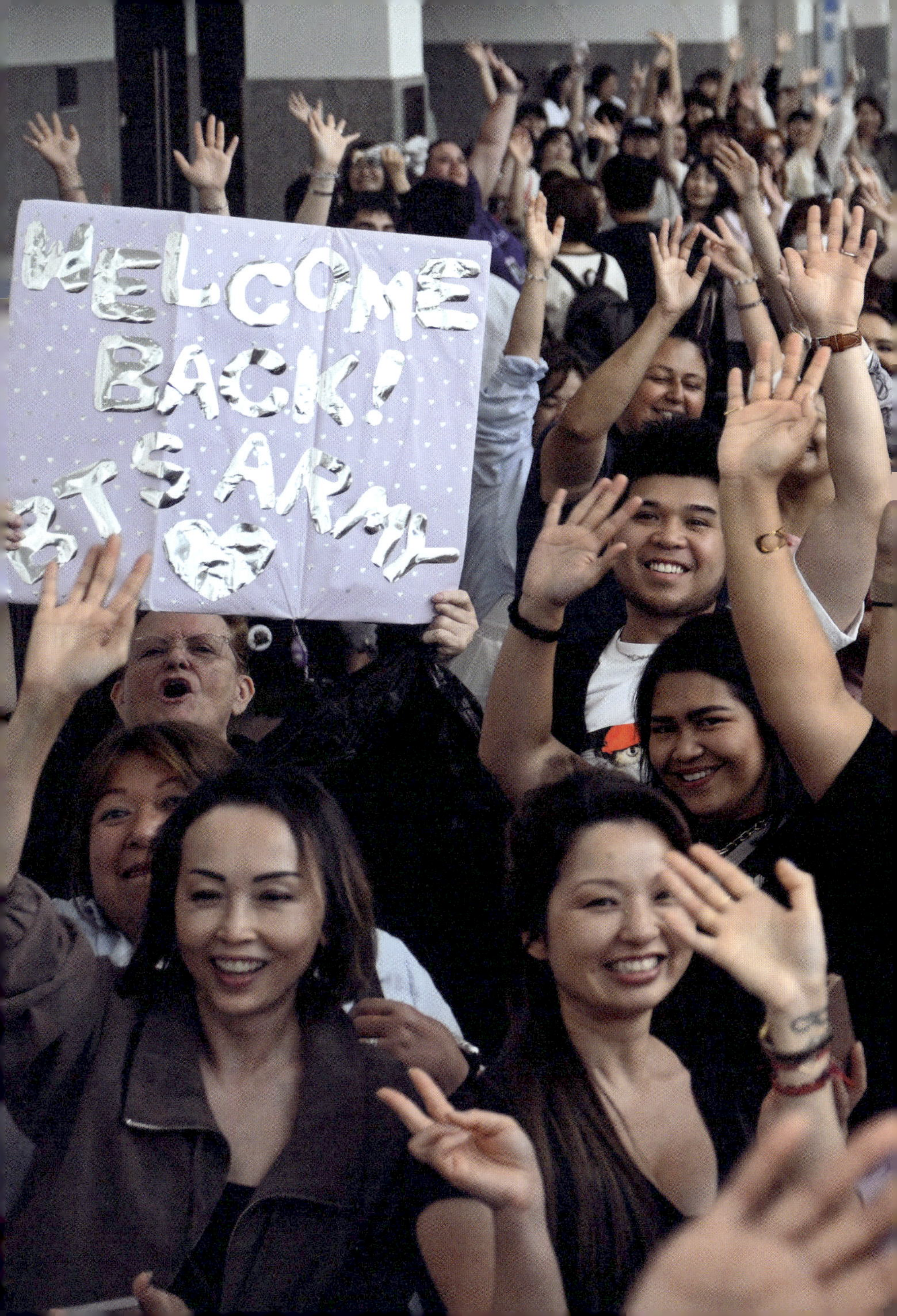
WELCOME
BACK!
BTS ARMY

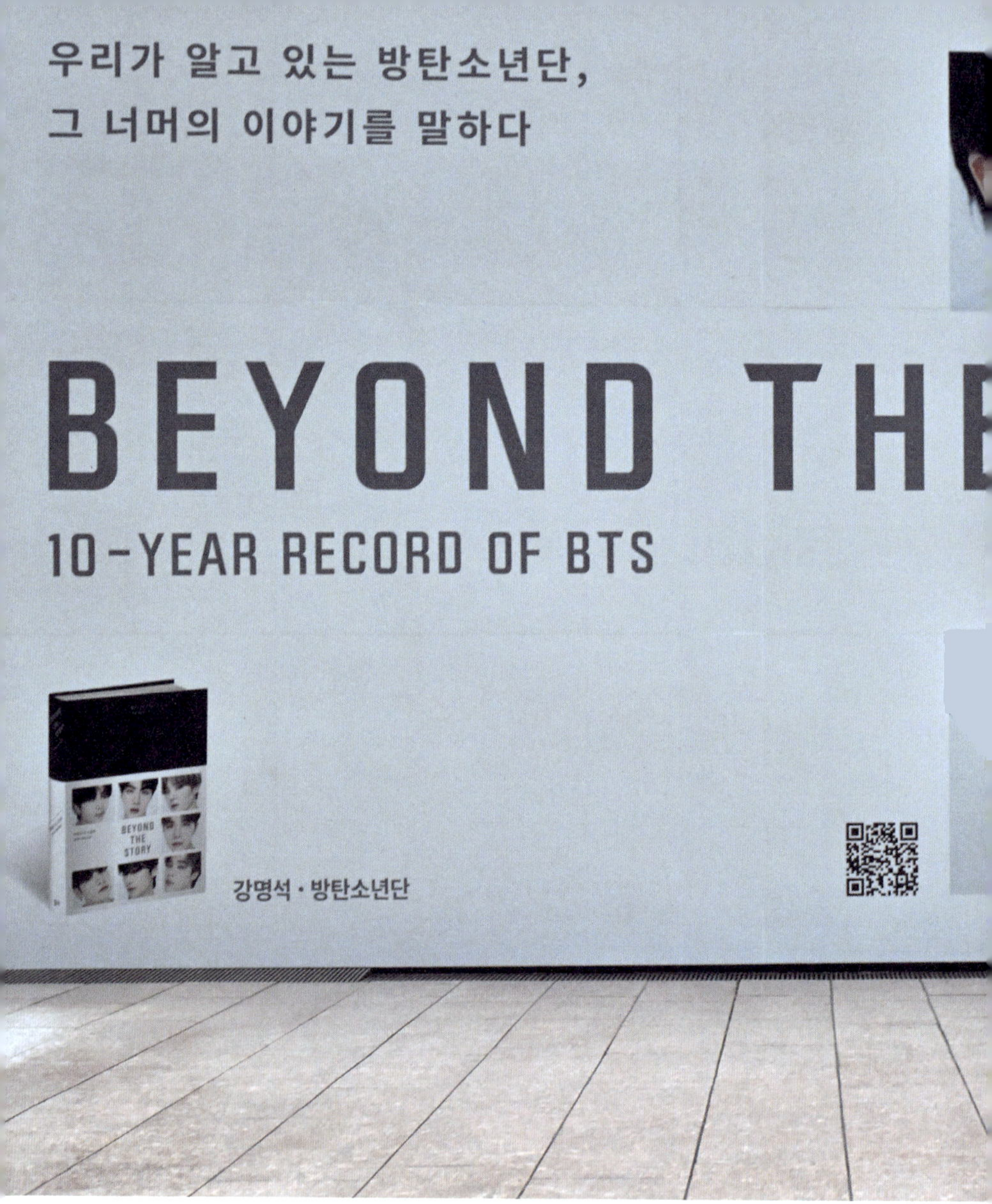

Advertising for the BTS memoir *Beyond the Story: 10-Year Record of BTS*. Released in July 2023, it marked their tenth anniversary.

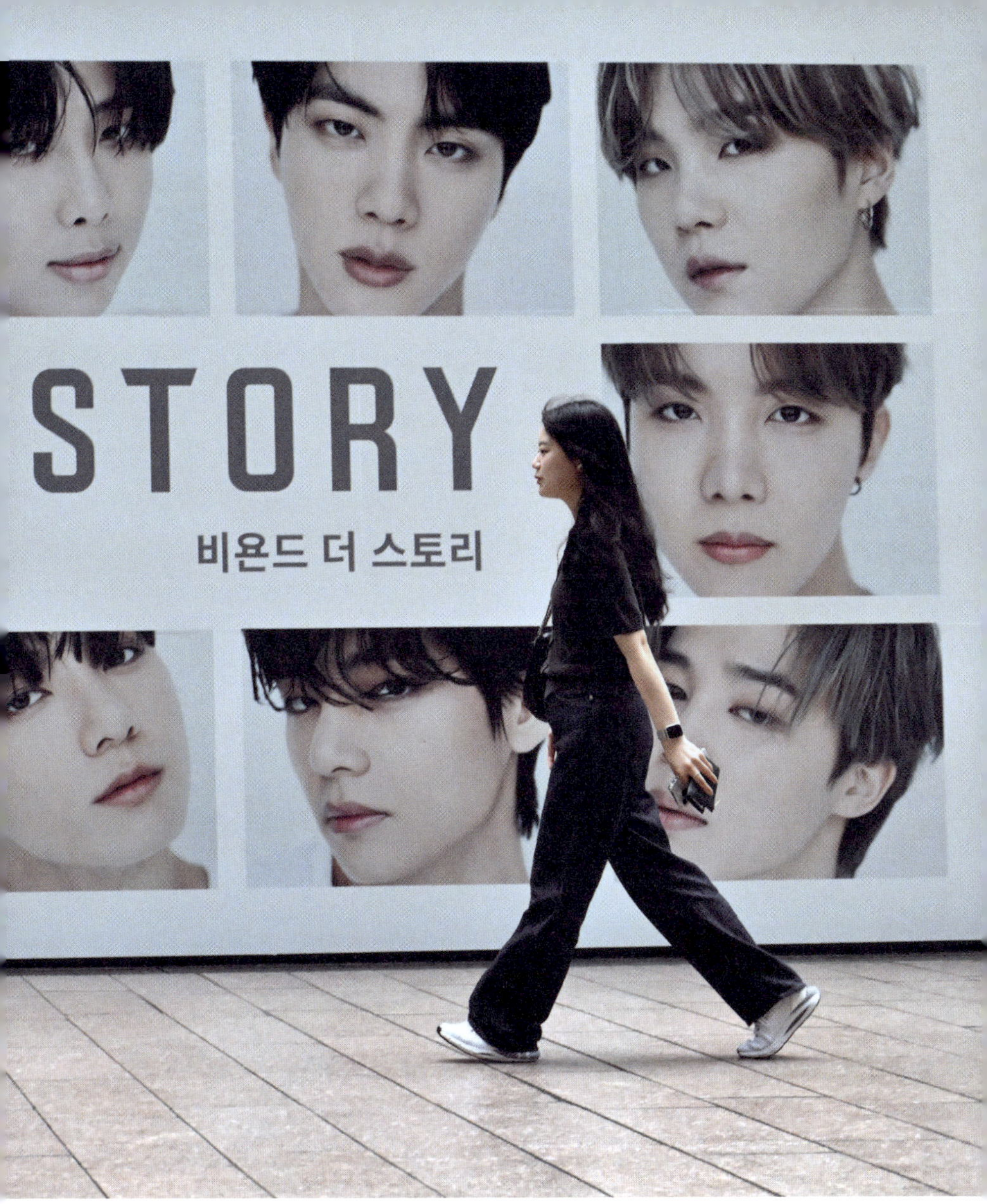
STORY
비욘드 더 스토리

There have also been several controversies in the sector, such as the headline-making dispute between the up-and-coming girl group NewJeans and their agency. Hallyu has also, at times, revealed a darker side that raises questions about South Korean attitudes towards mental health, sexual assault and exploitation, especially of women. In recent years, there have been a series of scandals – including revelations that some K-pop stars had secretly filmed themselves having sex with women without their consent – and high-profile suicides.

However, the Korean Wave shows no signs of breaking, with several historic wins throughout the year. At the 2025 Victoria's Secret Fashion Show, Twice became the first K-pop group to perform at the starry event. Meanwhile, Rosé won the 2025 MTV VMA for Song of the Year for her collaboration with Bruno Mars, "Apt.", marking the first time a K-pop artist had won the award. She also became the first solo K-pop artist to perform at the Grammys. And elsewhere, the Korean-produced musical *Maybe Happy Ending* won the Best Musical award at the 78th Tony Awards on New York City's Broadway, marking a new milestone for Korean creativity in Western theatre. Not to mention the 2025 animated film *Kpop Demon Hunters*, which became a worldwide hit for Netflix and their most-viewed film of all time with over 236 million views and counting. This prompted the *Washington Post* to name K-pop as "the hottest sound of the summer" in 2025, when many Western artists struggled to create a seasonal smash hit, let alone one with a lasting impact. It was also the first K-pop project to win a Grammy Award, with its popular track "Golden" taking home the prize for Best Song Written for Visual Media in 2026.

“Mega hits like Kpop Demon Hunters *really showed how deeply K-pop culture has entered the global mainstream.”*

RAY SEOL, ASSOCIATE PROFESSOR AT BERKLEE COLLEGE OF MUSIC IN BOSTON, 2026

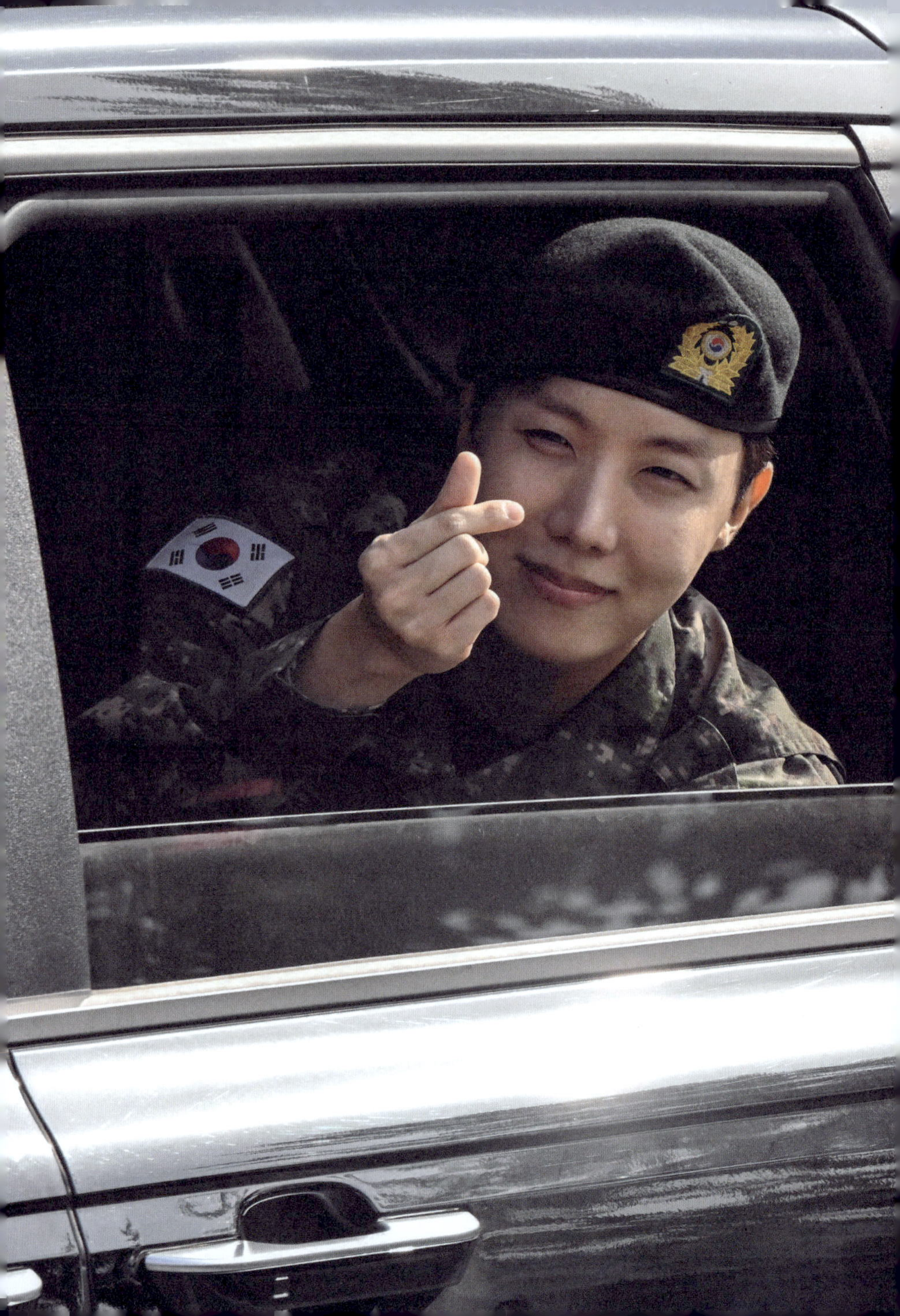

As K-pop continues to evolve, the biggest question surrounding it is "localization", said Yale University's IBM Professor of Sociology and Professor of Ethnicity, Race and Migration, Grace Kao, pointing to the fact that a growing number of K-pop artists are not ethnically Korean. Many also sing in Korean as well as English and Japanese. "I think Hybe and SM are moving in this direction. Already there is Katseye, the girl group from Los Angeles. There's Santos Bravos, a new boy group from Latin America. And there's also DearALICE, which is from the UK", she said. "The question then becomes, do you need Koreans to be K-pop? At what point is it no longer K-pop?"

Hye Jin Lee, clinical associate professor of communication at the USC Annenberg School for Communication and Journalism in Los Angeles, draws links between K-pop and K-beauty, the latter whose definition is also expanding. "We're seeing new K-beauty brands emerge without Korean founders," he said in an original interview for this book. "Whether such brands would still be considered 'K-beauty' is analogous to debates around whether songs like 'Golden' or tracks from *KPop Demon Hunters* should be classified as K-pop, which is an ongoing and often heated discussion among K-pop fans," Lee continued. "Ultimately, it depends on how we define the 'K' here – whether it refers to nationality, cultural affinity, or a powerful brand identity associated with certain aesthetics and values."

In Kao's view, "there's really something unique and special about K-pop in that it promotes Korea and Asia, and it helps

J-hope gestures to fans as he leaves after being discharged from his military service outside a base in Wonju in October 2024.

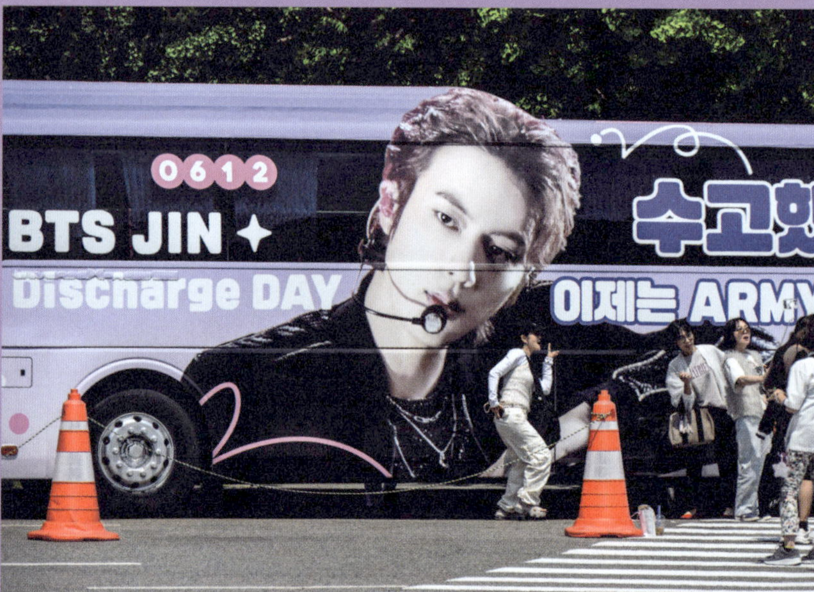

ABOVE In June 2024, fans eagerly awaited the release of Jin, who was the first member of BTS to finish the national service that put the whole band's musical career on hold.

OPPOSITE Jin (left) celebrated his discharge with fellow BTS member RM. He was the first in the band to complete the mandatory duty, freeing him up to fully resume musical activities.

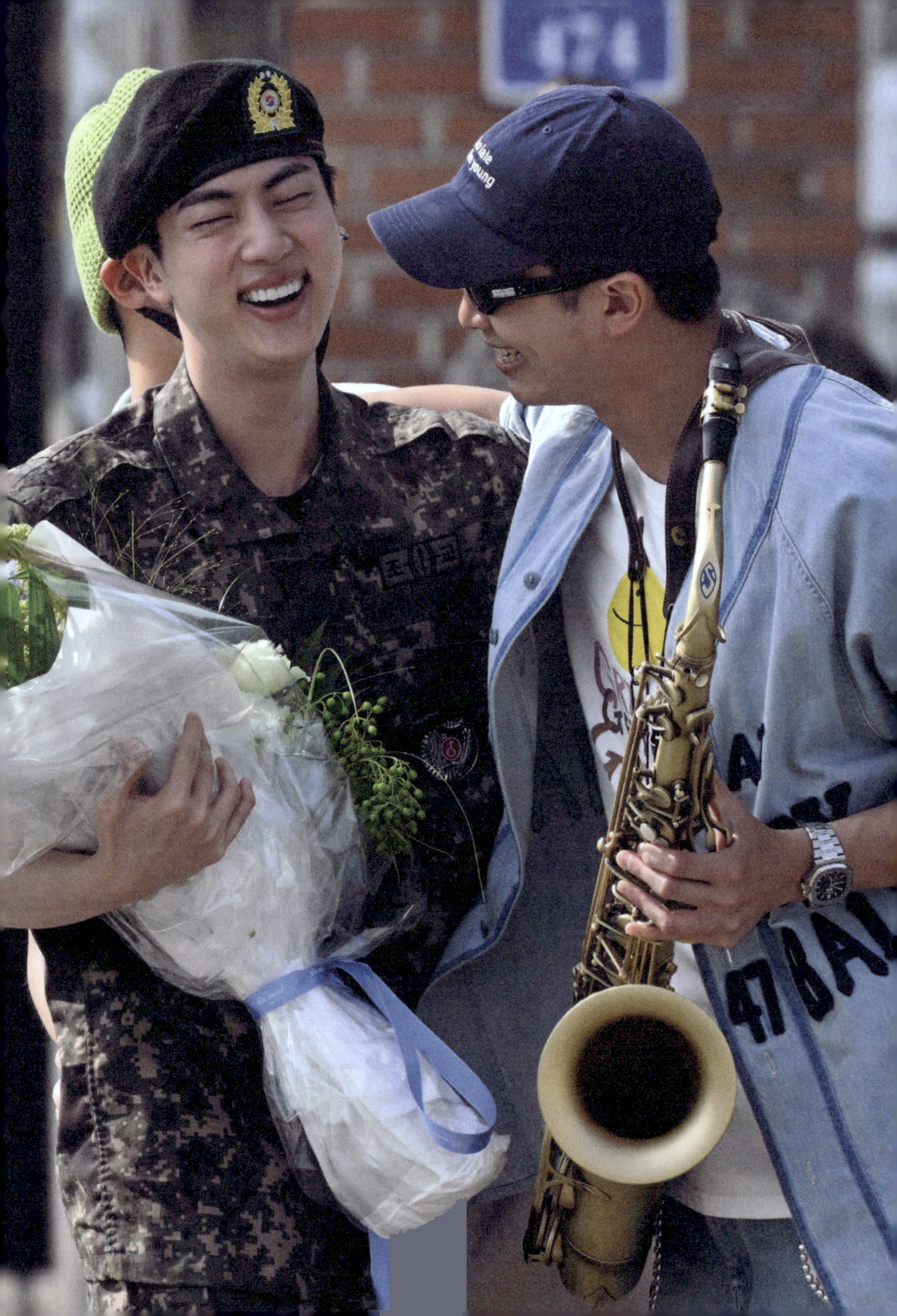

the status of the Asian diaspora all over the world", she explained. "It's great that you see representations of Asia from K-pop, K-dramas and so forth. So, I am not interested in a version that is completely absent from these things."

Those looking forward to the return of BTS may hope that the group may bring renewed energy – and maybe even a path forward for the industry. Shareholders viewed the group's reunion with such optimism that shares of Hybe surged 57 per cent in 2025 on expectations of a comeback. "Even during their military service, the BTS fandom kept growing", Im Soo-jin, an analyst at Daishin Securities, told the *Financial Times* in June 2025. "New boy bands like the Stray Kids, Seventeen [and] Enhypen partly filled the vacuum, but they have failed to replace BTS", Soo-jin said.

Each member wasted little time following their discharge from the army, hosting musical performances, shooting magazine covers, featuring in editorials and attending a variety of high-profile events. Jin, the first member to be discharged, in June 2024, has been releasing new music. In May 2025 he celebrated the launch of his second solo album, *Echo*, at the Empire State Building in New York City. The album contained seven songs, including the main track "Don't Say You Love Me", and was created with the intention of reconnecting with fans through music by exploring everyday emotions and experiences. The music reflects not only his musical evolution but also his personal aesthetic; there is a distinct change from the playful, boy-next-door styling seen in his first solo single, "The Astronaut", to the edgy punk-inspired look he embraced for his new work.

RM and V looked happy to be discharged after their compulsory 18-month military service

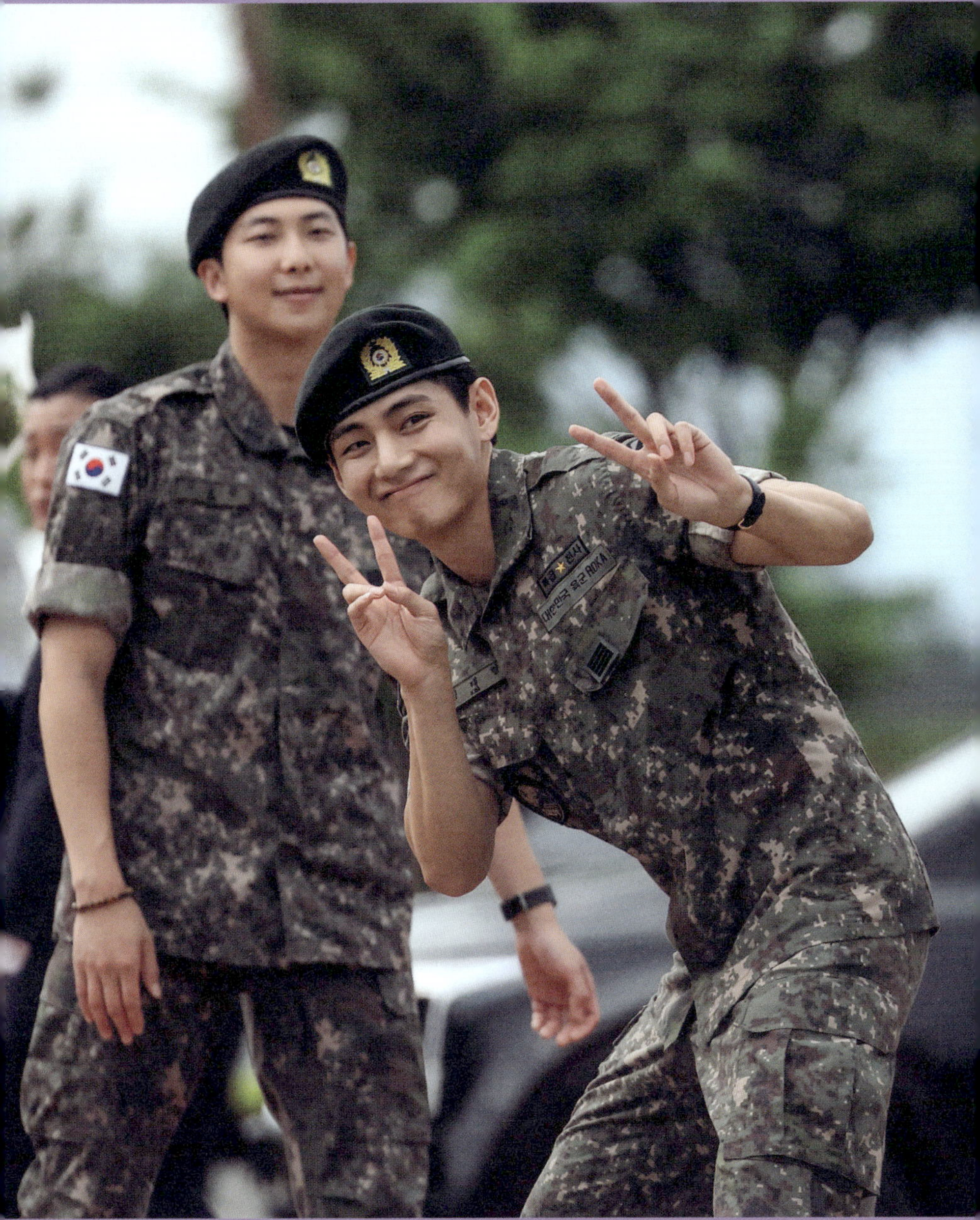
대한민국 육군 ROKA

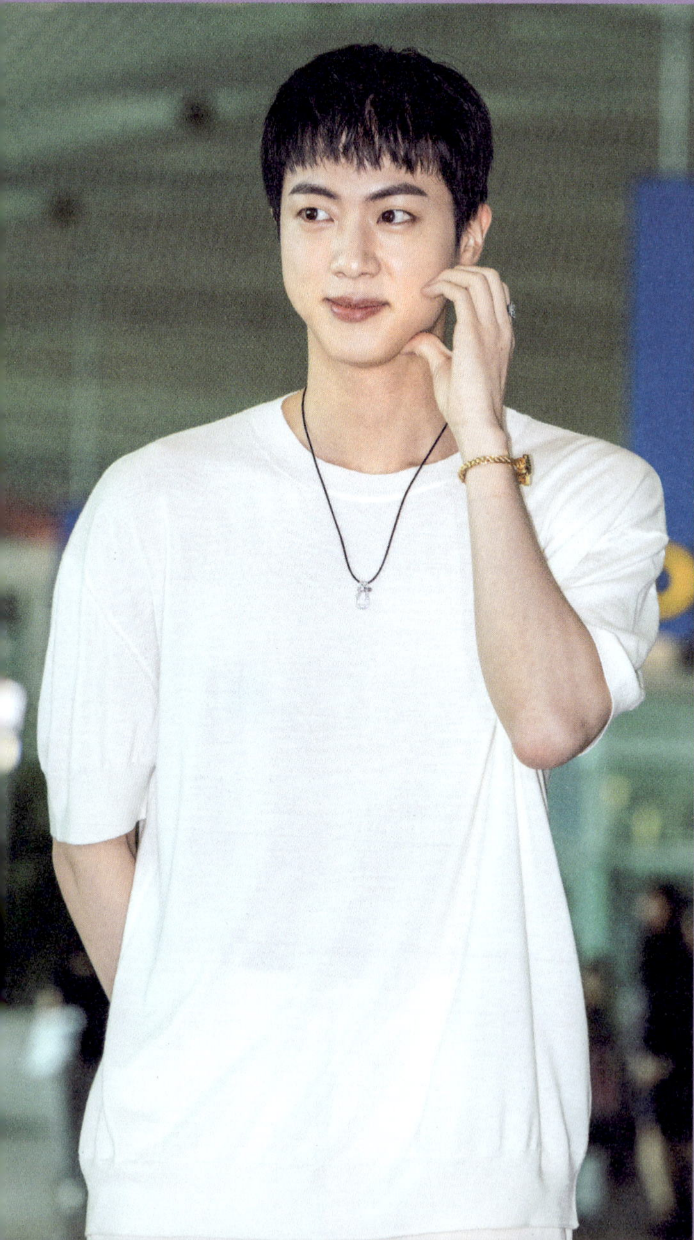

Jin has also been participating in events for *Kian's Bizarre B&B*, the Netflix show where he plays a staff member running an unconventional guest house, and fulfilling his duties at Alo, where he is global brand ambassador. In July 2025 he was present to support the opening of the activewear brand's first flagship store in Asia – Seoul – wearing a white long-sleeved top paired with a black shirt, black trousers and matching black baseball cap.

Monochromatic clothing appears to be his growing preference. He opted for a similar, albeit smarter, look when he arrived for the premiere of Gucci's Spring/Summer 2026 collection at Milan Fashion Week in September 2025. As Jin descended the Palazzo Mezzanotte, where the Gucci event took place, he was wearing a crisp white shirt with a plunging V-neck, styled with black trousers, black belt, black bag and black shoes.

OPPOSITE Free from military service, Jin left from Seoul's Incheon International Airport to attend the 2024 Paris Olympic Torch Relay in July 2024.

OVERLEAF In May 2025, Jin, wearing a Simone Rocha double carnation embellished blazer, celebrated the release of his second solo album, *Echo*, at the Empire State Building in New York.

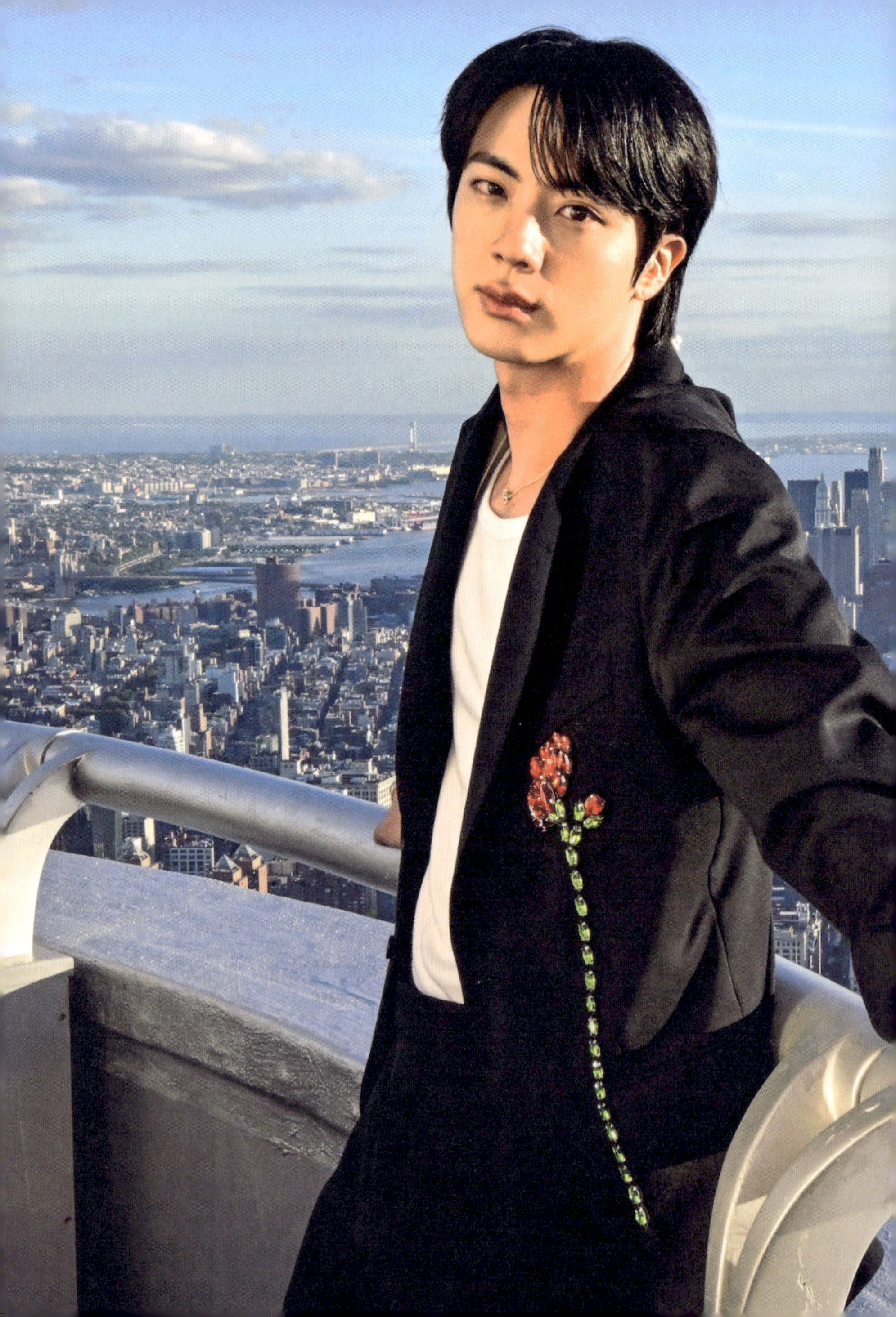

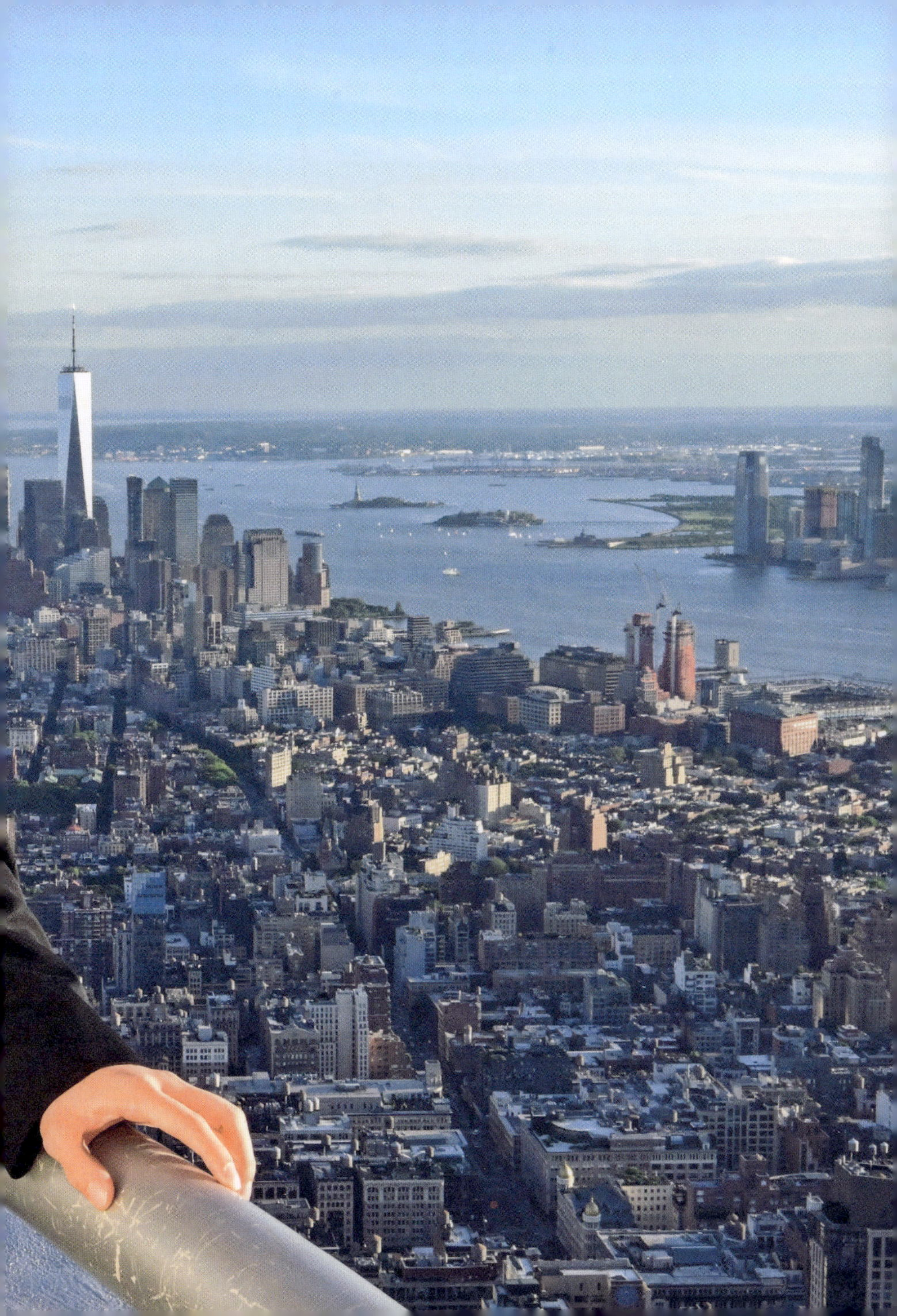

"I don't think I've ever **really thought** *of being not a part of this group... I can't imagine what I would do on my own."*

JIN,
ROLLING STONE**,**
2021

Jin wore a sage green suit from Gucci's pre-Fall 2025 collection at the press conference for the Netflix series *Kian's Bizarre B&B* in Seoul in April 2025.

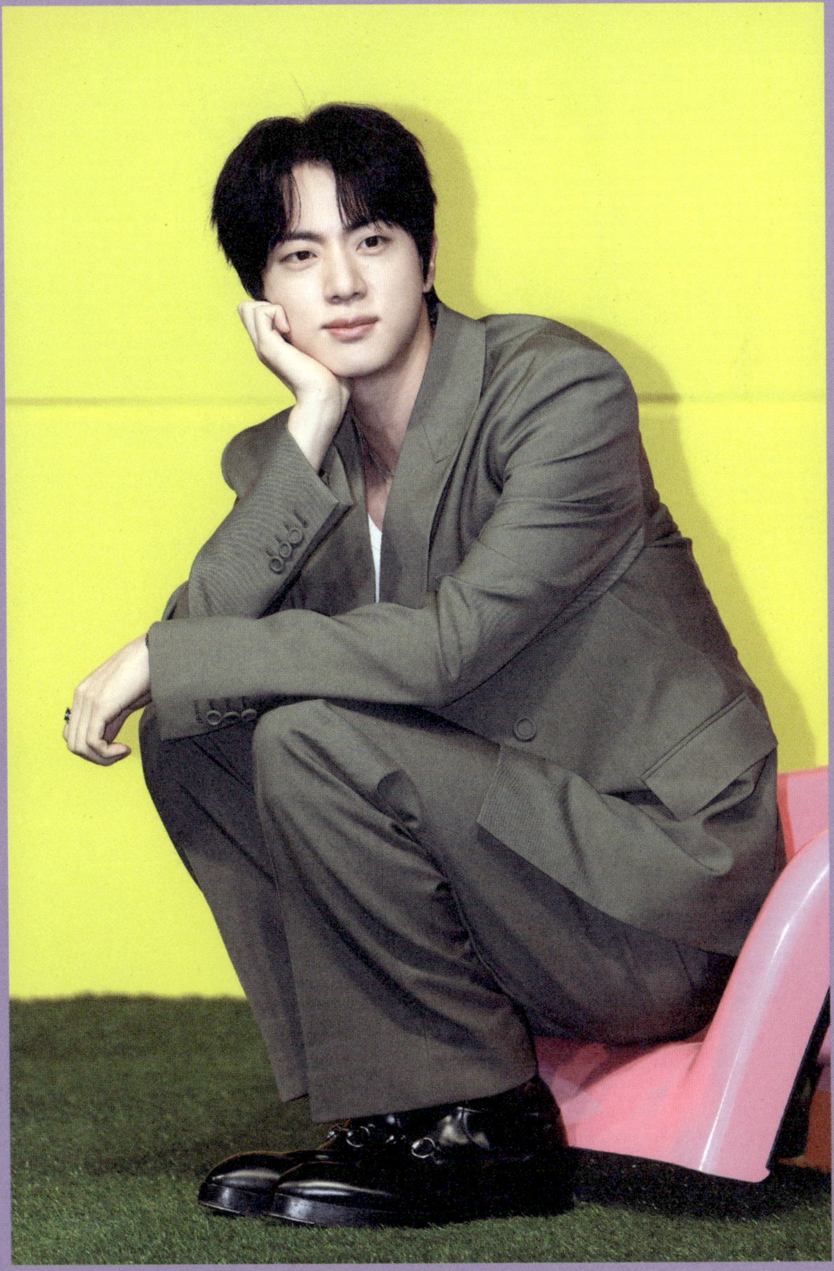

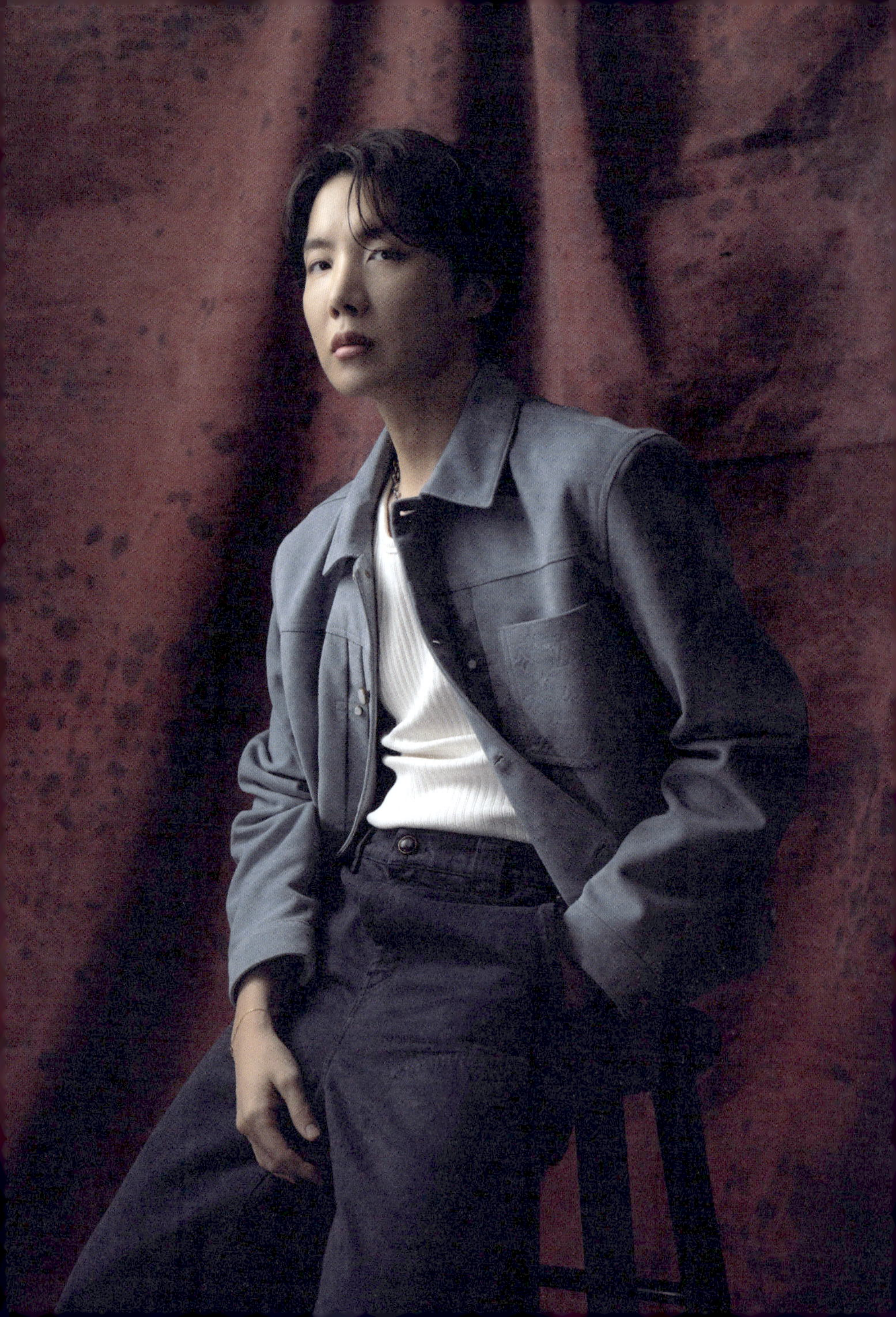

J-Hope, the second member to be released, in October 2024, also kept a busy schedule. The artist launched his first solo world tour, Hope on the Stage, which began in Seoul in late February 2025 and concluded in Osaka, Japan in June that year. J-Hope also released new music, including the singles "Sweet Dreams", "Killin' It Girl" and "Mona Lisa", which he performed to crowds of around 60,000 people who were present for his set at the Lollapalooza music festival in Berlin in July 2025. Marking his return to the Lollapalooza stage following a solo headline performance in Chicago in 2022, where he was the first South Korea artist to headline a main stage at a major US festival, J-Hope delivered a 90-minute performance of solo and BTS tracks. Many fans chanted and sang along; some participated in a fan gesture of holding up purple paper hearts as he performed his new singles.

Speaking with *Teen Vogue* in October 2025, Huh Yunjin, a member of Le Sserafim, described J-Hope as "an artist that I deeply admire and respect", which led to their collaboration on the new single, "Spaghetti". J-Hope was unveiled as a featured artist in a teaser just days before the song's release, and in the music video he can be seen wearing a sleek futuristic-looking outfit, fitting with the track's bold and campy visual language.

J-Hope was photographed for the *Los Angeles Times* in April 2025.

J-Hope and bandmates V and RM also made an appearance at *W Korea*'s "Love Your W" charity event for breast cancer awareness in October 2025. Dressed head-to-toe in Louis Vuitton, J-Hope's look featured a houndstooth jacket, an argyle jumper waistcoat and black trousers, accessorized with a necklace and ring also from the brand. V wore a custom-made navy military-style jacket with gold embroidery by Jaybaek Couture, a white ruffled shirt, layered Cartier necklaces and distressed denim jeans. RM wore a powerful yet understated charcoal grey double-breasted Bottega Veneta suit with a tie and black glasses.

Photos and videos of the trio quickly spread across social media and community sites such as Instagram and theqoo.net, where fans praised their individuality and sophisticated style. Several said they felt the looks reflected each member's personality while maintaining the group's overall sense of cohesion.

In the weeks preceding the event the BTS singers were also spotted on the front row at global fashion weeks, indicating their continued interest and commitment to high fashion.

J-Hope was a headliner at the Lollapalooza music festival in Berlin in 2025.

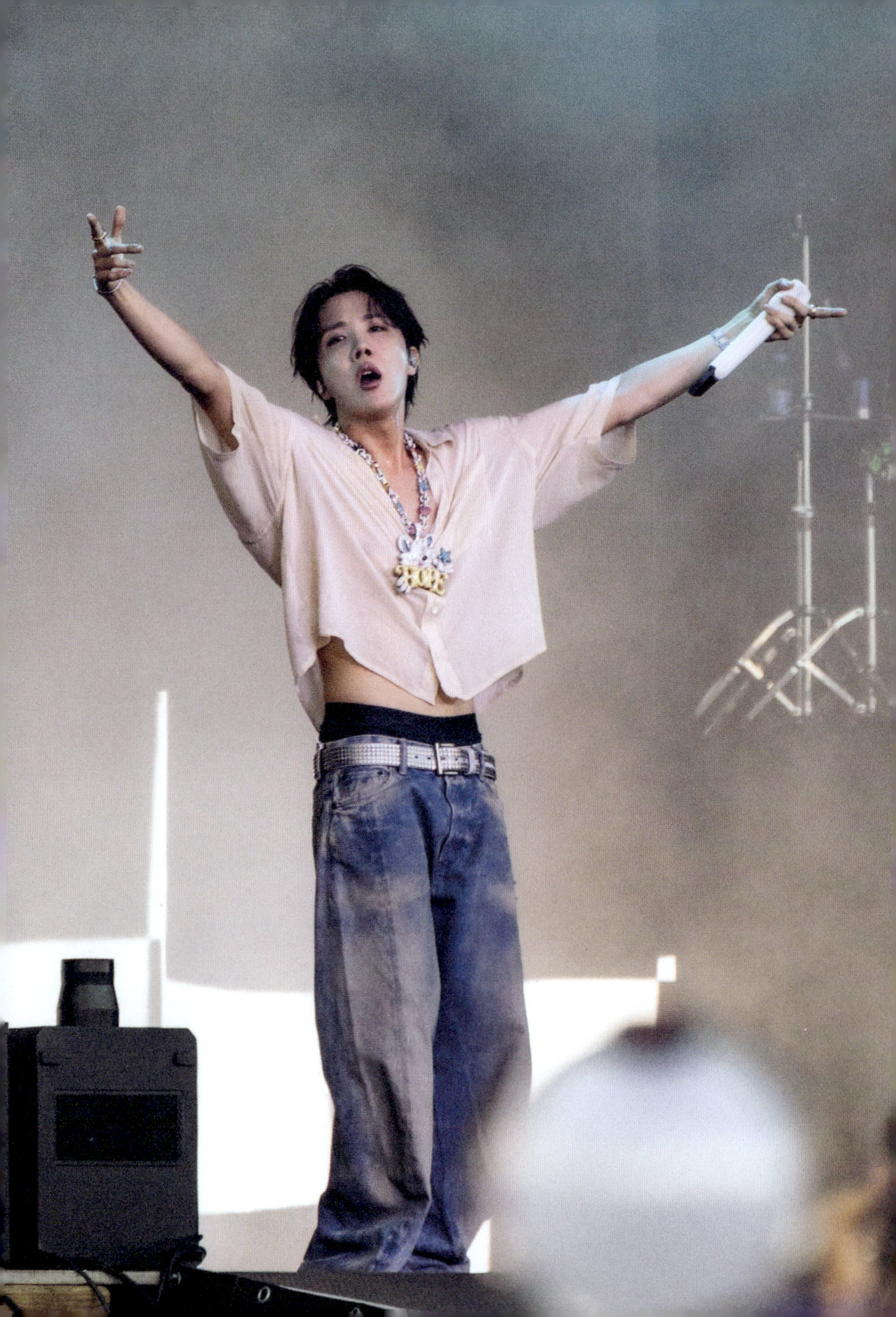
HOPE

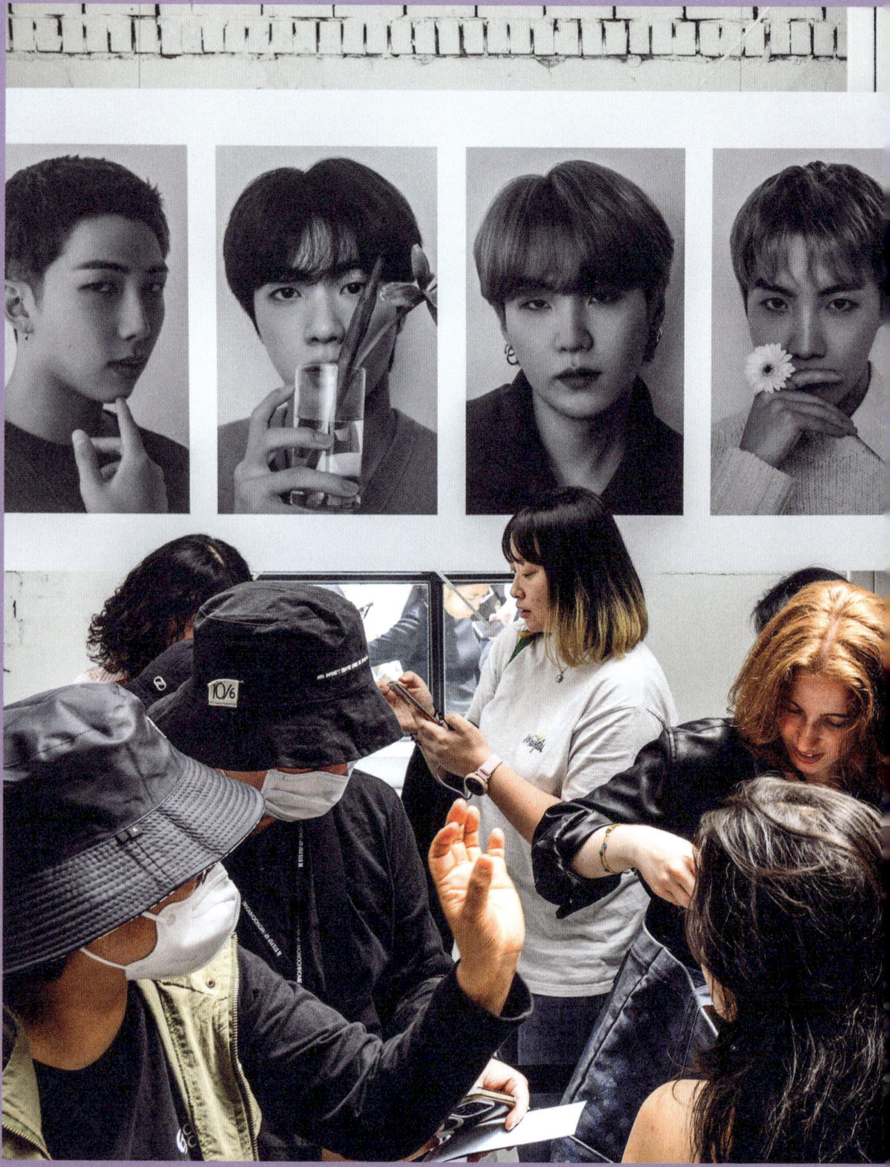

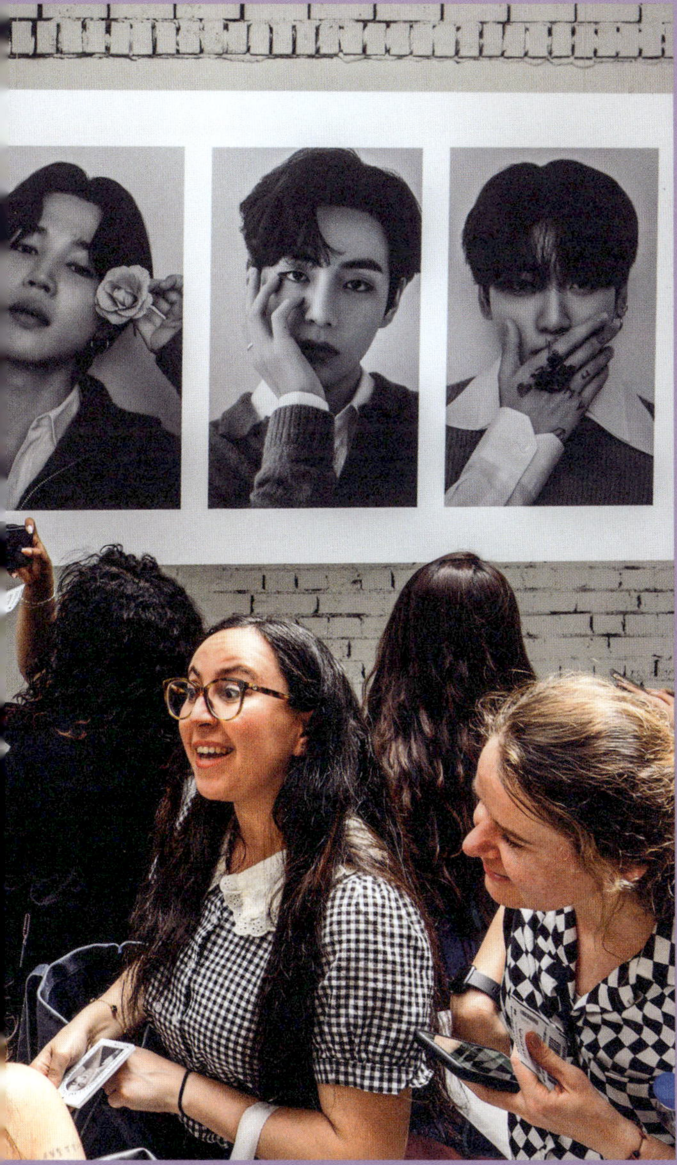

Fans at a BTS pop-up store in April 2024.

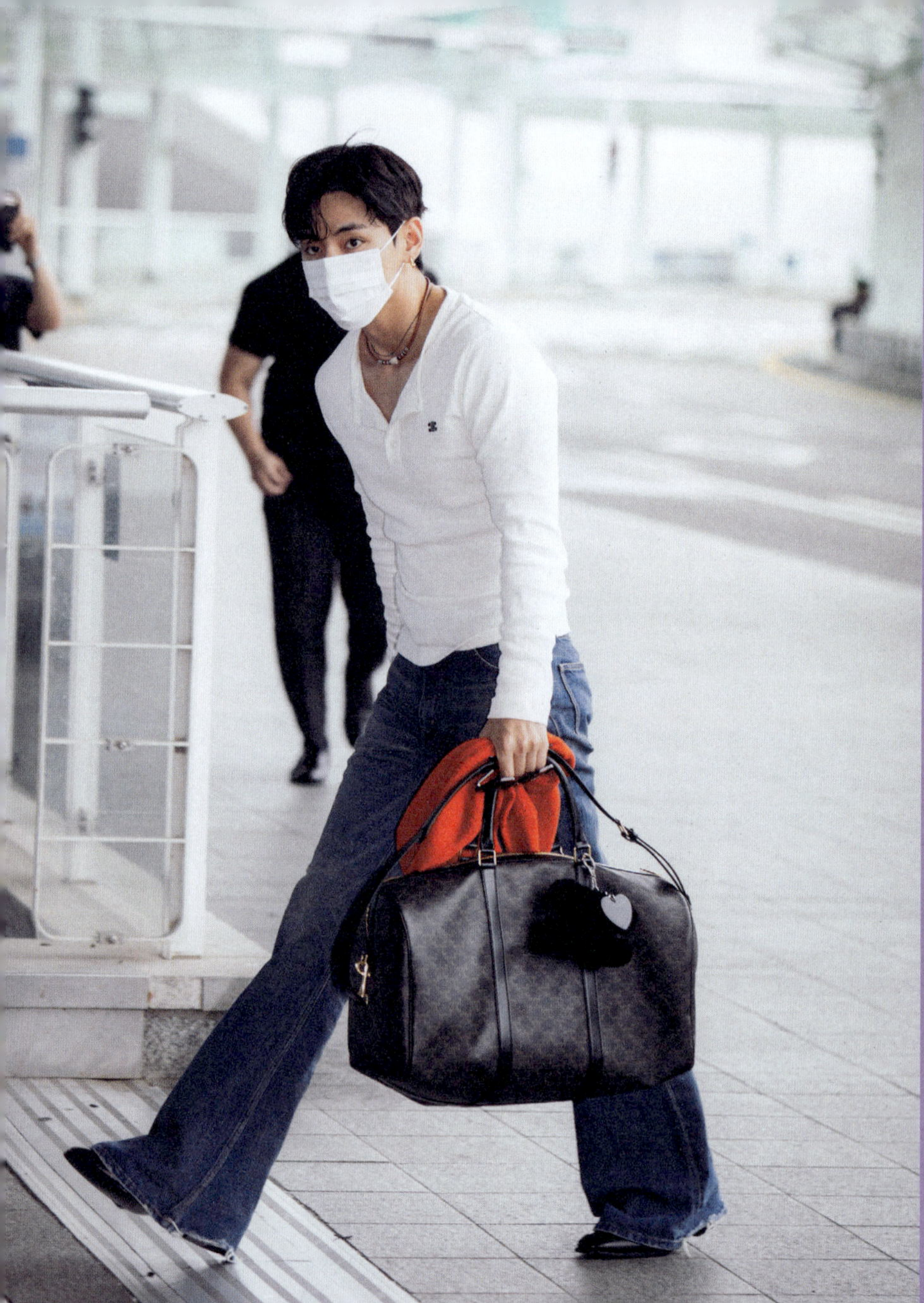

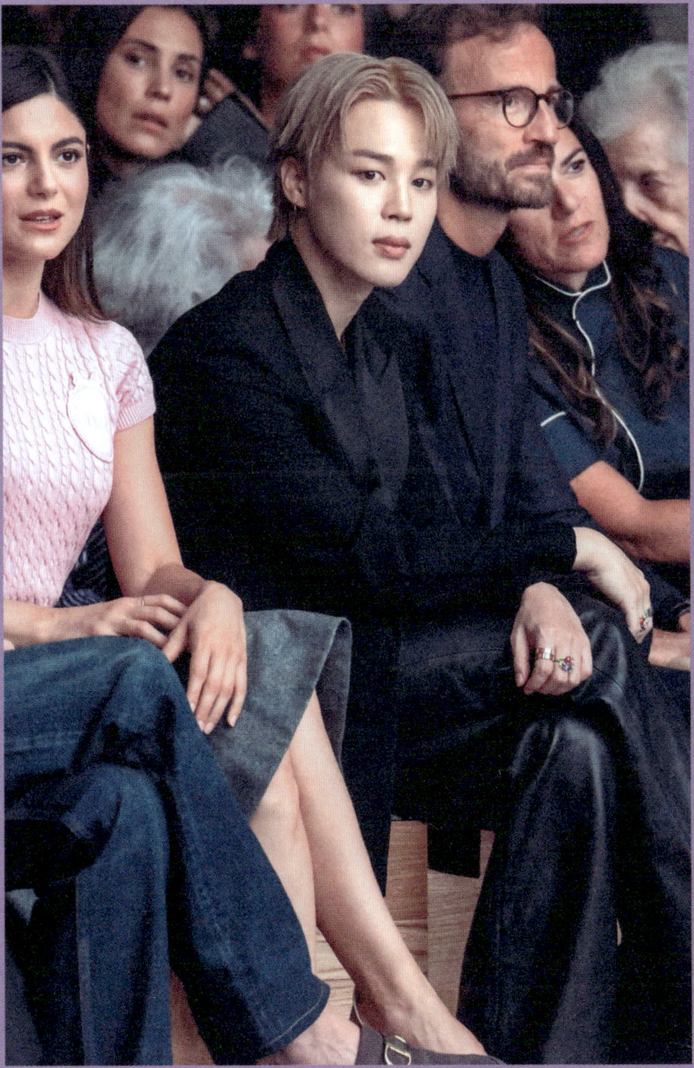

ABOVE Jimin at Dior's womenswear Spring/Summer 2026 show at Paris Fashion Week in October 2025.

OPPOSITE V, with Celine travel bag, long sleeved white T-shirt and Marco jeans at Incheon airport, Seoul, in July 2025.

V attended Celine's Spring/Summer 2026 runway show at Paris Fashion Week in October 2025 wearing a long knee-length brown coat over a white shirt and leopard-print tie. Later in the month, he attended the "Vogue World: Hollywood" event at Paramount Studios in Los Angeles, where he sat in the front row alongside Hollywood stars Nicole Kidman and Baz Luhrmann. On that day, V wore a long grey coat paired with a wide-brimmed grey fedora reminiscent of a traditional Korean "gat" hat. He accessorized with a red sash adorned with traditional Korean patterns and jade attached to his waist. The look was viewed by fans as a modern reinterpretation of traditional Korean aesthetics.

Also at Paris Fashion Week was Jimin, who attended Dior's womenswear Spring/Summer 2026 show – one of the most highly anticipated runways of the season as it marked designer Jonathan Anderson's debut for the French luxury house. Jimin turned heads as he bared his abs in a black Dior suit worn without a shirt, and his hair was styled in a centre-parted wet-look effect.

Meanwhile, RM made an appearance during Milan Fashion Week at the Bottega Veneta show, where designer Louise Trotter presented her first collection for the Italian label. He chose a relaxed outfit consisting of a cream knit jumper and beige trousers, which complemented his fresh blond hair dye. The look was accessorized with silver chains and sleek sunglasses.

RM and Uma Thurman on the front row of Bottega Veneta's Spring/Summer 2026 show at Milan Fashion Week.

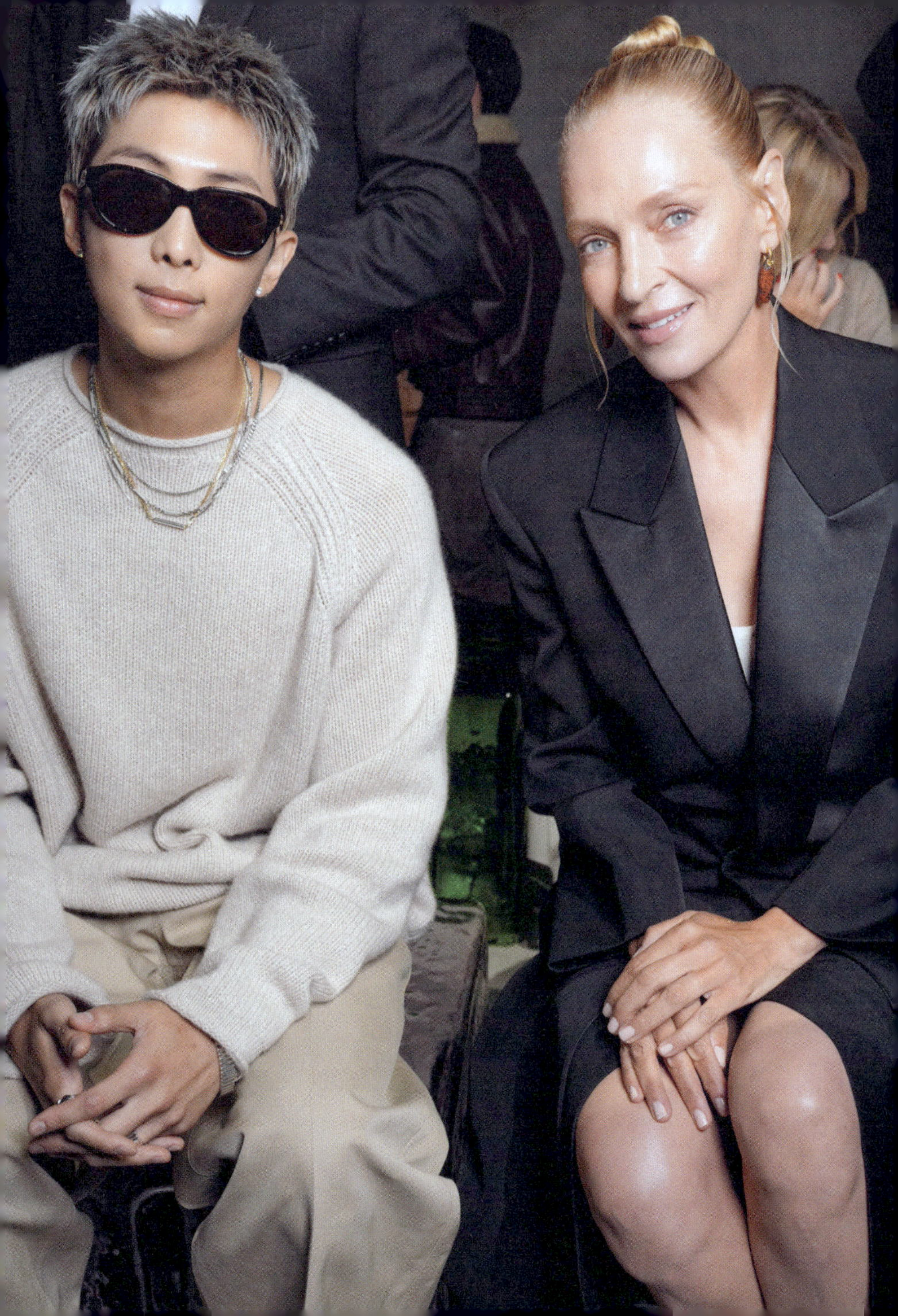

"There's really something unique *and* special *about* K-pop *in that it promotes Korea and Asia,*

and it helps the status of the Asian diaspora all over the world."

GRACE KAO, YALE UNIVERSITY'S IBM PROFESSOR OF SOCIOLOGY AND PROFESSOR OF ETHNICITY, RACE AND MIGRATION, 2025

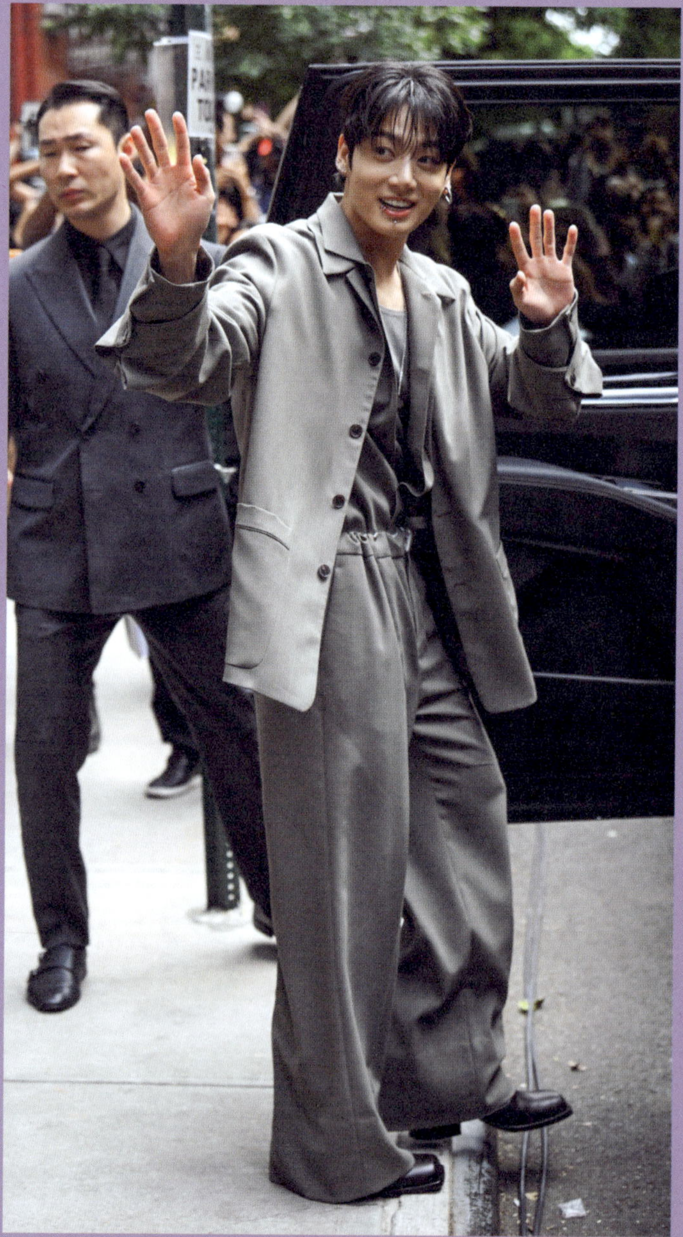

Jung Kook was spotted at New York Fashion Week attending the Calvin Klein show in a grey jacket with matching grey shirt and trousers. In the month following the show, Jung Kook appeared in a new campaign for the brand, posing in denim and other 1990s-inspired garments in his preferred all-black colour palette. With his toned chest on display, one Korean news site, koreaboo.com, called it his "sexiest photoshoot yet", indicating a maturation in some sense of the band's youngest member and showing how far the group has come since their debut as young adults and teenagers.

From the humble beginnings of the first generation to the global domination of the third, each K-pop era has left an indelible mark on history and shaped the genre into the phenomenon it is today. New talents and groups are continually being nurtured and formed, but if the hubbub around their reunion is anything to go by, BTS will continue to captivate audiences with their electrifying music, performances and creativity. Fans eagerly await to see how their new-found maturity might translate into their professional work and personal style and what the next chapter of their evolution might look and sound like.

For now, one thing is certain: whether you're a fan of BTS or K-pop at large, there's no denying the impact both have had on the world.

OPPOSITE Jung Kook on his way to the Calvin Klein fashion show during New York Fashion Week in September 2025.

OVERLEAF Fans make their feelings clear on the tenth anniversary of the band's debut, Seoul, 2023.

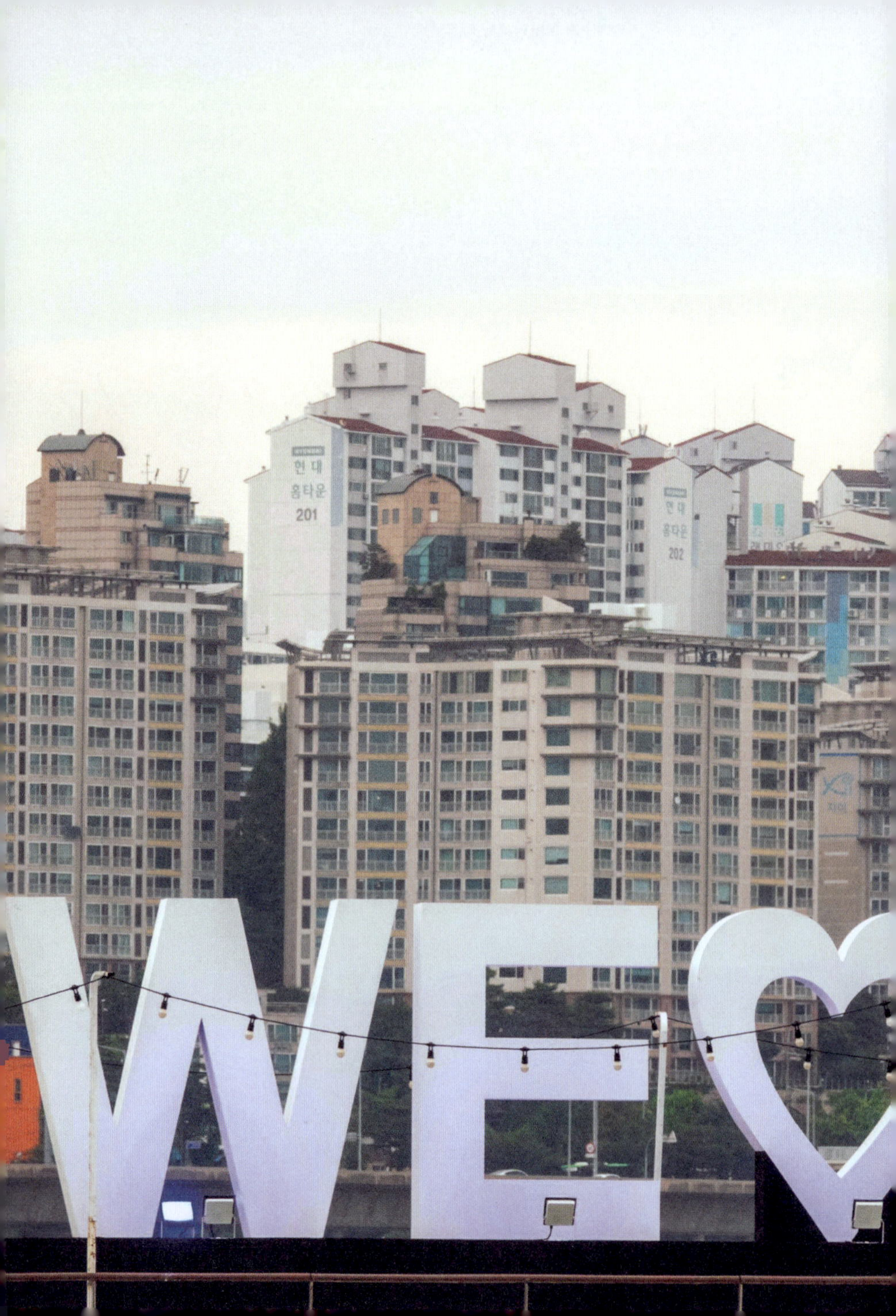
현대
홈타운
201
현대
홈타운
202
WE

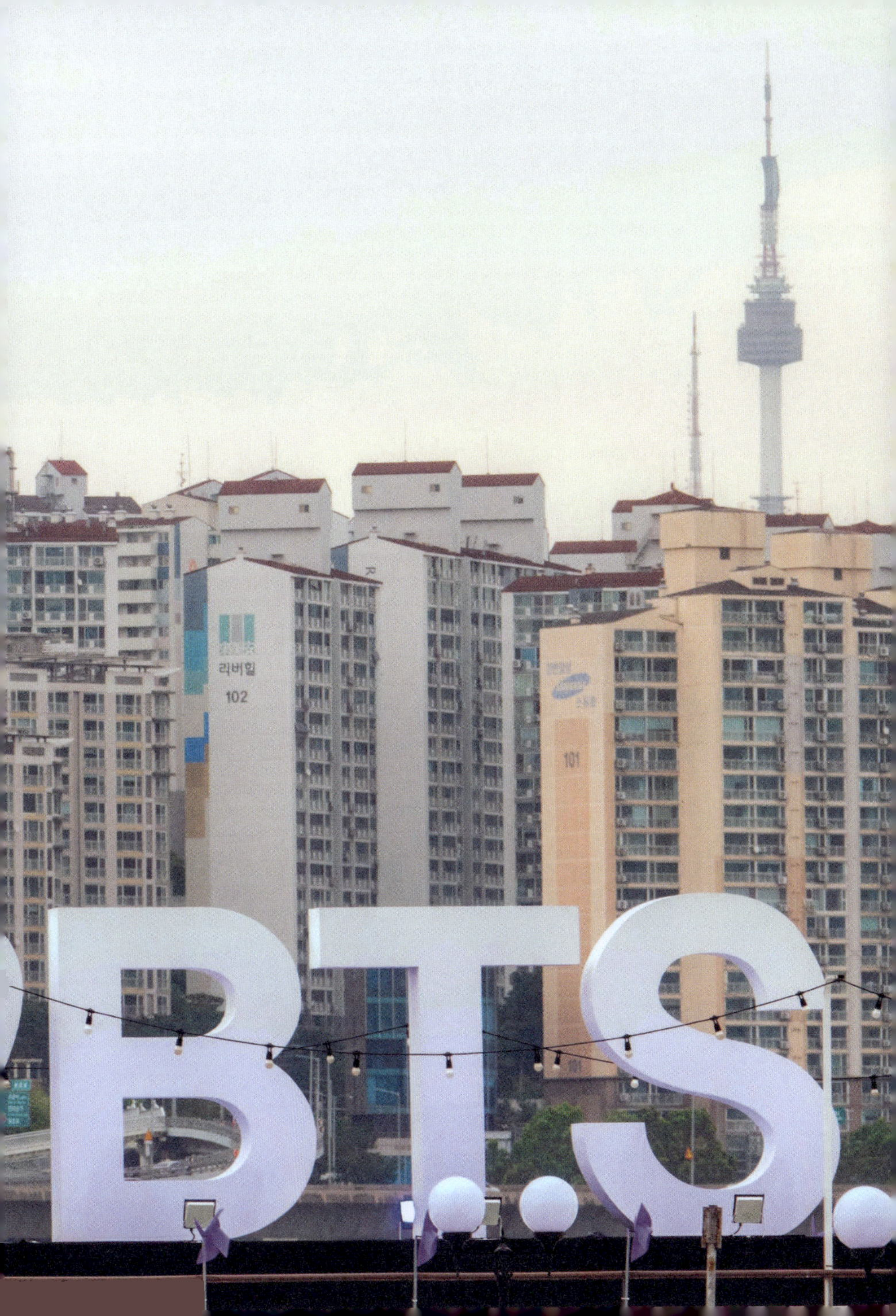
B.T.S.
리버힐
102
101

INDEX

CREDITS

The publishers would like to thank the following sources for their kind permission to reproduce the pictures in this book.

Alamy: Aflo Co. Ltd 79, 122, 136-137, 138; /Everett Collection Inc 20, 83, 84, 96; /Lee Jae-Won/AFLO 218; / MediaPunch Inc 113; /Newscom 74-75; /Erik Pendzich 50-51; /Lev Radin 101; / Top Photo Corporation 104-105; / Getty Images: John Angelillo/POOL/ AFP/AFP via Getty Images 159; / Jason Armond/Los Angeles Times via Contour RA by Getty Images 204; /Axelle/Bauer-Griffin/FilmMagic 10; /Pedro Becerra/Redferns 207; / Allen Berezovsky 174, 177; /Edward Berthelot 126; /Big Hit Entertainment/ BBMA2020 7; /Billboard Music Awards 2021 via Getty Images 102; / Tommaso Boddi 166; /Frederick M. Brown/Getty Images for dcp 92, 115; /Vittorio Zunino Celotto/Getty Images for Gucci 153; /SeongJoon Cho/Bloomberg via Getty Images 86-87; /The Chosunilbo JNS/Imazins via Getty Images 22, 39, 40, 41, 56, 57, 60, 63, 69, 94-95, 108, 130, 142, 198, 203; /Lester Cohen/Getty Images for The Recording Academy; /Oliver Contreras/Sipa/Bloomberg via Getty Images 156; /Rich Fury/Getty Images for iHeartMedia 44; /Swan Gallet/WWD via Getty Images 213; / Eugene Gologursky/Getty Images for Empire State Realty Trust 200-201; / Taylor Hill 133; /Erin Hooley/Chicago Tribune/Tribune News Service via Getty Images 72; /lgan Sports/Multi-Bits via Getty Images 14-15, 27; /Lee Jeong Mu/Imazins via Getty Images 150, 210; /Arnold Jerocki/Getty Images for Bottega Veneta 146; /JTBC PLUS/ ImaZinS Editorial 64, 66, 107; /Michael Kovac/Getty Images for The Recording Academy 80; /Jeff Kravitz/FilmMagic 47; /Juan Mabromata/AFP via Getty Images 23; /Kevin Mazur/Getty Images for The Recording Academy 125; / Emma McIntyre/Getty Images for The Recording Academy 55; /Han Myung-Gu/WireImage 32-33, 65, 141, 149, 165; /NDZ/Star Max/GC Images 48, 140; / Johnny Nunez/Getty Images for The Recording Academy 45, 81, 170-171; / PG/Bauer-Griffin/GC Images 216; / Marc Piasecki/WireImage 129, 132, 134; /Michael Regan - FIFA/FIFA via Getty Images 13; /THE FACT/Imazins via Getty Images 21, 28, 34, 119; /Rebecca Sapp/WireImage 31; /Choi Soo-Young/ Multi-Bits via Getty Images 58-59; /Chung Sung-Jun 184-185, 197; / Daniele Venturelli/Getty Images for Gucci 152; /Anthony Wallace/AFP via Getty Images 161, 183, 194, 208-209; / Theo Wargo/Getty Images for The Recording Academy 43, 76; /Peter White 211; /Kevin Winter/Getty Images for dcp 19; /Kevin Winter/Getty Images for MRC 91; /Jung Yeon-je/AFP 169, 180, 187, 188-189, 192, 195

Shutterstock 8-9, 218-219